Equality, Moral Incentives, and the Market

Equality, Moral Incentives, and the Market

An Essay in Utopian Politico-Economic Theory

Joseph H. Carens

The University of Chicago Press
Chicago and London

The University of Chicago Press, Chicago 60637
The University of Chicago Press, Ltd., London

©1981 by The University of Chicago
All rights reserved. Published 1981
Printed in the United States of America
85 84 83 82 81   5 4 3 2 1

JOSEPH H. CARENS, assistant professor of politics at Lake Forest College, is currently the Charles E. Culpeper Postdoctoral Fellow in the Department of Government at Wesleyan University.

Library of Congress Cataloging in Publication Data

Carens, Joseph H
  Equality, moral incentives, and the market.

  Includes index.
  1. Income distribution.   2. Incentives in industry.
3. Capitalism.   4. Utopias.   I. Title.
HB523.C37   335'.12   80-36774
ISBN 0-226-09269-0

To Gay Gullickson

Contents

Preface ix

1 Efficiency and Equality 1
2 Logically Necessary Prerequisites 23
3 Empirically Necessary Prerequisites 94
4 Implications 178

Appendix: Saving from Equal Income Shares 213

Notes 221

Index 247

Given five fat sheep and ninety-five thin, how induce the ninety-five to resign to the five the richest pasture and the shadiest corners? By convincing them, obviously, that if they do not, they will die of rot, be eaten by wolves, and be deprived in the meantime of such pasture as they have.

R. H. Tawney

Preface

The subject of this book initially attracted my interest as a result of my reading on three different topics during my first year in graduate school. The most compelling of these topics was the issue of moral incentives in Cuba. That was my first real exposure to socialist theory and to socialist practice. I was strongly drawn to the Cuban vision of an egalitarian society in which people were motivated primarily by the desire to serve the common good rather than by a concern for self-aggrandizement. Better still, the Cubans were actively engaged in an attempt to build that ideal society. The Cubans had serious economic problems, however, and many observers were inclined to attribute these problems directly to the Cubans' reliance on moral incentives. My own hypothesis was that the economic difficulties resulted more from a failure of administration than from a lack of motivation. For example, factory workers were often idle because raw materials had been sent to the wrong places. This was obviously a problem of inefficient resource-allocation, not of ineffective incentives to work. Unfortunately, it often proved impossible to distinguish the issues of motivation and administration so clearly on the basis of the limited empirical data available from Cuba at the time. Moreover, I quickly became interested in the broader questions raised by the Cuban case. Many of the critics assumed that the Cuban experiment was doomed to failure from the beginning because widespread, systematic reliance on moral incentives conflicted with basic self-interest in human nature. To consider this issue it was essential to distinguish between the obstacles which the Cubans faced because of particular historical, cultural, economic, and political constraints and the obstacles which they faced because of inherent limits on the patterns of human motivation and social organization. If the earlier distinctions had been difficult to draw on the basis of available empirical data, these proved impossible.

The second topic I was investigating at this time was the debate among functionalist sociologists over the inevitability of stratification. This satisfied my craving for a broader theoretical framework within which I could investigate questions about inequality. It also drew my attention both to the crucial importance of socialization in determining motivational patterns and to the need for any efficient social system to find ways of inducing those with scarce and valued talents and skills to use their abilities in ways that the society considered important. But the debate brought its own frustrations. In particular, both sides in the debate seemed uninterested in questions about possible mechanisms for acquiring and communicating information about the relative importance of various social tasks and for allocating available resources (human and physical) among those tasks in accordance with their importance.

My reading on a third topic—alternative politico-economic mechanisms—addressed these questions about the communication of information and the allocation of resources in a much more satisfactory way. In particular, when I read *Politics, Economics, and Welfare* by Robert Dahl and Charles E. Lindblom, I was struck for the first time by the extraordinary organizational advantages which the market offered as a mechanism for decentralized calculation and control. But despite its valuable general discussion of the advantages and disadvantages of a wide range of politico-economic arrangements, the book focused primarily on incremental alternatives within the American politico-economic system. More important, Dahl and Lindblom seemed to assume that economic inequality was inextricably linked to the market, an assumption which was shared by both critics and advocates of the market.

At this point it occurred to me that the conventional assumption about the market might be wrong. Perhaps moral incentives could be used as a lever to pry the organizational advantages of the market from the distributional disadvantages. If so, such a system might ultimately provide a way for societies like Cuba to combine their commitment to equality with an efficient nonbureaucratic system of administration. And merely showing that such a system was theoretically possible might help to weaken the position of those in our own society who used claims about the inevitability of inequality to justify perpetuation of the status quo. With these things in mind, I set out to identify the prerequisites of a politico-economic system which could combine efficient utilization of the market with equal distribution of income by making effective use of moral incentives. The result is this book.

One feature of the argument requires special mention. In the bulk of the work (Chapters 1–3) I have focused on an egalitarian model which resembles a market capitalist system in most respects. This is not because I consider market capitalism to be an ideal politico-economic system apart from the unequal distribution of income. Indeed, I consider market capitalism to be seriously defective in many important respects. Nevertheless, I think that the market mechanism has great advantages over its major alternative, central planning, as a device for allocating resources. In developing the argument, therefore, I thought that it was important to take the case for pure market capitalism at its strongest point, by assuming that all of the features of such a system (such as inequalities in power and prestige) contribute in some way to economic efficiency. I have tried to show that, even under this extreme assumption, it would still theoretically be possible to achieve the same level of economic efficiency in a system which distributed income equally. Because of the extreme assumption, however, my initial egalitarian model retains many of the undesirable features of a conventional market capitalist system. In the final chapter, I have considered alternative assumptions about the causes and the importance of efficiency, and I have shown how my egalitarian model can be modified to fit a range of alternative politico-economic ideals more in keeping with the egalitarian socialist tradition.

In pursuing this investigation over several years I have benefited from the advice and help of many people. Charles

E. Lindblom served as the advisor for an earlier version of the work which was submitted as a doctoral dissertation at Yale University. He read each of the several drafts with great care, and he consistently challenged me to develop the analysis more fully. At the time I was not always appreciative of the demands, but when I look back at earlier drafts, I am very glad that he persisted. Robert Dahl read an early draft and made valuable comments. Dan LeMahieu and Robert Baade read parts of the manuscript at a crucial stage and made helpful suggestions. Charles Miller gave me the idea of setting the arguments about logical prerequisites in the context of a thought experiment. Ellen Comisso, John Echols, James Fishkin, Douglas Rae, and David Miller all read the manuscript carefully and raised important questions and criticisms. I have attempted to answer most of these in my discussion of the implications of the egalitarian system in the final chapter. I have ignored a few of them at my peril. David Braybrooke read the final version and offered valuable comments.

Several individuals and organizations gave me administrative and financial help. Peggy and Van Quinn provided some logistical assistance at a time when it was badly needed. Nancy Allen typed the dissertation and Florence Meyer typed the revised version. A fellowship from the Danforth Foundation enabled me to switch from religious studies to political science while in graduate school. Lake Forest College provided a supportive and collegial atmosphere as well as financial support for the final stage of research and for preparation of the manuscript.

My greatest debt is to my wife, Gay Gullickson, who took time from her own research to read every draft and to offer just the right combination of criticism and support.

1 Efficiency and Equality

It has been said that the modern age is an age of equality. Some have argued that there is a historical tendency towards equality in all spheres of social life and that this tendency is inevitable. For example, Tocqueville says

> The gradual development of equality of conditions is ... a providential fact, and it possesses all the characteristics of a Divine decree: it is universal, it is durable, it constantly eludes all human interference, and all events as well as men contribute to its progress.[1]

The accuracy of Tocqueville's claim about the tendency of history may be disputed, but there are few who would disagree with Kristol's observation that the idea of equality has for some time enjoyed a kind of moral authority in discussions of how social arrangements ought to be ordered:

> It is generally accepted—it is, indeed, one of the most deeply rooted conventions of contemporary political thought—that the existence of inequality is legitimate provocation to social criticism. Every inequality is on the defensive, must prove itself against the imputation of injustice and unnaturalness. And where such proof is established, it never asserts itself beyond the point where inequality is to be tolerated because it is, under particular conditions, inescapable.[2]

Despite the general allegiance which equality seems to command as an ideal, there are certain inequalities which are widely believed to be inescapable in modern society, at least in the sense that the elimination of these inequalities would require a greater cost in terms of the sacrifice of other valued goals than the benefit to be gained by the elimination of the inequalities. Inequality of income distribution is often thought to be inescapable in this sense. It is widely believed that no large industrial politico-economic system could ever distribute income equally without greatly reducing economic efficiency and/or limiting human freedom. Some significant degree of income inequality is seen as a permanent, inevitable, necessary feature of any politico-economic system with a high level of productive efficiency and of human freedom.

George Halm argues, for example, that equal distribution is inherently incompatible with freedom of occupation and of consumption. If consumer choices are to be effective in determining what is produced, labor will have to shift from one industry to another in response to changes in preferences. If income is equally distributed, Halm argues, this shifting could be achieved only by a command allocation of labor. And if free choice of occupation were combined with equal distribution, consumers would have no say in what was produced.[3]

Even those who explicitly endorse income equality as an abstract ideal concede that its attainment would require too high a price, even in principle. Arthur Okun, for example, has written a book with the title *Equality and Efficiency: The Big Tradeoff*. On one page he indicates that he thinks the ideal distribution from an ethical perspective would be highly egalitarian.[4] On the next page he asserts that the ideal is one which could be achieved only at great cost to economic efficiency because "society would forego any opportunity to use material rewards as incentives to production."[5] Moreover, Okun warns of the dangers of trying to rely on alternative sources of motivation such as altruism or collective loyalty. These types of incentive either would not work or would reduce freedom or would do both.[6]

Okun's views are widely shared, and not only by economists. For example, Brian Barry, a political philosopher, expresses approval of the goal of income equality in theory but declares that equal distribution would be incompatible with the organizational requirements of a large, complex politico-economic system.[7] Thomas Nagel, another philosopher, suggests that people "deserve to be treated equally" with respect to distribution but does not see how this can be done "without a gigantic increase in total social control."[8]

I believe that this conventional view about the inevitable costs of income equality is based on a limited set of assumptions about the possible sources of human motivation and about the possible types of politico-economic organization. Although these assumptions may be accurate with respect to existing conditions in many societies, they are inappropriately restrictive in an analysis of the *necessary* relationship between income equality on the one hand and freedom and efficiency on the other. I shall show in this book that, given certain conditions, an equal distribution of income need not reduce efficiency or limit freedom.

This is not just a critical exercise, however, in which I shall attempt to refute the conventional view on the costs of income equality. As the subtitle indicates, this is an essay in utopian politico-economic theory. It is a positive attempt to sketch an aspect of the ideal state by identifying the conditions under which income equality can coexist with freedom and efficiency. In his previously cited article Nagel expressed the hope that

> someone will discover a way in which the socially produced inequalities (especially the economic ones) between the intelligent and the unintelligent, the talented and the untalented, or even the beautiful and the ugly, can be reduced without limiting the availability of opportunities, products, and services and without resort to increased coercion or decreased liberty in the choice of work or style of life.[9]

That is precisely what I shall try to do here. I shall not pretend that my analysis could be directly applied for policy purposes to any existing society, but I do think that even a theoretical investigation of utopian possibilities has important implications for alternatives in existing politico-economic systems.

The Question

In inquiring how equal distribution of income might be combined with efficiency and freedom, I shall be concerned primarily with answering the following question: What are the prerequisites for a politico-economic system which would:

1. distribute annual after-tax income for consumption equally among adult individuals, at least for the most part;
2. utilize moral incentives as a major source of motivation for economic activities;
3. rely heavily on the market mechanism;
4. perform economic functions as efficiently as a private-property market system;
5. provide virtually the same freedoms as a private-property market system.

Henceforth, in this essay I shall use the phrase "the egalitarian system" as the term for a politico-economic system which would satisfy these five requirements. For purposes of this essay, therefore, the phrase "egalitarian system" refers to a system with all of the above characteristics and not merely to one with equal-income distribution. This is merely a terminological device adopted to avoid excessive repetition of these characteristics. For the same reason, I shall use the phrase "PPM system" as an abbreviation for "private-property market system."[10]

The specific question which I propose to address contains several elements which were not explicitly included in the initial discussion of the alleged conflict between income equality on the one hand and freedom and efficiency on the other. Let me explain why I have included these new elements.

The First Requirement: Equal Distribution

Three technical qualifications. The first requirement of the egalitarian system contains three qualifications—"annual," "for the most part," and "among adult individuals"—which were not included in the initial discussion of income equality. All three qualifications have been introduced for technical reasons.

The term "annual" was introduced in order to make it clear that income must be equalized within a relatively short-run period. Thus the egalitarian system requires a much higher degree of short-run income equality than would be required, for example, by a system which aimed only at the equalization of lifetime incomes. On the other hand, the choice of a year as the time period within which income must be equalized is somewhat arbitrary. I have adopted it simply because it is a convenient and familiar short-run period and because it might be impractical, even in theory, to require equalization within a shorter time period such as a month or a week.

The qualification "for the most part" was introduced because there are certain technical constraints on the possibilities of measuring income (particularly income in kind) and certain practical limits to the control of deviance which might make it impossible ever to achieve an absolutely equal distribution of income. In order to avoid rejection of arguments about the fundamental tendency of the system on the basis of minor deviations, I introduced the qualifying phrase "for the most part."

The phrase "among adult individuals" was introduced in order to avoid consideration of the question of how much income (if any) should be given to children. I am avoiding consideration of this question in order to simplify the task of the investigation. Questions about how to treat family units greatly complicate both theoretical and practical discussions of income inequality,[11] and yet these issues are not central to questions about the tradeoff between equality on the one hand and efficiency and freedom on the other. If equal distribution among adults could be achieved without sacrificing efficiency or freedom, it would presumably also be possible to provide income grants to children if that were thought desirable. For similar reasons, I am ignoring the principle of distribution according to needs throughout most of this essay. If equal distribution could be achieved without sacrificing efficiency, it should also be possible to base distribution on need without sacrificing efficiency. I shall develop this argument in more detail in the final chapter where I will show how the egalitarian system could be modified to take account of the principle of distribution according to needs.

For stylistic reasons I shall often leave out these three qualifying phrases when referring to the requirement of equal income distribution, but in principle the qualifications apply throughout the essay.

Income in kind. The simple phrase "equal distribution" might suggest that each individual would receive the same amount of money income. The phrase "after-tax income for consumption" is intended to broaden the scope of what is equally distributed in one respect and to narrow it in other respects.

If equal distribution required only that *money* be equally distributed, there would be a glaring loophole in the egalitarian system. Some individuals might be able to acquire much more *income in kind* than others. One obvious type of income in kind in PPM systems is a job-related fringe benefit (such as free or subsidized housing) which increases a person's level of consumption. Other examples would be goods received through barter and goods produced for one's own consumption. In principle the market value of any income in kind which an individual acquires in the egalitarian system must be counted as part of that individual's income for consumption. If after-tax income for consumption is to be equally distributed, those who receive more income in kind must receive less money to spend on consumption and vice versa. Taxes and transfers in the egalitarian system should not simply provide each individual with the same amount of money to spend on consumption. Rather, taxes and transfers must be used to ensure that each individual enjoys the same total amount of income for consumption once the value of his income in kind (if any) is added to whatever money income he has available for consumption. I shall use the term "equal income share" for the total amount of income for consumption which each individual would receive after taxes and transfers in the egalitarian system.

Business expenses. Not all goods and services which an individual acquires without paying for them should be considered income in kind. Employers often provide employees with goods and services which are necessary to enable the employee to fulfill his occupational responsibilities. For example, the chair, desk, typewriter, etc. provided to a secretary would fit in this category. Since the purpose of such goods and services is not to increase the employee's personal level of consumption, they should not be treated as income in kind and should not count as income for consumption. To distinguish them from income in kind, I shall call them "business expenses."

Sometimes individuals bear business expenses directly. For example, a carpenter might have to purchase his own tools. Again, the primary purpose of such expenditures is not to increase the individual's personal level of consumption but to enable him to do his job. Thus money which an individual spends for business expenses should not count as money which is available to him for consumption. In other words, money spent on business expenses should not count as part of one's equal income share.

The line between "business expenses" and "income in kind" is not always as easy to draw in practice as it is in theory. It is clear, however, that the category of "business expenses" would have to be narrowly defined in the egalitarian system in order to avoid the introduction of unequal distribution under another name. In the fictional politico-economic system described in Michael Young's *The Rise of the Meritocracy,* for example, there is complete equality of incomes in theory, but in practice goods and services for consumption are differentially dispensed, to the benefit of the managerial class, on the grounds that all aspects of the life of a manager affect his performance at work.[12] This would obviously violate the principle that business expenses be narrowly defined. Even the more modest consumption advantages gained under the heading of "business expenses" in existing PPM systems would be ruled out by our principle that such expenses be narrowly defined.[13]

Other inequalities. The requirement that after-tax income for consumption be equally distributed clearly does not imply that before-tax income must be equally distributed. Indeed, it is essential that before-tax income *not* be distributed equally, as I shall explain in my discussion of the role of the market mechanism in the egalitarian system. Moreover, it is only income for consumption that must be equally distributed after taxes.[14] In other words, control over resources (whether money or goods and services) may be unequally distributed so long as those controlling the resources are not permitted to use them for personal consumption purposes. For example, bank presidents in PPM systems control the use of a great deal of money which they are not permitted to use to enhance their own personal consumption. Such an arrangement would be quite compatible with the egalitarian system so long as the bank president received no more income for consumption than anyone else. Finally, the requirement that after-tax income for consumption be equally distributed does not imply that leisure or power or prestige or anything other than income for consumption must be equally distributed in the egalitarian system.

The Second Requirement: Moral Incentives

The second requirement of the egalitarian system is that it use moral incentives as a major source of motivation for economic activities. By "moral incentives" I mean incentives based on the desire to serve society or to perform one's duty to society. I have included the requirement that the egalitarian system utilize moral incentives because they seem to me to be the key element needed to make it possible for a politico-economic system to combine equal distribution of income with efficient use of the market mechanism.

Reliance on moral incentives has been an important element in many models of ideal politico-economic systems, especially in the socialist tradition. Contemporary Western social scientists frequently suggest, however, that moral incentives could not be an effective source of motivation for economic activities in large, complex, politico-economic systems, at least over the long run.[15] They believe that reliance on income incentives is inevitable for any large, complex system which seeks to induce a consistently high level of effort from its members. In the third chapter of this essay, however, I shall show that under certain conditions moral incentives could provide a strong and powerful source of motivation for economic activity in the egalitarian system, even over the long run.

The requirement that the egalitarian system use moral incentives as a major source of motivation for economic activities raises not only the question of whether or not moral incentives could provide a powerful and reliable source of motivation but also the question of how moral incentives could be integrated with the market mechanism. The answer to this latter question is by no means obvious. Goodwill does not always lead to good results. To lead to good results, the goodwill must be channeled in the right direction. Even if people are anxious to serve society, their actions will not necessarily benefit society unless the roles which they fill and the structures within which they act enable them to act in society's interest. It has been argued that individuals in a PPM system who pursue what they consider to be the "public interest" rather than their private, pecuniary interests may simply interfere with the socially beneficial coordination which the "invisible hand" ordinarily achieves and may undermine both the freedom of consumers and the efficiency of the system.[16] Hayek expresses the dilemma as follows:

> The problem of adequate incentives ... is commonly discussed as if it were a problem mainly of the willingness of people to do their best. But this, although important, is not the whole nor even the most important aspect of the problem.... What is more important is that if we want to leave them the choice, if they are to judge what they ought to do, they must be given some readily intelligible yardstick by which to measure the social importance of

the different occupations. Even with the best will in the world, it would be impossible for anyone intelligently to choose between various alternatives if the advantages they offered him stood in no relation to their usefulness to society. To know whether as a result of a change a man ought to leave a trade and an environment which he has come to like and exchange it for another, it is necessary that the changed relative value of these occupations find expression in the remunerations they offer.[17]

Thus one crucial task for the analysis is to show how moral incentives, in a politico-economic system which relies heavily on the market, could theoretically substitute for income incentives without destroying the ability of the market to function. I shall focus on this task in the second chapter.

The Third Requirement: Reliance on the Market

The third requirement of the egalitarian system is that it rely heavily on the market mechanism. By "market" (or "market mechanism") I mean that individual economic units such as individuals and corporations generally make decisions about production and consumption on the basis of their own preferences rather than on the basis of directions from a central authority, that these individual economic units enter into exchange with other economic units, and that money is widely used as a medium of exchange. I have included the requirement that the egalitarian system rely heavily on the market because I believe that decentralized coordination of individuals and resources through the use of prices and exchange is an extremely efficient method of economic organization for many purposes. Moreover, I want to meet head-on the argument that society can have the advantages of the market only if it tolerates income inequalities.

Reliance on the market has many disadvantages as well as advantages. Nevertheless I intend to ignore those disadvantages in the first three chapters and to assume that reliance on the market is desirable. Since the market *appears* to require income inequality for structural as well as motivational reasons, I shall confront the hardest possible case for combining efficiency and equality by assuming that reliance on the market is desirable. In the final chapter, however, I shall discuss possible objections to the egalitarian system which focus on its link to the market mechanism.

Market socialism. Many socialists have also come to perceive the economic advantages of the market mechanism. Both in theory and in practice, they have attempted to use the market as a major component in socialist politico-economic systems.[18] My egalitarian system differs from market socialist models in two important respects.

First, despite their reliance on the market, most market socialist models entail a higher degree of centralized direction of the economy than is characteristic of PPM systems. This leads some critics to suggest that individuals in these models would not be as innovative or as sensitive to change as individuals in PPM systems. Polanyi argues, for example, that "Government investors are not likely to probe as quickly and completely as private investors into all avenues of advantageous investment and to react as sensitively to changing circumstances by an appropriate re-shifting of investments all over the field of enterprise."[19] I intend to show that the egalitarian system could theoretically provide virtually the same degree of decentralization in control over resources as is found in PPM systems as well as provide equally effective incentives for individual initiative and individual entrepreneurial activity. Thus I shall show that criticism of the kind that Polanyi offers would not apply to the egalitarian system.

Second, and more important, no market socialist models have managed to show how inequalities in income from labor could be eliminated without substantially reducing the efficiency of their systems.[20] Most simply treat inequality in incomes from labor as a necessary cost of efficiency.[21] In this respect, their views coincide with those of nonsocialist economists and conflict directly with the position which I am advocating in this essay.

The Fourth Requirement: PPM-like Efficiency

This leads to the fourth requirement, that the egalitarian system perform economic functions as efficiently as a PPM system. The PPM system is the obvious standard to use for judging the efficiency of any politico-economic system that relies upon the market because most nonsocialist economists since Adam Smith have argued that a PPM system is the most efficient possible politico-economic system. Even market socialists use the PPM system as a standard of efficiency and try to show that their models would equal or surpass the efficiency of the PPM system.

The definition of efficiency. The term "efficiency" can be used in many different ways. For my purposes, there are two dimensions of the concept which are of particular importance. First, a system is efficient to the extent that it produces as much as possible from a *given* set of resources in response to a given pattern of demand. The ideal is to allocate resources so that it is impossible to increase the output of one desired commodity without decreasing the output of some other desired commodity.[22] Second, a system is efficient to the extent that it increases the amount of resources available for production.[23] This includes the ability of a system to induce people to work hard, to save, and to invest in the creation of new productive resources.

These two types of efficiency are important in this essay because many people believe both that PPM systems are highly efficient in these two respects and that any politico-economic system which distributed income equally would be highly inefficient in these two respects, especially if that politico-economic system relied heavily on the market. There are many specific arguments which could be cited here, but the major ones can be grouped under four headings: (1) allocation; (2) effort; (3) saving and investment; and (4) risk. It can be argued that equal distribution would have negative effects on each of these economic functions.

The efficiency of PPM systems. The argument that a PPM system tends to allocate available resources efficiently is the most familiar and most highly developed aspect of economic theory. It also provides essential background for all four objections to equal distribution. In highly simplified form the argument runs as follows.[24]

In a PPM system everything has a price. The price of labor is called its "wage rate," and different kinds of labor have different prices. People receive money for what they sell. This is their income. People use this money to buy what they want.

The price of any good or service is determined by the interaction of supply and demand. If people want more shoes than are being produced, the price of shoes will go up and producers will have an incentive to produce more, other things being equal. The increased price will lead people to purchase fewer shoes than they would have at the lower price. If demand falls, the price will go down. Producers will then produce somewhat fewer shoes than they would have at the higher price and consumers will buy somewhat more shoes than they would have at the higher price. Thus equilibrium will be restored. It can be seen that responsiveness to price changes is at the heart of arguments about the efficiency of PPM systems.

Producers have an incentive to produce what consumers want because it is only by selling what they produce that they can acquire an income. They have an incentive to make what they produce as cheaply as possible and to sell it as dearly as possible because that is the way they can make the most income. Each producer, however, has to compete with other producers who have the same incentives as he to produce cheaply and sell dearly, and he must compete with the others both in purchasing the factors of production and in selling the final product. The supplier of any factor has an incentive to seek as high a price as he can for the use of his resources since this will increase his income, but he has to compete with other suppliers of the same factor who have the same incentive. The interaction of competition among producers seeking to buy a given factor of production, and competition among suppliers seeking to sell a given factor of production, ensures that each factor of production will be priced at the value of its marginal contribution to production. Similarly, competition among producers together with competition among consumers who have an incentive to buy as cheaply as possible ensures that each final product will be sold at its marginal cost of production.

In short, prices in the PPM system provide individuals with information about the relative scarcity of goods and services, and simultaneously they provide individuals with incentives to act on this information. When changes in supply or demand alter relative scarcities, they alter prices as well and thus alter incentives.

Equality and allocation. It can be argued that prices must play the same role in any market system that they play in a PPM system and that in the case of wages, at least, this role is inseparable from differences in personal income distribution.[25] Suppose, for example, that we simply equalized all wages by fiat. Then the prices of different kinds of labor would no longer reflect their relative scarcities. A producer would have an incentive to hire highly skilled labor where less skilled labor would do, since it would not cost him any more to do so.[26] Clearly, this would be an inefficient use of resources in the first sense I gave to the term "efficient." This argument is correct. In any market system, prices must reflect relative scarcities, or people will not have the information they need to use their resources efficiently. Differences in the relative scarcity of different kinds of labor must be reflected in different wage rates.

Suppose now that differences in wage rates are permitted but that taxes and transfers are used to equalize the actual incomes individuals have to spend on consumption. This is the technique employed by the egalitarian system. The goal clearly is to separate functional distribution (differential wage rates reflecting different relative scarcities) from personal distribution (the income an individual acquires for consumption). According to Halm this would not work either: "this separation of personal and functional distribution would mean that labor would no longer be automatically pulled in the right direction, because the elimination of (after-tax) differentials has simultaneously eliminated the inducement on which the allocation of labor rests in a market economy."[27] In other words, even if prices still provided accurate information about relative scarcities and about changes in relative scarcities, the taxes and transfers would have eliminated the incentives for individuals to act on that information.

If this argument were correct I would have to conclude that the egalitarian system would necessarily lead to a more inefficient use of available resources than the PPM system. Clearly it is true that equal distribution through taxes and transfers would eliminate income incentives to respond to wage differentials. Thus one key task for my argument is to show how moral incentives could substitute for income incentives in inducing people to respond to wage differentials.

Equality and effort. The argument about effort is basically concerned with the second dimension of efficiency, the amount of resources available for production. The argument is quite straightforward. The more people are willing to work, the more resources there are available for production. In PPM systems individuals receive the value of their marginal product as income which they can spend on consumption. Other things being equal, the more they work, the more income they acquire. Thus the desire for income provides a strong incentive for them to work hard.

It is frequently argued that any tax on income is inefficient precisely because it removes some of the income incentive to work. Progressive income taxes are regarded as the worst offenders because they reduce income most at the margin.[28] The case against the taxes and transfers of the egalitarian system is obviously far stronger. Equal distribution would completely remove income as an incentive to work hard. The key question therefore is whether moral incentives could provide equally effective incentives for work.

Equality and the saving/investing functions. The question of saving and investment concerns both dimensions of efficiency. Resources which are not consumed but instead are invested in new capital goods increase the productive resources available in a system (the second dimension of efficiency), and a given quantity of resources saved for investment may be more productively invested in one use than in another (the first dimension of efficiency). Note also that the general topic "saving and investment" includes under the heading of "investment in human capital" the question of how successfully a system enables and induces people to increase their own productive capacities (e.g., through the acquisition of new skills).

The fact that people can increase their incomes by investing their savings gives them an incentive first to save and then to invest where the return is greatest (i.e., where the marginal productivity of their investment is greatest). Similarly, the desire for more income provides every individual with an incentive to develop his own personal talents and skills so as to increase his marginal productivity and thus increase his income.

Again, a system providing equal distribution could not use the desire for more income as an incentive for individuals to save or to invest. While socialist market models offer some structural alternatives to provide for saving and investing in nonhuman capital, it is debatable whether these alternative structures would be as efficient as the income incentives available to individuals in PPM systems.[29] Moreover, equal distribution would eliminate any income incentive for individual self-improvement.[30] Thus the question for the egalitarian system is whether these functions of saving and investing can be performed as efficiently through reliance on moral incentives.

Equality and risk. Finally, there is the question of risk. Most decisions about allocation and investment in real-world PPM systems involve some degree of risk, because many things can alter relative scarcities and thus reduce the prices people are willing to pay for particular goods and services. Some choices entail much more risk than others. In PPM systems, people may be induced to take great risks when there are opportunities of great gain. It is frequently argued that greater equalization of incomes through taxes and transfers would reduce incentives to take risks since the possibility of great gains would be eliminated while the possibility of great losses would remain.[31] Thus allocations and investments would be directed only towards low-risk, low-return activities, and efficiency would be reduced.

It is not entirely clear whether these arguments are actually applicable to the egalitarian system, since a completely equal distribution would eliminate the possibility that an individual could reduce his personal income for consumption by taking risks. Of course, an equal distribution would also eliminate the possibility that an individual could increase his personal income for consumption by taking risks. The situation is sufficiently puzzling that something will have to be said about the incentives to take risks in the egalitarian system.

The Fifth Requirement: PPM-like Freedoms

The fifth and last requirement of the egalitarian system is that it provide virtually the same freedoms as a private-property market system. I introduced this requirement because of the widespread belief cited at the beginning of the chapter that equal distribution of income would necessarily entail severe restrictions on personal freedoms. Again, the PPM system provides a convenient standard by which to measure the availability of freedoms in an egalitarian system, especially since the PPM system is the standard which the critics of equal distribution usually have in mind, either explicitly or implicitly.

There are two major kinds of issues which arise under this heading of "freedom." The first concerns economic freedoms. The question here is how much choice the individual has about how much he will work, about the kind of work he will do, about what he will consume, etc. I shall show that reliance on the market mechanism would ensure that individuals would enjoy extensive economic freedoms in the egalitarian system. The second issue concerns the degree of centralized direction and overall social control which would be required to make moral incentives effective and to keep income distribution equal. I shall show that the egalitarian system would not require much more centralized direction and social control than the PPM system.

The Method

From time to time, social scientists advocate the pursuit of utopian inquiries such as the one I am undertaking here, but they rarely specify how such an inquiry is to be conducted.[32] This raises a fundamental methodological problem: How does one identify a "prerequisite" of a politico-economic system? What counts as a "prerequisite"? I propose to identify two different kinds of prerequisites: those that are logically necessary and those that are empirically necessary.

Logically Necessary Prerequisites

In order to identify the logically necessary prerequisites of the egalitarian system I shall construct a "rational-choice" model of the egalitarian system.[33] The defining characteristic of a rational-choice model is the assumption that every individual always chooses among available alternatives according to a consistent set of preferences.[34] This assumption, which I shall call the assumption of rationality, is purely formal. It does not specify either the nature of the available alternatives or the character of the individual's preferences. If one makes specific assumptions about the conditions within which choice is exercised (i.e., the available alternatives) and about individuals' sources of motivation (i.e., their preferences) then the behavior of individuals in the rational-choice model can be described, or, more accurately, deduced.[35]

In the context of a rational-choice model, a prerequisite

is simply an assumption which is logically necessary in order for one to deduce validly that individuals will behave in a particular way and that certain systemic consequences will follow. Rational-choice models have been used most extensively in the field of economics in order to predict how individuals will respond to price signals, but, as Harsanyi has pointed out, rational-choice models may also be used to determine whether various goals of a politico-economic system are consistent with one another.[36] It is this latter function which the rational-choice model will serve here. I shall identify a set of assumptions about the conditions within which choice is exercised and about individuals' sources of motivation from which it is possible to deduce that after-tax income for consumption would be equally distributed, that moral incentives would be a major source of motivation for economic activity, that the market would be the principal mechanism for coordinating economic activity, that economic functions would be performed as efficiently as in a PPM system, and that virtually the same freedoms would be available as in a PPM system. These assumptions will constitute the logically necessary prerequisites of the egalitarian system.

There is one further point which should be clarified about the nature of this first set of prerequisites. The phrase "logically necessary assumption" may be used in both a strong sense and a weak sense. In the strong sense, an assumption would be logically necessary if one needed it in order to deduce that individuals would behave in a particular way, regardless of whatever other assumptions were adopted about motivations and conditions of choice. In the weak sense, an assumption would be logically necessary if one needed it in order to deduce that individuals would behave in a particular way, *given* the other assumptions about motivations and conditions of choice. I shall attempt only to identify prerequisites which are logically necessary in the weak sense. That is, I shall identify a set of assumptions from which it is possible to deduce the appropriate conclusions about the behavior required by the egalitarian system and I shall show that each of these assumptions is logically necessary given the other assumptions. However, I shall not attempt to prove that this is the only possible set of assumptions from which such conclusions could be drawn.

The nonempirical character of logically necessary prerequisites. It must be emphasized that the analysis at this initial stage will be purely logical. I shall not make any claims about the "plausibility" or "realism" of the assumptions which I identify. I shall seek only to show that the assumptions are consistent with one another and that one can in fact deduce the appropriate conclusions from them (i.e., equal distribution, moral incentives, reliance on the market, and PPM-like efficiency and freedom). Nevertheless, the identification of these assumptions will be an important first step for my analysis since, as we have seen, it is by no means obvious that the elements of the egalitarian system can be consistently combined in a politico-economic system under *any* conditions. Moreover, the identification of the logically necessary prerequisites will set the stage for the identification of the second kind of prerequisites, the empirically necessary ones.

Empirically Necessary Prerequisites

The empirically necessary prerequisites of the egalitarian system are those conditions which we can infer from empirical social theory to be essential prior conditions for the existence of the logically necessary prerequisites of the egalitarian system. The empirically necessary prerequisites are, therefore, second-order prerequisites. They are the prerequisites of the first-order (logically necessary) prerequisites. Unlike the logically necessary prerequisites, however, the empirically necessary prerequisites are not assumptions in a self-contained logical system. Rather they are conditions which are identified as prerequisites on the basis of what can be known about the possibilities and requirements of human social organization from contemporary empirical social theory. Thus the empirically necessary prerequisites are based on theories which have been developed from the observation and analysis of actual societies and of politico-economic systems in the real world. It is in discussing them that I shall address questions about the plausibility of the logically necessary prerequisites. Nevertheless, I should emphasize the word "theory" in the phrase "empirical theory." An egalitarian system of the kind I am considering has never actually existed. In discussing the empirically necessary prerequisites for such a system, therefore, I must rely on arguments by analogy and on the application of concepts and models which have been developed in empirical investigations to a system which cannot itself (at this time, at least) be the subject of empirical investigation.

Limits on the Investigation

In order to keep the investigation within somewhat manageable bounds, I shall place three important limits on the issues to be discussed.

First, I shall not attempt to discuss what might be required for a *transition* to the egalitarian system. In other words, I shall not try to identify the conditions which would have to be satisfied in order for some existing politico-economic system (e.g., an existing PPM system) to be transformed into an egalitarian system.[37] Rather, I shall proceed as though it were a question of constructing the egalitarian system *ab initio et ex nihil*. As Tumin has remarked in a similar context,

> we are considering what is possible in human affairs assuming the availability of a population with a fresh slate on which no major cultural themes have yet been written.
>
> This distinction between the immediately probable and the theoretically possible form of social arrangements must be kept in mind if we are not to confuse practical social planning with theoretical specification of limits and possibilities.[38]

Second, I shall assume that there are no exogenous variables which can affect the operation of the egalitarian system. In other words, I shall not discuss the question of what effect interaction with other politico-economic systems might have on the egalitarian system.

Third, I shall pay relatively little attention to normative questions. In the second and third chapters I shall simply assume that equal distribution and PPM-like efficiency are desirable. In the fourth chapter, I shall consider objections to these goals, but my primary aim will be to show either that the egalitarian system is sufficiently flexible to take account of the alternative goals proposed by the critics or that these alternative goals are inherently unattainable in any large, complex, politico-economic system. The egalitarian system does presuppose certain moral principles, and in the fourth chapter I shall indicate what these are and how arguments might be constructed to justify these principles. Nevertheless, the basic approach is analytical and empirical rather than normative. I wish ultimately to show what the egalitarian system has to offer to those who share a range of values within what might broadly be called the egalitarian tradition. But I attempt no fundamental justification of the tradition itself.

2 Logically Necessary Prerequisites

In this chapter I shall conduct an extended thought experiment. Imagine that we have two politico-economic systems. Assume that individuals in both these systems maximize their satisfactions, i.e., that they are "rational" in the sense described in Chapter 1. Thus both of the imaginary politico-economic systems are more properly described as rational-actor *models* of politico-economic systems, though for the sake of convenience, I shall continue to refer to them simply as politico-economic systems. Now, imagine that the first politico-economic system is a PPM system with some given set of physical resources, some given set of individuals with particular abilities and preferences. Then imagine that the second politico-economic system is exactly the same as the first in all respects except one: In this second system incomes are taxed and money is redistributed so that each year after taxes every adult receives the same total income for consumption as every other adult. In saying that the second system is exactly the same as the first, I mean that in both systems there is the same set of physical resources, the same set of individuals with the same abilities and preferences, the same set of conditions, rules, etc. regarding the control and disposition of resources, except for the distribution of after-tax income for consumption.

Given these basic conditions, the experimental task is that of answering the following question: In what other ways (besides the equal distribution of income) would one have to assume that the second system differed from the first in order to conclude that the second politico-economic system would be as efficient as the first? By answering this question, I shall ultimately identify the logically necessary prerequisites of the egalitarian system.

It is important to see that the assumption of identical individuals, resources, rules, etc. allows control of irrelevant variables in answering this experimental question and thus in answering the more basic questions about the conditions under which it is possible to combine efficiency and equality in a politico-economic system. There are many factors which can affect the efficiency of a politico-economic system (individual characteristics, available resources, property laws, and so on). What the assumption does is to eliminate the effects of any such factors which are not caused or required by the equal distribution of income. Thus this thought experiment will enable us to isolate the requirements for combining efficiency with equality—at least in the imaginary rational-actor model and in using the imaginary PPM model as the standard of efficiency.[1]

I should perhaps note that the investigation imposes no a priori limits on what is assumed about the imaginary PPM system which is used as the standard of efficiency. Indeed one could imagine many different PPM systems and for each of them one could imagine a parallel system in which income is distributed equally. In what follows I shall assume particular details about a PPM system to provide concrete illustrations for arguments about what would be required by a parallel egalitarian system, but the details themselves are not essential to the arguments or to the logically necessary prerequisites which I shall identify. The flexibility which this implies will prove important when I assess the significance of the egalitarian system in the final chapter.

Given the need to control for irrelevant variables, one additional assumption must be made about the identity between the two systems. I shall assume that there is the same pattern of demand in both systems. This assumption is not implied by the general assumption regarding identity precisely because the pattern of demand would be influenced by the requirement that incomes be distributed equally. An equal distribution would presumably generate a different pattern of demand from an unequal distribution, since the same individuals would have different amounts to spend in the two cases. Nevertheless, my central concern here is to compare the efficiency of the second system with that of the first system. I wish to focus in particular on the question of how resources would be allocated in response to some given pattern of demand in the second system as opposed to the first system. In order to make this comparison, the given pattern of demand has to be the same in both cases. It is quite irrelevant what that particular pattern happens to be. In other words, the fact that the pattern of demand would be different in the second system from what it would be in the first is an irrelevant variable for the purposes of this inquiry. The difference in the patterns of demand is a difference caused by the requirement that incomes be distributed equally, but it is the one difference caused by equal distribution which must be ignored in order to conduct the inquiry. For this reason I shall assume that there is the same pattern of demand in both systems.

The Three Initial Prerequisites of the Egalitarian System

As the first step in answering the question asked in my thought experiment, I shall assume the following modifications of the second system.

First, individuals in the second system believe they have a social duty to earn as much pre-tax net income as they are capable of earning.[2]

Second, individuals in the second system derive satisfaction from performing this social duty to earn as much pre-tax income as they can.[3]

Third, individuals in the second system place the same relative value on the satisfactions derived from performing their social duty to acquire pre-tax income (hereafter called social-duty satisfactions) as individuals in the first system (the PPM system) place on the satisfactions derived from acquiring income for consumption (hereafter called income-consumption satisfactions).

These three modifications may seem odd and unrealistic. After all, one may assume anything, and the politico-economic systems in this discussion are purely imaginary.

Nevertheless, I must ask the reader's forbearance and defer discussion of such objections until the next chapter. The first task is to understand the logic of the egalitarian system. Only then can the plausibility of the assumptions on which it is based be considered.

These three assumed modifications introduce moral incentives (i.e., satisfactions derived from the performance of social duty) into the second system, which I shall henceforth simply call the egalitarian system. As I indicated in the first chapter, the goal of the egalitarian system is to rely on moral incentives in place of income-consumption satisfactions as a basic source of motivation for economic activity. The moral incentives which I have just assumed are intended to supply a *mechanism* which would lead people to respond to prices and price changes in the egalitarian system as efficiently as people respond to prices and price changes in the PPM system.

In the first chapter of this essay I identified four major allegations about the inefficiencies which would be caused by equal distribution. In this chapter, I propose to address each of these arguments in turn, showing why each is not applicable to the egalitarian model.

To facilitate the exposition of the argument, I shall adopt the following procedures. First, I shall abstract from issues to be discussed in a later argument when discussing an earlier one. I shall begin by discussing the questions of resource allocation in the egalitarian system, assuming that effort is constant and that there is no saving, investing, or risk to be considered. When I turn to the question of effort, I shall abstract from saving, investing, and risk. And when I first discuss saving and investing, I shall assume the absence of risk.

Second, I shall begin by assuming that income-consumption satisfactions play no role in the egalitarian system. This assumption is *not* a logically necessary prerequisite of the egalitarian system. Indeed, when I have completed the discussion of the four arguments about efficiency, I shall show that income-consumption satisfactions would be integral to the egalitarian system and I shall analyze the effects of income-consumption satisfactions in the egalitarian system.

The initial assumption that income-consumption satisfactions play no role is purely a procedural device which will enable me to structure the argument more clearly.

Moral Incentives and Resource Allocation

My assumptions about social-duty satisfactions are unconventional and their meaning may not be obvious. The easiest way to proceed is to introduce examples of individuals in the imaginary systems facing prices and price changes. I shall compare what can be inferred about the behavior of individuals in the imaginary PPM system with what can be inferred about the behavior of individuals in the imaginary egalitarian system. I can then use these examples as the basis for more theoretical discussions of the assumptions. Through these theoretical discussions I should be able to spell out the implications of my assumptions and eliminate any uncertainty as to their meaning.

The Case of Sam Smith, Property Owner

I shall begin by assuming that an individual named Sam Smith exists in my imaginary PPM system and that he owns a factory. I shall further assume that Sam is an old-fashioned profit-maximizer and that his sole goal in life—at least in business life—is to acquire as much income for consumption as he can from his property. Of course, few people (if any) really are profit-maximizers. Fewer still are single-minded about their reasons for pursuing profits. However, economists have frequently found it useful to assume profit-maximization as a goal of property owners (or of firms) in order to explore certain features of the logic of the PPM system. I will use my assumption here for similar purposes.

From the fact that Sam is a profit-maximizer, one can infer a number of things about the way he will respond to prices. For example, one can infer that he will always buy the cheapest raw material, other things being equal (equal quality, equal supply availability, etc.). One can also infer that he will hire the cheapest available labor, given the skills he needs. If one oversimplifies a bit, one can infer that he will determine how much to produce by making the marginal cost of the last unit produced equal to the marginal revenue to be gained by selling that unit. I could add many examples of what can be inferred about Sam's behavior but these should suffice. They are common, familiar assertions about the behavior of profit-maximizing firms or individuals.

Now turn to the imaginary egalitarian system. Since my thought experiment assumes identical individuals, resources, rules, demand, and the like in the imaginary PPM system and the imaginary egalitarian system, Sam Smith would exist in the imaginary egalitarian system, too, and would own the same factory. It is worth pausing here to emphasize the last point. Sam owns the factory in the egalitarian system in the same way that he owns it in the PPM system except that he cannot keep the profits for consumption purposes. (I will leave open here the question of whether he might be able to keep the profits for other purposes such as investment. This will be discussed later in the chapter.) Obviously the one restriction placed on property owners is a very big restriction. Nevertheless, it is important to see that this egalitarian system contains no inherent constraints on economic institutions, methods of organization, property rules, fiscal mechanisms, and so on apart from the requirement that after-tax income for consumption be distributed equally.[4] For example, an egalitarian system could without logical self-contradiction have decentralized control of resources through privately owned corporations, banks, and insurance companies, so long as after-tax income[5] was equally distributed.[6] This organizational flexibility is one factor which distinguishes my egalitarian model from many market socialist models. Of course, the key question is whether the economic institutions, organizations, property rules, and fiscal mechanisms of a PPM system would *work*, given the requirement that after-tax incomes be distributed equally. Why would such things exist in an egalitarian system and, if they did exist, why would they lead the system to function efficiently? To answer these questions we turn back to Sam Smith, the factory owner.

What can one infer about the behavior of Sam Smith from the assumptions I have adopted about the imaginary egalitarian system? It is stipulated in the third assumption that Sam places the same relative value on social-duty satisfactions in the egalitarian system as he placed on income-consumption satisfactions in the PPM system. While the concept "same relative value" will have to be clarified in later contexts, its meaning here is obvious. Sam's sole goal in the PPM system was to maximize income-consumption satisfactions. Therefore his sole goal in the egalitarian system is to maximize social-duty satisfactions, and he can do this by earning as much pre-tax income as possible. And how can he earn as much pre-tax income as possible? By maximizing profits. Therefore in the egalitarian system, too, Sam will be a profit-maximizer. All of the things inferred about his behavior in response to prices in the PPM system will also be true of his response to prices in the egalitarian system. That is, he will buy the cheapest raw material available, hire the cheapest labor available, equate marginal cost to marginal revenue for the last unit. In short, his behavior will be exactly the same in both systems, despite the fact that in the egalitarian system the profits that he acquires will not affect the amount of his income for consumption, except indirectly and in a small way through its effect on the amount of everyone's equal income-share.

The trustee analogy. This idea may still seem strange and perplexing. What is the point of Sam's maximizing profits when it doesn't affect his after-tax income? The answer is that the way Sam and other property owners allocate resources does affect the income of society as a whole. By maximizing profits, Sam is maximizing his contribution to the total social income. Consider, as an analogy, the position of a trustee in a PPM system. The trustee's responsibility is to use the resources which he holds in trust to earn as much income as possible for the individual or institution to whom these resources belong. In effect, the assumptions adopted in the egalitarian model make everyone a trustee for society (or, more precisely, for oneself and one's fellow members in society). Each individual has a responsibility to use the resources he controls—whether property as in Sam's case or labor as in other cases—to earn as much income as he can for society. In the PPM system, the trustee's motive for using the resources to generate income for others is a feeling of duty, not personal gain in income. (Indeed the law forbids trustees from using resources held in trust for personal gain.) In the egalitarian system, the individual's motive for using the resources he controls to generate pre-tax income is a feeling of duty, not personal gain in income, since the effect of one's own pre-tax income on the size of one's after-tax income is bound to be slight in any large society.[7] The tax laws of the egalitarian system prohibit the individual from using the resources he controls for personal gain in income (beyond the gain accorded everyone).

The trustee image is only an analogy intended to help people think about the egalitarian model. Like all analogies it should not be pushed too far. Moreover, it is not intended to provide evidence in support of the plausibility of the egalitarian model. As an aid in understanding the model, however, the analogy can be quite useful.

Other sources of motivation. In the earlier discussion I assumed that, in the PPM system, Sam's only reason for maximizing profits was to acquire income for consumption. I noted then that this assumption was unrealistic, and it may be useful to point out that there could be other motives besides that of acquiring income for consumption which would lead property owners to seek profits. For example, assume now that Sam also derives satisfaction from exercising power over people and over resources in his business, from the prestige he acquires as a successful businessman and from the prospect of passing control over his business to his descendants. Note that these sources of satisfaction are analytically distinct from the acquisition of income for consumption and do not depend upon the expenditure of income for consumption. Assume further that Sam believes that the best way to continue to enjoy all of these satisfactions is to maximize profits. In other words, these are simply additional reasons for Sam to maximize profits. These new goals therefore do not alter Sam's behavior in responding to prices but they do make the motivation behind his behavior less monolithic.

This leads to an important point about the kinds of satisfactions available in the egalitarian system. This system does not require a monolithic motivational structure. Indeed my thought experiment excludes monolithic motivation in the egalitarian system if motivation is not monolithic in the PPM system. I have assumed that individuals in the two systems are identical in all respects except those spelled out by the modifying assumptions. Therefore I must now assume that, in the egalitarian system, Sam derives satisfaction from exercising power over people and over resources in his business, from the prestige he acquires as a successful businessman and from the prospect of passing control over his business to his descendants, *as well as* from performing his social duty to earn as much pre-tax income as possible. All of these new satisfactions are as available to Sam in the egalitarian system as in the PPM system because of the basic assumption that all property rules, other individuals, and so on are identical between the two systems. Equal distribution of after-tax income is logically quite compatible with the inequalities in power, prestige, and opportunity which Sam's other satisfactions entail.

It might be argued that inequalities in power, prestige, and opportunity would be likely in practice to lead to inequalities in the distribution of after-tax income. This is a hypothesis which I shall consider in the next chapter. It might also be argued that inequalities in power, prestige, and opportunity are intrinsically undesirable. This is an important question but it goes beyond the scope of this essay. What is important to note here is that the egalitarian system formally requires only equal distribution of after-tax income, not elimination of all (or any) other social inequalities and that in the imaginary egalitarian model of this chapter this equal distribution of after-tax income can coexist with other important inequalities. What I am emphasizing again is the flexibility of the egalitarian system as a social system.[8]

In the egalitarian system, as in the PPM system, these new motivations would not alter Sam's behavior since here too Sam would believe that the best way to continue to enjoy all of these satisfactions would be to maximize profits. Thus these new motivations would simply provide him with additional reasons to do what his desire for social-duty satisfactions already inclines him to do—to maximize profits.

Property Owners and Relative Values
Arnold and Benedict

Not all motivations are as mutually reinforcing as the ones I have assumed for Sam. Property owners may sometimes find there is conflict among the goals they wish to achieve through the use of their property.[9] For example, assume that there exist in my imaginary PPM system two individuals, Arnold and Benedict, who own widget factories. To simplify matters assume that both Arnold and Benedict have only two sources of satisfaction in life (at least in business life): acquiring income for consumption; making widgets. (If the second assumption seems too implausible, imagine that the widget factories have been in their respective families for generations. Making widgets is a family tradition for both of them.) Now assume that there is a falling demand for widgets. Assume further, that there is an increasing demand for gadgets and that it would be technologically possible to transform both factories into gadget factories. (Assume also that the widget and gadget markets are sufficiently large that whatever Arnold does or does not do has no impact on the prices Benedict faces, and vice versa.)

In this situation, Arnold and Benedict both face a conflict between their goals. Assume, however, that Arnold and Benedict have *different* relative values so that they resolve their conflicts differently. Arnold places a higher relative value on the additional income-consumption satisfactions to be gained from making gadgets than he does on the satisfactions to be gained from continuing in the widget business. Therefore, he transforms his factory and earns as much income for consumption as it is possible for him to do. By contrast, Benedict places a higher relative value on the satisfactions to be gained from making widgets than he does on the satisfactions to be gained from the additional income for consumption he would earn if he produced gadgets. Therefore, he continues making widgets. Each is maximizing his satisfactions, but, because of the different values they place on various satisfactions, only Arnold is maximizing his income-consumption satisfactions. On the other hand, Benedict is still acquiring some income for consumption. He has not foregone this source of satisfactions entirely. He has merely traded the additional satisfactions to be gained from more income for consumption for the satisfactions of continuing in the family business.

Now transpose Arnold and Benedict to the egalitarian system. Social-duty satisfactions replace income-consumption satisfactions as one source of satisfactions.[10] The other source—making widgets—remains the same. The situation Arnold and Benedict face is, of course, the same (declining demand for widgets, rising demand for gadgets). What can be inferred about their behavior in the egalitarian system? To answer this, it is necessary to turn to the third modifying assumption of the egalitarian model: "Individuals in the (egalitarian) system place the same relative value on the satisfactions derived from performing their social duty to acquire pre-tax income as individuals in the PPM system place on the satisfactions derived from acquiring income for consumption.

The meaning of the phrase "same relative value" is quite clear in this context. Arnold places a higher relative value on the additional social-duty satisfactions to be gained from making gadgets, and thus making more pre-tax income, than he does on the satisfactions to be gained from continuing in the widget business. He transforms his factory and earns as much pre-tax income as he can, thus maximizing his social-duty satisfactions. Benedict places a higher relative value on the satisfactions to be gained from making widgets than he does on the additional social-duty satisfactions he could gain from the additional pre-tax income he would earn if he produced gadgets. He continues to produce widgets. Note that Benedict is still earning *some* pre-tax income and is thus still acquiring some social-duty satisfactions. He has merely traded the additional social-duty satisfactions to be gained from more pre-tax income for the satisfactions of continuing in the family business. Again, each of them is maximizing his satisfactions even though only Arnold is maximizing social-duty satisfactions.

Two lessons about the egalitarian system. There are two important points about the egalitarian model to be noted from this case. First, moral incentives perform the same function in the egalitarian system here as income-consumption incentives perform in the PPM system, and the moral incentives operate through the price mechanism. It is the fall in demand for widgets and the rise in demand for gadgets that creates an incentive for Arnold to transform his factory in the egalitarian system as well as in the PPM system.

Second, it should now be clear that the assumption that individuals believe they have a social duty to earn as much pre-tax income as they can does not mean that fulfillment of this duty is an all-or-nothing proposition. The more an individual earns, relative to what he is capable of earning, the more fully he performs this duty and the more of this kind of satisfaction he acquires. In this respect, having a duty to earn as much pre-tax income as one can is no different from having a duty to be as good a parent or citizen as one can or from having an indefinitely great desire for income for consumption in a PPM system. It is perfectly reasonable to feel such duties or desires and yet to find, at some point, that there is conflict among them. Given the variety and complexity of duties and desires which real people have, virtually no one ever maximizes any one kind of satisfaction. The principle of declining marginal utility is well known. At some point one must trade off the satisfactions to be gained from further pursuit of one duty or desire against the satisfactions to be gained from pursuit of another duty or desire. It is perfectly consistent, therefore, to assert both that Benedict believes he has a social duty to acquire as much pre-tax income as he is capable of acquiring and that he places a lower relative value on the additional social-duty satisfactions to be gained by maximizing his pre-tax income than he does on the satisfactions to be gained from staying in the family business.

Price Changes and Trade-offs among Satisfactions

In the case of Arnold and Benedict the meaning of the phrase "same relative value" was obvious, as I said earlier. But this was a very simple case in which I assumed that there were only two sources of satisfaction and that individuals faced a single either-or choice. Most trade-offs which individuals face in the real world are far more complicated than that. Moreover—and this is the key point—the trade-offs individuals face in a PPM system do not remain constant but frequently change as a result of price changes. The key question is whether the three initial assumptions about moral incentives in the egalitarian system really do provide a mechanism such that price changes affect trade-offs between social-duty satisfactions and other satisfactions in the same way that price changes in the PPM system affect trade-offs between income-consumption satisfactions and other satisfactions. The answer to this question will determine whether resource allocation is as efficient in the egalitarian system as it is in the PPM system.

To answer this question I will turn from cases focusing on property owners to cases involving workers, that is, people who must decide how to allocate their labor. Both kinds of cases raise similar questions about resource allocation. The one advantage to cases involving the allocation of labor is that the need for individuals to make trade-offs is more apparent than it is in cases which involve only the allocation of property. Economists do sometimes assume that entrepreneurs and firms maximize profits on the grounds that there are few kinds of important satisfactions sought by entrepreneurs and firms which conflict with maximizing profits. Economists almost always assume, however, that individuals in PPM systems maximize satisfactions, not income. Income is only one source of satisfactions, and individuals may have other conflicting sources of satisfactions such as the satisfactions derived from leisure.[11] Thus the necessity of making trade-offs among satisfactions is more obvious here than in cases which involve only the allocation of property.

Earning capacity. Before considering how price changes affect such trade-offs in the PPM and egalitarian systems, I must clarify one feature of my assumptions about social-duty satisfactions in the egalitarian system. The individual's social duty to earn pre-tax income is defined in terms of what he is capable of earning. ("Individuals . . . believe they have a social duty to earn as much pre-tax income as they are capable of earning.") The amount of social-duty satisfactions an individual acquires thus depends on the amount of pre-tax income that he earns relative to what he is capable of earning, not on the absolute amount of pre-tax income that he earns.

It may be helpful to think of each individual as having an earning capacity (EC), which I shall define as the maximum amount of pre-tax income that he can acquire (max p-t I). This earning capacity may change as a result of price changes and other factors. An individual's full earning capacity would include the pre-tax income he could acquire both from the use of his property and from the use of his labor.[12] For the sake of simplicity, I wish to focus only on the allocation of labor in the following discussion. I shall therefore exclude property from consideration. Let me note in advance, however, that the same principles which govern the allocation of labor resources would also govern the allocation of property resources. If property is excluded, earning capacity is a product of the maximum number of hours a person could work (max H), which could be limited by physical capacity, legal restrictions, available work, and so on, and the highest available wage per hour a person could acquire (max W). His pre-tax income is, of course, a product of the actual hours worked (H) and the actual wage per hour received (W). Finally, the amount of social-duty satisfactions he acquires (SDS) depends on the extent to which he utilizes his earning capacity or, in other words, on the percentage of earning capacity (% EC) at which he performs. To summarize these relationships:

$$EC = \max \text{ p-t } I = \text{Max } H \cdot \max W$$
$$\text{p-t } I = H \cdot W$$
$$SDS = f(\% \ EC) = f(H \cdot W/\max H \cdot \max W)$$

Just as trade-offs between income-consumption satisfactions and other satisfactions (especially leisure) are virtually inevitable in a PPM system, trade-offs between social-duty satisfactions and other satisfactions (especially leisure) are virtually inevitable in an egalitarian system. Almost no one works flat-out. Virtually everyone works at some percentage of earning capacity below 100. The key point is that the amount of social-duty satisfactions an individual acquires depends on the extent to which he utilizes his earning capacity, rather than on the absolute amount of pre-tax income he acquires.

It is important to see how this differs from the PPM system. Individuals in PPM systems do have earning capacities, of course, since "earning capacity" is, by definition, an individual's highest income possibility, and some highest possibility has to exist for everyone. Moreover, individuals in PPM systems do usually work at some percentage of capacity below 100, forgoing possible income-consumption satisfactions for the sake of other satisfactions such as leisure. Nevertheless, the income-consumption satisfactions (I-CS) which individuals do acquire are not tied to earning capacity in the way that social-duty satisfactions are. More income for an individual means more income-consumption satisfactions (other things being equal), regardless of the relation between this increased income and his earning capacity. For example, if a change in demand and/or supply enabled an individual in a PPM system to earn $10 for work for which he had previously been paid $5, he would enjoy more income-consumption satisfactions than before, for any given amount of this work. There is no need to refer to his earning capacity to determine this. By contrast, to determine the effect of such a change on an individual's social-duty satisfactions in the egalitarian system, one would have to know what his earning capacity had been both before and after the change. To put the contrast another way:

In the PPM system I-CS = f(I)
In the egalitarian system SDS = f(p-t I / max p-t I)

Thus the relationship between pre-tax income and social-duty satisfactions in the egalitarian system is more complicated than the relationship between income and income-consumption satisfactions in the PPM system.[13] Pre-tax income dollars are not simply points indicating the amount of social duty done or the amount of social approval gained. The link between social-duty satisfactions and earning capacity may seem to create an unwelcome and unnecessary complication. But this link is essential if the egalitarian system is to avoid replacing the inequality of income-consumption satisfactions in the PPM system with an equivalent inequality of social-duty satisfactions. I shall be able to develop this point only at the end of Chapter 3, after I have identified all of the prerequisites of the egalitarian system. Later in this chapter, however, I will show that the link to earning capacity offers the additional advantage of inducing individuals in the egalitarian system to respond to inflation in the same way that individuals in the PPM system would. Moreover, I will show now that social-duty satisfactions would perform the same functions with respect to resource allocation in the egalitarian system as income-consumption satisfactions perform in the PPM system despite the fact that social-duty satisfactions are tied to pre-tax income differently from the way in which income-consumption satisfactions are tied to income in the PPM system.

The initial trade-off position. Let us return to the question of how prices affect trade-offs among satisfactions in the PPM and egalitarian systems. I shall begin the discussion with another imaginary case. Assume that there is an individual, Jane Jones, who is a bricklayer in my imaginary PPM system and that she earns $5 an hour and works forty hours a week. In this initial position she is presumably making certain trade-offs between the satisfactions derived from acquiring income for consumption and the satisfactions derived from leisure. If she worked more, she could earn more income but she would have less leisure. If she worked less, she would have more leisure and less income. She may also be making other trade-offs as well. For example, assume both that she has the skills to be a plumber or a carpenter as well as a bricklayer and that she likes carpentry better than bricklaying and both of them better than plumbing. Assume, however, that she can earn $6 an hour as a plumber, $5 an hour as a bricklayer, and $4 an hour as a carpenter (see table 1). It follows that she is trading off fewer work satisfactions in favor of more income-consumption satisfactions in choosing to be a bricklayer rather than a carpenter and that she is trading off more work satisfactions in favor of fewer income-consumption satisfactions in choosing to be a bricklayer rather than a plumber. I could assume other kinds of trade-offs as well but these should suffice.

Table 1: Initial Trade-off Position in PPM System

	Carpentry	Bricklaying	Plumbing
Work preference	1	2	3
Wages/hour	$4	$5	$6

Now transpose Jane to the imaginary egalitarian system. Since she places the same relative value on social-duty satisfactions in the egalitarian system that she placed on income-consumption satisfactions, one can infer that she will be a bricklayer in the egalitarian system earning $5 an hour in pre-tax income and working forty hours a week. Again, the meaning of the phrase "same relative value" seems clear in this context. The relative value an individual places on a given satisfaction can be measured by the other satisfactions the individual is willing to give up for the given satisfaction. Thus to assert that Jane places the same relative value on social-duty satisfactions in the egalitarian system as she placed on income-consumption satisfactions in the PPM system is to assert that she will give up the same alternative satisfactions for social-duty satisfactions in the egalitarian system that she gives up for income-consumption satisfactions in the PPM system (and that she will insist on acquiring the same alternative satisfactions at the expense of social-duty satisfactions that she insists on acquiring at the expense of income-consumption satisfactions). The heuristic assumption of identity between the egalitarian and PPM system allows me to construct a situation in which her other possible satisfactions are identical in both cases. It is essential, however, that these other satisfactions be *alternative* to social-duty satisfactions when they are *alternative* to income-consumption satisfactions. That is, it is essential to see that her initial position in the egalitarian system represents a trade-off, although this time the trade-off is between social-duty satisfactions and other satisfactions.

It is easy to see that such a trade-off exists. Take the decision to work forty hours a week. She is making a trade-off between the satisfactions derived from performing her social duty and the satisfactions derived from leisure. If she worked more, she would earn more pre-tax income, she would be utilizing her earning capacity to a higher degree, and she would therefore enjoy more social-duty satisfactions, but she would have less leisure. If she worked less, she would have more leisure but fewer social-duty satisfactions since she would be utilizing less of her earning capacity. Similarly, in choosing to be a bricklayer rather than a carpenter (since I assume the same work options are open to her), she is trading more social-duty satisfactions for fewer work satisfactions. In choosing to be a bricklayer rather than a plumber, she is trading more work satisfactions for fewer social-duty satisfactions. As a bricklayer, she utilizes less of her earning capacity than she would as a plumber and more than she would as a carpenter, keeping hours worked constant (see table 2).

The meaning of "same relative value." It may be objected that my use of the phrase "same relative value" and my description of Jane Jones's position in the egalitarian system assume

Table 2: Initial Trade-off Position in Egalitarian System

	Carpentry	Bricklaying	Plumbing
Work preference	1	2	3
Wages	$4	$5	$6
% EC	4·H/6·max H	5·H/6·max H	6·H/6·max H

Note: H and max H are assumed to be constant.

precisely the point which I ought to prove, namely, that social-duty satisfactions can provide incentives which are as effective as income-consumption satisfactions in inducing efficient economic behavior despite the differences between the two kinds of satisfactions. This is not the case, however.

The phrase "same relative value" was introduced as part of the third assumed modification of the PPM system in my thought experiment. The basic purpose of this assumption was to introduce the idea that social-duty satisfactions were an important source of motivation as an explicit element in the egalitarian model. Obviously there are other possible ways of expressing that point. For example, I could have said "Individuals in the egalitarian system place a great deal of value on the satisfactions derived from performing this social duty." Phrasing the assumption in terms of "same relative value" has two advantages over such alternative formulations, however.

First, it avoids the danger of suggesting that the egalitarian system requires a monolithic motivational pattern. In a PPM system different people place different amounts of value on income-consumption satisfactions. A PPM system would not function efficiently (as I have defined "efficiency") unless most people placed a fairly high value on income-consumption satisfactions, but the value particular individuals place on such satisfactions can vary a great deal within this general constraint. The same is true of the egalitarian system. The egalitarian system would not function efficiently unless most people placed a fairly high value on social-duty satisfactions, but the value particular individuals place on these satisfactions can vary a great deal within this general constraint. The "same relative value" phrase makes clear that the motivational variety characteristic of a PPM system is also compatible with the egalitarian system.

Second, and more important, the phrase "same relative value" serves a similar function to that of the basic assumption of identity between the PPM and egalitarian systems. It serves the function of controlling for irrelevant variables. In this chapter, differences between the potential strengths of income-consumption satisfactions and social-duty satisfactions as basic sources of human motivation would be an irrelevant variable because I am concerned only to explore the *logic* of integrating social-duty satisfactions with the market mechanism. I wish therefore to *assume* here that social-duty satisfactions can be as strong a source of motivation as income-consumption satisfactions. I am able to make this assumption precisely by asserting that individuals in the egalitarian system place the "same relative value" on social-duty satisfactions that individuals in the PPM system place on income-consumption satisfactions.

This leads to the question of whether my description of Jane Jones's position may beg some important questions about the *logic* of the egalitarian system. It would not be correct to use the phrase "same relative value" to avoid questions about the connections between social-duty satisfactions and prices. The question is whether social-duty satisfactions would function differently in a price system from income-consumption satisfactions because social-duty satisfactions are tied to earning capacity while income-consumption satisfactions are not. I did not intend to avoid this question in assuming an initial position in which Jane's trade-off between social-duty satisfactions and other satisfactions in the egalitarian system leads her to the same point as her trade-off between income-consumption satisfactions and other satisfactions in the PPM system. Some such comparable initial position needs to be established precisely so that this question about how social-duty satisfactions work can be faced. For the fundamental question here is whether price *changes* affect behavior in the egalitarian system in the same way that they affect behavior in the PPM system. To put it another way, would changes in supply and demand affect resource allocation through the price mechanism in the egalitarian system in the way that they affect resource-allocation through the price mechanism in the PPM system? To answer that question, one must begin with both systems at the same equilibrium point, in order to see what effects (if any) price changes might have on the equilibrium in each system. Now this is precisely what my description of Jane's initial position in both systems provides, that is, a comparable equilibrium point from which to judge the effects of price changes. My analysis of the trade-offs implicit in Jane's initial position in the egalitarian system is fully justified, given this context. What must be determined now is whether similar price changes in both systems would lead to similar alterations in Jane's incentives in both systems.

Price changes and resource allocation. Since I am concerned primarily with the issue of resource allocation in this section of the chapter, I shall assume that the number of hours Jane is willing and able to work at any given job remains constant at forty hours a week. In the next section, I shall consider how price changes might affect effort in the egalitarian system. In this section I shall focus only on the question of how price changes would affect Jane's willingness to allocate her labor among alternative occupations. By addressing this question I can complete the exposition of the logic which governs resource allocation in the egalitarian model.

First, recall that, at the equilibrium point which I have assumed in the PPM system, Jane is receiving $5 an hour from a firm for working as a bricklayer and that she has the option of working for $6 an hour as a plumber and for $4 an hour as a carpenter. Recall as well that, other things being equal, she would prefer bricklaying to plumbing and would prefer carpentry to both.

Now, suppose that a rival firm which also used to pay bricklayers $5.00 an hour begins to pay $5.50 an hour and that there are openings for bricklayers in this firm. How will this price change affect Jane's behavior? Other things being equal, she will take the new job because by doing so she can increase her income-consumption satisfactions while maintaining her work satisfactions at the current level. Of course, other things might not be equal. For example, she might have friends in the old plant and none in the new, or she might like the location of the old plant better. If one wishes to include the possibility of such other unspecified factors playing a role, one can simply say that the price change will increase the attractiveness of working for the other firm in terms of income-consumption satisfactions and will create an incentive for Jane to shift jobs. (The question of whether she actually shifts can be left open.)

Now, starting with the same equilibrium point in the egalitarian system, consider the effect of the same price change. How will it affect Jane's behavior? Other things being equal, she will take the new job in the firm paying $5.50 an hour because by doing so she can utilize more of her earning capacity and thus increase her social-duty satisfactions while maintaining her work satisfactions at the current level. Again, other things may not be equal, so that, if one wishes to leave open the possibility of other factors playing a role, one can simply say that the price change will increase the attractiveness of working for the other firm in terms of social-duty satisfactions and will create an incentive for Jane to shift jobs. (Again, the question of whether she actually shifts can be left open.)

As a second example, suppose that the wages of plumbers increase from $6 to $7 an hour while those of bricklayers and carpenters remain the same. How will this affect Jane's incentives in the PPM and egalitarian systems? In the PPM system it will clearly increase the incentives for her to work as a plumber because the difference between what she can earn as a plumber and what she can earn as a bricklayer will now be greater than it was before. Whether these increased incentives will be sufficient to induce her to become a plumber depends on how much she likes money and how much she dislikes plumbing. To put it more formally, it will depend on the relative value she places on the additional income-consumption satisfactions to be acquired from work as a plumber as over against the relative value she places on the additional work satisfactions to be gained from working as a bricklayer. Note that my earlier assumption about the relative value she placed on work satisfactions and income-consumption satisfactions when the plumber's job paid $6 an hour does not permit one to draw any conclusion about what her choice would be now that the price of plumbers' wages has changed. She still might think the difference in income was not worth the more unpleasant character of the work, and she might continue to work as a bricklayer. Alternatively, she might think that the difference in income was now sufficient to overcome the disadvantages of the work, and she might decide to work as a plumber. What one can conclude, however, is that the price change has created stronger incentives for her to work as a plumber than previously existed (see table 3).

Table 3: Wage Increase in Alternative Job in PPM System

	Carpentry	Bricklaying	Plumbing
Work preference	1	2	3
Wages before change	$4	$5	$6
Wages after change	$4	$5	$7
Effect on incentives	−	−	+

What conclusions can be drawn about the effects of this price change in the egalitarian system? One can conclude exactly the same thing, that the price change will create stronger incentives for Jane to work as a plumber. The fact that Jane can now earn $7 an hour in pre-tax income if she works as a plumber means that the difference between the pre-tax income she can earn as a plumber and the pre-tax income she can earn as a bricklayer will now be greater than before. Thus the difference between the percentage of her earning capacity that she will utilize if she works as a plumber and the percentage of her earning capacity that she will utilize if she works as a bricklayer is now greater than it was before. Thus the difference between the amount of social-duty satisfactions she will receive if she works as a plumber and the amount of social-duty satisfactions she will receive if she works as a bricklayer is now greater than before. In terms of social-duty satisfactions, the option of working as a plumber has been made relatively more attractive in comparison with the option of working as a bricklayer. Again, one cannot conclude anything definite about whether she will choose to work as a plumber. This depends on the relative value she places on the difference in social-duty satisfactions between the two jobs as over against the relative value she places on the difference in work satisfactions between the two jobs. As in the PPM system, the terms of trade have changed as a consequence of the price change, but without some additional assumptions about her relative values one cannot determine what choice she will make. What one can conclude, however, is that the price change in the egalitarian system has increased the relative attractiveness of working as a plumber, just as the price change in the PPM system increased the relative attractiveness of working as a plumber (see table 4).

Table 4: Wage Increase in Alternative Job in Egalitarian System

	Carpentry	Bricklaying	Plumbing
Work preference	1	2	3
Wages before change	$4	$5	$6
% EC before change	4·40/6·max H	5·40/6·max H	6·40/6·max H
Wages after change	$4	$5	$7
% EC after change	4·40/7·max H	5·40/7·max H	7·40/7·max H
Effect on incentives	−	−	+

Note: max H is assumed to be constant.

Both of the price changes I have considered so far have been price increases. It may be useful to consider the effects of a price decrease. Suppose that the wages of bricklayers drop from $5 an hour to $4 an hour. How does this price change affect incentives in the PPM system? First, it makes the option of working as a bricklayer relatively less attractive in comparison with the options of working as a carpenter or as a plumber. In fact, one can definitely infer that Jane will not work as a bricklayer. I assumed earlier that she preferred working as a carpenter to working as a bricklayer. This price change has made the income-consumption satisfactions to be had from working as a carpenter equal to those to be had from working as a bricklayer. Other things being equal, Jane can now gain more satisfactions working as a carpenter than as a bricklayer since she can gain the same amount of income-consumption satisfactions from both and more work satisfactions from carpentry. One cannot conclude, however, that Jane will necessarily take up work as a carpenter. The same price change which has decreased the relative attractiveness of bricklaying in relation to carpentry has decreased the relative attractiveness of bricklaying in relation to plumbing. There is now a $2 an hour wage differential between plumbing on the one hand and both carpentry and bricklaying on the other. It is impossible to say whether Jane will value the greater work satisfactions to be gained from carpentry more than the greater income-consumption satisfactions to be gained from plumbing, or vice versa. Therefore, while one can infer that she will not work as a bricklayer, one cannot determine which of the other two options she will choose (see table 5).

Table 5: Wage Decrease in Current Job in PPM System

	Carpentry	Bricklaying	Plumbing
Work preference	1	2	3
Wages before change	$4.00	$5.00	$6.00
Wages after change	$4.00	$4.00	$6.00
Effect on incentives	+	−	+

In the egalitarian system the price change has equivalent effects. It makes the option of working as a bricklayer relatively less attractive in comparison with the options of working as a carpenter or as a plumber. The price change makes the social-duty satisfactions to be had from working as a carpenter equal to those to be had from working as a bricklayer. Again, since it is known that Jane prefers the work of carpentry to that of bricklaying, one can infer that she will no longer work as a bricklayer. However, the price change which has decreased the relative attractiveness of bricklaying in relation to carpentry in terms of social-duty satisfactions has also decreased the relative attractiveness of bricklaying in relation to plumbing. The gap between them in pre-tax income and thus in social-duty satisfactions has been made greater. Again, it is impossible to say whether Jane will value the greater work satisfactions to be gained from carpentry more than the greater social-duty satisfactions to be had from plumbing, or vice versa. One cannot determine which of these options she will choose, although one can conclude that she will no longer be a bricklayer (see table 6).

Table 6: Wage Decrease in Current Job in Egalitarian System

	Carpentry	Bricklaying	Plumbing
Work preference	1	2	3
Wages before change	$4	$5	$6
% EC before change	4·40/6·max H	5·40/6·max H	6·40/6·max H
Wages after change	$4	$4	$6
% EC after change	4·40/6·max H	4·40/6·max H	6·40/6·max H
Effect on incentives	+	−	+

Note: max H is assumed to be constant.

Conclusions About Resource Allocation in the Egalitarian System

In trying to generalize on the basis of these three cases, it may be useful to recall that the rational-actor framework adopted for this chapter assumes that each individual ranks the options available to him on the basis of their relative attractiveness. I would suggest that we can extrapolate from these cases to the following general principles. Any price change which increases the relative attractiveness of a job in terms of income-consumption satisfactions in the PPM system will increase the relative attractiveness of the job in terms of social-duty satisfactions in the egalitarian system. Any price change which decreases the relative attractiveness of a job in terms of income-consumption satisfactions in the PPM system will decrease the relative attractiveness of that job in terms of social-duty satisfactions in the egalitarian system.

These principles are of great importance. If the market is functioning properly, any relative increase in the wages paid for a particular occupation reflects an increase in the relative scarcity of workers in that occupation, either because the demand for such workers has increased or the supply of such workers has decreased, or both. If workers respond to such increases, the allocation of labor resources will be more efficient for two reasons. First, workers already in that occupation will work for those firms where their marginal productivity is highest, since these firms will be the ones which can afford the greatest increase. Second, workers from other occupations will be drawn into the occupation whose wages are increasing, thus increasing the supply of labor within that occupation. Similarly any relative decrease in the wages paid for a particular occupation reflects a decrease in the relative scarcity of workers in that occupation. If resources are to be allocated efficiently, such a decrease should create incentives for workers to leave that occupation.

The cases I have just discussed and the principles that I have extracted from them show that moral incentives in the egalitarian system function like income incentives in the PPM system in inducing workers to allocate their labor in accordance with the relative scarcity of that labor. The earlier discussion of cases of property owners in the egalitarian system showed that, for them too, moral incentives functioned like income incentives in providing inducements for them to allocate their property to its most productive use as indicated by relative prices. Thus I have shown that the three assumptions of the egalitarian model do provide a mechanism comparable to that of the PPM model for one critical factor affecting the efficiency of politico-economic systems, namely, the allocation of resources according to relative scarcity. Given these assumptions, the forces of supply and demand would work through the price mechanism to control the allocation of resources in the egalitarian system just as they do in the PPM system.

Price Changes and Effort

Allocation of available resources in accordance with their relative scarcity is not the only factor affecting the efficiency of politico-economic systems. I turn now therefore to the question of how the amount of resources available for production would be affected by the egalitarian model which I have constructed. I shall focus first on the question of effort and later on the question of saving and investment. For my purposes, effort can be measured simply in terms of the number of hours worked.[14]

The three assumptions about the egalitarian system which I adopted at the beginning of this chapter permit one to infer, as a starting point for analysis, some equilibrium point at which individuals in the egalitarian system are working as hard as individuals in the PPM system. In other words, if the various trade-offs that an individual in the PPM system makes among his alternative satisfactions lead him to work forty hours a week (at a given job) in the PPM system, then the trade-offs the same individual makes among his alternative satisfactions in the egalitarian system will lead him to work forty hours a week (at the same job) in that system. In this section, for the sake of simplicity, I shall treat the question of trade-offs among satisfactions as though it were simply a question of the trade-off between income-consumption satisfactions and leisure satisfactions in the PPM system and of the trade-off between social-duty satisfactions and leisure satisfactions in the egalitarian system. (All other satisfactions and preferences are identical in the two systems anyway, given my basic assumption of identity between the two systems.) Moreover, in my discussion of effort I shall not consider the option of changing from one job to another, since the principles governing such cases have been adequately discussed in the preceding section.

The discussion of the "same relative value" assumption in the last section spelled out the rationale for beginning analysis at an identical equilibrium point in the two systems. Of course, most of those who argue that equal distribution would reduce effort are arguing that moral incentives would be a less powerful source of motivation than income incentives. In assuming an identical equilibrium point, I am inevitably ignoring this argument. The neglect is merely temporary, however. In the next chapter, I will discuss the conditions which would have to be satisfied in order for social-duty satisfactions to be as powerful a source of motivation in the egalitarian system as income-consumption satisfactions are in the PPM system. Here I am only concerned with the problem of how moral incentives can be integrated with the market mechanism. As we shall see, however, this logical inquiry can also raise questions about whether the level of effort would tend to decline more in the egalitarian system than in the PPM system. The fundamental question which I must address here is how price changes would affect effort in the two systems.

Inflation and Effort

One kind of price change which is familiar to everyone in contemporary society is a price increase caused by inflation. It is frequently important to try to determine how much of a price increase is "purely inflationary." For example, if one asks whether we are spending more or less today than we did ten years ago on military weapons or education, it is essential not to compare expenditures in 1967 dollars with expenditures in 1977 dollars, since there has been considerable inflation during that time. If the cumulative inflation rate for those ten years has been 50 percent and if we spent $100 billion on military weapons in 1967 and are spending $150 billion on them in 1977, then it is fair to say that the increase in dollar spending is purely inflationary. The real cost has not changed. By contrast, if we now spend $200 billion, we would conclude that there has been a 33⅓ percent increase in the size of expenditures. Of the $100 billion price increase, the first $50 billion is a purely inflationary component. The remaining $50 billion is a real increase but is worth only as much as $33⅓ billion in 1967. For the same reason an increase in dollar spending to $125 billion would represent a decrease in real spending.

Analytically it is useful to try to isolate the purely inflationary component of price changes in order to see what effect (if any) purely inflationary price changes would have on effort in the PPM and egalitarian systems. The way I will do this is to assume that there is a general inflation which affects all goods and services equally so that all prices double in the imaginary PPM and egalitarian systems. Thus there are no changes in any *relative* costs in the systems. This assumption is obviously quite unrealistic. Various factors contribute to inflation, but any one factor will tend to affect some goods and services more than others. For example, an increase in oil prices affects goods and services which utilize oil most directly, though it may affect others as well through a ripple effect. Nevertheless, economists frequently adopt unrealistic assumptions (e.g., that of perfect competition) in order to explore the logic of particular features of politico-economic systems. I am engaged in a similar task here in isolating the purely inflationary component of a price increase from its effect on relative costs. Moreover, the assumption that there is a general inflation will provide an opportunity to spell out some of the reasons for linking social-duty satisfactions to earning capacity in the egalitarian system.

In the PPM system an inflationary price change of the kind I am assuming would have no effect on anyone's willingness to work, if one assumes that individual preferences with regard to satisfactions remain unchanged. Prior to the inflation, each individual would have made certain trade-offs among the satisfactions available to him, including income-consumption satisfactions and leisure satisfactions. For example, in the earlier discussion I assumed that Jane Jones had chosen to work forty hours a week at the rate of $5 an hour. The inflationary price change which I have assumed here would not alter the terms on which alternative satisfactions would be available to Jane or anyone else. Consider the trade-off between income-consumption satisfactions and leisure. Jane would now be earning $10 an hour since the price for her services would have doubled, but the goods and services on which she would spend her income would also have doubled in price. To maintain the same level of consumption, she would still have to work forty hours a week. Since I have assumed that preferences with regard to satisfactions have not changed, I can infer that she would continue to work forty hours a week. In short, the level of effort in the PPM system would remain the same despite the price change.

In the egalitarian system I can also infer that this inflationary price change would have no effect on willingness to work if one assumes that individual preferences with regard to satisfactions remain unchanged. Again, prior to the inflation, each individual would have made certain trade-offs among the satisfactions available to him, including social-duty satisfactions and leisure satisfactions. Under my earlier assumptions, Jane Jones had made these trade-offs by choosing to work forty hours a week for $5 an hour in pre-tax income. Again, the inflationary price change which I have assumed would not alter the terms on which alternative satisfactions would be available. Consider the trade-off between social-duty satisfactions and leisure satisfactions. Jane would now be earning $10 an hour in pre-tax income but her earning capacity would also have doubled (since the price of all services would have doubled). Thus to work at the same percentage of her earning capacity, she would still have to work forty hours a week. Since social-duty satisfactions depend upon the percentage of earning capacity at which one works and not upon the dollar amount of one's pre-tax income, Jane would still have to work forty hours a week to maintain her previous level of social-duty satisfactions. And since I have assumed that preferences with regard to satisfactions have not changed, I can infer that she would continue to work forty hours a week. In short, the level of effort in the egalitarian system would remain the same despite the price change.

The importance of the link to earning capacity. It is important to see how the conclusion regarding level of effort in the egalitarian system would have been altered if I had adopted somewhat different assumptions about the nature of social-duty satisfactions in the egalitarian system. Suppose that I had assumed that social-duty satisfactions depended simply upon the amount of pre-tax income that one earned, so that the more pre-tax income one acquired, the more social-duty satisfactions one received. If I had adopted this assumption I could not have concluded here that the assumed inflation would have had no effect upon effort in the egalitarian system. Under the proposed assumption, the only measure an individual would have of the extent to which he would be doing his social duty would be the dollar amount of his pre-tax income. Thus a purely inflationary increase in pre-tax income would theoretically increase everyone's social-duty satisfactions. The inflation I assumed earlier *would* change the terms on which social-duty satisfactions were available. For example, under the proposed assumption and given the hypothetical inflation, Jane Jones could work only twenty hours a week and receive the same social-duty satisfactions that she had previously gained from working forty hours a week since her pre-tax income in both cases would be $200 a week. It does not follow that she would necessarily reduce her effort since she might prefer to continue working forty hours in order to earn more pre-tax income than before and to enjoy more social-duty satisfactions, but it is possible that she would reduce her effort.

The major point is this. In the PPM system, an individual who bases his work effort on the desire for income-consumption satisfactions will automatically[15] take into account not only the money amount of his income but the actual amount of goods and services which the money can buy. This does not ensure that individuals will never reduce their work effort in PPM systems, as we shall see, but it does ensure that they will not reduce effort in response to purely inflationary price changes, if their preferences remain constant. In the egalitarian system, by contrast, the link between effort and consumption is necessarily cut by the requirement that income be distributed equally. However, in constructing a mechanism which can substitute for income-consumption satisfactions in inducing individuals in the egalitarian model to respond to prices, one should try to build in some feature which would lead individuals to disregard purely inflationary price changes when deciding how much effort to put forward. Now this is precisely what my original assumption about social-duty satisfactions accomplishes. In this respect the link between social-duty satisfactions and earning capacity is able to affect effort in the egalitarian system in the same way that consumption affects effort in the PPM system. I shall point out in Chapter 3 that there are also egalitarian reasons for linking social-duty satisfactions to earning capacity, but for the moment the automatic adaptation to inflation which this linkage provides seems sufficient justification.

Other Price Changes: The Income and Substitution Effects

Turn now to the question of how price changes which are not purely inflationary might affect willingness to work in the PPM and egalitarian systems. I indicated earlier that I would regard the number of hours an individual chooses to work in the PPM system as a trade-off between income-consumption satisfactions and leisure satisfactions. There are two kinds of price changes which might affect income-consumption satisfactions and therefore might affect an individual's willingness to work in the PPM system: a change in the price paid for his labor (an increase or decrease in his wage rate) and a change in the total price which he pays for the goods and services he consumes (an increase or decrease in his cost of living). I shall consider the effects of both separately and then consider their interaction.

Wage increase and effort in the PPM system. Begin by assuming that Jane Jones receives a raise from $5 an hour to $7.50 an hour and that all other prices remain constant. How will this raise affect Jane's effort in the PPM and egalitarian systems?

In the PPM system a wage increase of this kind has two contradictory effects. On the one hand, it creates incentives for individuals to reduce their efforts and to devote more time to leisure, since they can do so without foregoing any of the income-consumption satisfactions they have enjoyed before. For example, Jane could cut her working hours from forty hours a week to thirty hours a week, thus gaining ten more hours of leisure, and yet she would still have more income for consumption than she had before she received the raise. In other words, she can afford more leisure. Economists call this the income effect.

On the other hand, the wage increase creates incentives to increase effort and to devote less time to leisure since each additional hour of work is rewarded with more income for consumption than before. Jane is giving up $7.50 instead of $5 for each hour when she could work but chooses not to. In other words, the price of leisure has risen in relation to the price of other goods, which creates an incentive to substitute other goods for leisure. Economists call this the substitution effect.

Without knowing an individual's preferences with respect to leisure and consumption, one cannot tell whether the income effect will be more powerful than the substitution effect, or vice versa. Thus one cannot determine whether the wage increase will induce Jane to work more hours or fewer hours. Indeed the income and substitution effects could balance each other perfectly and she could continue to work the same number of hours, but again there is no way to determine this without adopting additional assumptions regarding her preferences.

Wage reduction and effort in the PPM system. If Jane were to receive a reduction in her hourly wage rather than an increase, the income and substitution effects would work in exactly the opposite direction though the net result would still be indeterminate.[16] On the one hand, she would have an incentive to increase her effort in order to maintain her income-consumption standards at the established level. For example, at $4 an hour Jane would have to work fifty hours a week to acquire as much income for consumption as she had acquired from forty hours of work at $5 an hour (the income effect). On the other hand, the reduction would provide her with an incentive to decrease effort and to devote more time to leisure since she would forgo only $4 of income-consumption satisfactions instead of $5 for each additional hour of work. In other words, the price change would create an incentive to substitute leisure satisfactions for income-consumption satisfaction (the substitution effect). As in the previous case, it is impossible to determine the net impact of these contradictory effects without assuming some additional knowledge about Jane's preferences.

Cost of living price change and effort in the PPM system. Like a change in the wage rate, a change in the total price of the goods and services which one consumes can affect income-consumption satisfactions and therefore effort in the PPM system. In effect, a change in one's cost of living works in exactly the opposite way as a change in the wage rate. That is, an increase in the cost of living functions like a decrease in the wage rate and a decrease in the cost of living functions like an increase in the wage rate. Let us assume that Jane's wages are held constant at $5 an hour but that she finds that she would have to pay $220 for the goods and services she used to be able to purchase each week for $200. Obviously this creates an incentive for her to increase the number of hours she works in order to acquire sufficient income to maintain her current level of consumption (income effect), but it also creates an incentive for her to reduce effort since leisure has become less costly in relation to the goods and services she consumes (substitution effect).[17] By contrast, if the cost of goods and services she consumes decreases from $200 to $180 and if wages remain constant, she could reduce her working hours and still enjoy the same level of consumption (income effect), or she could increase her working hours and acquire even more goods and services than she could have before (substitution effect). Again, one cannot determine what the net impact of these two contradictory effects will be without assuming something more about Jane's preferences with regard to the trade-off between income-consumption satisfactions and leisure satisfactions.

Interaction of wage change and cost of living change. The two kinds of price changes could occur simultaneously with the effects of a wage increase (decrease) counteracting the effects of a cost of living increase (decrease) to the extent that they coincide. Therefore, an individual receiving a wage increase must subtract any increase in the cost of living from this wage increase to determine whether he is receiving a net gain or loss in his income for consumption. If there is no net gain or loss (as in the case of a purely inflationary price change), his effort will remain unchanged for the reasons given in the discussion of purely inflationary price changes. If there is a net gain or loss, the change in his effort (if any) depends on what is assumed about the relative strengths of the income and substitution effects.

Price Changes and Effort in the Egalitarian System

Turn now to the question of how price changes which are not purely inflationary affect effort in the egalitarian system. In this system, the number of hours an individual works reflects a trade-off between social-duty satisfactions and leisure satisfactions (rather than between income-consumption satisfactions and leisure satisfactions). Like effort in the PPM system, effort in the egalitarian system can be affected by changes in two kinds of prices, but one of the prices which can affect effort in the egalitarian system is different from one of the prices which can affect effort in the PPM system. In the PPM system, as we have just seen, the income-consumption satisfactions an individual enjoys can be affected not only by a change in the wage rate for his job but also by a change in the cost of living. By contrast, social-duty satisfactions cannot be affected by any change in the cost of living since they depend only on the percentage of earning capacity at which one works.

The only price changes which can affect social-duty satisfactions and thus affect the trade-off between them and leisure satisfactions are a change in the wage rate for the job an individual currently holds and/or a change in the wage rate for the most highly paid position open to him, since either kind of change can affect the percentage of earning capacity at which he is working. These two kinds of price changes which can affect effort in the egalitarian system both have contradictory effects which are quite similar to the income and substitution effects of price changes in the PPM system, although there are some important differences, as we shall see.

Wage increase and effort in the egalitarian system. I will begin by considering the effect of a wage raise which would increase the percentage of earning capacity at which an individual works. For example, assume that Jane Jones is working forty hours a week as a bricklayer and earning $5 an hour in pre-tax income and that she could work as a plumber and earn $7 an hour. Now assume that she receives a wage increase to $6 an hour while the wage she could earn as a plumber remains constant at $7 an hour. If she continued to work forty hours a week as a bricklayer she would be working at a higher percentage of earning capacity than she was before (see table 7).

Table 7: Wage Increase with Effort Constant

	Before Change	After Change
Wages	$5	$6
Hours	40	40
% EC	$5 \cdot 40/7 \cdot \max H = 200/7 \cdot \max H$	$6 \cdot 40/7 \cdot \max H = 240/7 \cdot \max H$

Note: max H is assumed to be constant. The 7 in the denominator = max W = wage for working as plumber.

On the one hand, a price change of this kind creates incentives for individuals to reduce their efforts and to devote more time to leisure, since they can do so without foregoing any of the social-duty satisfactions they enjoyed previously. Jane could cut her working hours from forty a week to thirty-five, thus gaining five more hours of leisure, and yet she would still be working at a higher percentage of earning capacity than before (see table 8). Since she would be working at a higher percentage of earning capacity, she would be receiving more social-duty satisfactions despite the cutback in effort. In other words she could "afford" more leisure (measuring affordability in terms of social-duty satisfactions). This effect of the price change is obviously similar to the income effect in the PPM system, and so I shall label it the "social-duty income effect."

On the other hand, the same wage increase creates incentives to increase effort and to devote less time to leisure, since the pre-tax income received for each additional hour of work represents a higher percentage of one's earning capacity than before and thus provides more social-duty satisfactions than before. The $6 in pre-tax income which Jane would give

Table 8: Wage Increase with Effort Reduced

	Before Change	After Change
Wages	$5	$6
Hours	40	35
% EC	$5 \cdot 40/7 \cdot \max H =$ $200/7 \cdot \max H$	$6 \cdot 35/7 \cdot \max H =$ $210/7 \cdot \max H$

Note: max H is assumed to be constant. The 7 in the denominator = max W = wage for working as plumber.

up for each hour she did not work would be closer to her $7 per hour maximum than the $5 she was giving up before. In other words, the cost of leisure has risen as measured by social-duty satisfactions foregone for each hour of leisure.

$$[\text{SDS before change} = f(5 \cdot H/7 \cdot \max H)] < [f(6 \cdot H/7 \cdot \max H) = \text{SDS after change}]$$

This effect of the price change is obviously similar to the substitution effect in the PPM system, and so I shall label it the "social-duty substitution effect."

Just as the net impact of the income and substitution effects cannot be determined in the PPM system without adopting additional assumptions, so too one cannot determine whether the social-duty income effect or the social-duty substitution effect will be more powerful unless one adopts some additional assumptions regarding preferences.

Wage reduction and effort in the egalitarian system. If Jane were to receive a wage reduction which decreased the percentage of earning capacity at which she worked, the social-duty income effect and the social-duty substitution effect would work in the opposite direction from that of the wage increase. On the one hand, she would have an incentive to increase her effort in order to maintain her social-duty satisfactions at the established level. For example, at $4 an hour in pre-tax income Jane would have to work fifty hours a week to perform at the same percentage of capacity and to receive the same social-duty satisfactions as she had from forty hours of work at $5 an hour, assuming that the alternative of working as a plumber for $7 an hour remained constant ($4 \cdot 50/7 \cdot \max H = 5 \cdot 40/7 \cdot \max H$). This is the social-duty income effect. On the other hand, the reduction would provide her with an incentive to decrease effort and to devote more time to leisure, since the pre-tax income foregone for each hour of leisure represents a lower percentage of her earning capacity than before and thus would provide fewer social-duty satisfactions than before ($4 \cdot H/7 \cdot \max H < 5 \cdot H/7 \cdot \max H$). This is the social-duty substitution effect. Again the net impact of these two contradictory effects cannot be determined without additional assumptions about preferences.

Earning capacity, price change, and effort in the egalitarian system. Like a change in the wage rate of the job in which an individual is employed, a change in the wage rate of the highest-paid occupation open to him can affect the social-duty satisfactions he receives in the egalitarian system. Like the cost-of-living price change in the PPM system, a change in the wage rate of the highest-paid occupation open to an individual works in exactly the opposite way as a change in the wage rate of the job in which the individual is employed. That is, an increase in the wage rate of the highest-paid occupation open to an individual affects social-duty satisfactions like a decrease in the wage rate of the job in which the individual is employed, and vice versa.

For example, assume that Jane's wages as a bricklayer are held constant at $5 an hour but that wages for plumbers increase from $7 an hour to $8 an hour (in pre-tax income). Each hour that she works as a bricklayer now provides a lower return in social-duty satisfactions than before because her earning capacity has increased and $5 represents a lower percentage of that earning capacity than before.

[SDS before change = $f(5 \cdot H/7 \cdot \max H)] > [f(5 \cdot H/8 \cdot \max H)$ = SDS after change]

On the one hand, this creates an incentive for her to increase effort in order to maintain her previous level of social-duty satisfactions (social-duty income effect). On the other hand, it creates an incentive for her to reduce effort since leisure has become less costly in relation to the social-duty satisfactions she can obtain by working as a bricklayer (social-duty substitution effect).

To consider the effects of a decrease in the highest-paid occupation open to an individual, assume that Jane's wages as a bricklayer are held constant at $5 an hour but that wages for plumbers decrease from $7 an hour to $6 an hour (in pre-tax income). Each hour that she works as a bricklayer now provides more social-duty satisfactions than before.

[SDS before change = $f(5 \cdot H/7 \cdot \max H)$] < [$f(5 \cdot H/6 \cdot \max H)$ = SDS after change]

She could reduce her working hours and still enjoy the same level of social-duty satisfactions as before (social-duty income effect) or she could increase her working hours and acquire even more social-duty satisfactions than she could have before (social-duty substitution effect).

In both of these examples, one cannot determine what the net impact of the two contradictory effects will be without assuming something more about Jane's preferences with regard to the trade-off between social-duty satisfactions and leisure satisfactions. The behavioral impact of either change is indeterminate.

Price changes which do not change % EC. There is one important kind of case which I have not considered in the examples, namely, the case in which an individual is already working at the job which pays him the highest wage rate he can obtain and in which the price change, whether it is an increase or a decrease, does not alter the fact that he is working at his highest wage rate. In such a case, the price change would have no effect upon the amount of effort the individual would put forth since the price change would not affect the percentage of capacity at which the individual was working. For example, suppose that Henry Jones is working as a secretary for $6 an hour and that this is the highest wage he can obtain in any occupation that is open to him. The percentage of capacity at which he is working would be calculated as follows: % EC = 6·H/6·max H. Now suppose that he receives a wage increase to $7 an hour and that this is still his highest wage possibility. His percentage of earning capacity would now be calculated: % EC = 7·H/7·max H. But 6·H/6·max H = H/max H =7·H/7·max H. Therefore, his percentage of capacity has not changed. Similarly, a wage reduction would not alter the percentage of capacity at which he worked so long as the reduced wage remained his highest wage possible. For example, suppose his wage were reduced to $5 per hour. Then, % EC = 5·H/5·max H = H/max H. But H/max H = 6·H/6·max H. In other words, in this kind of case, the price change has no impact on the trade-off between social-duty satisfactions and leisure satisfactions because the effects of the wage change counteract exactly the effects of the earning capacity change (and vice versa). If Henry worked forty hours before the price change, he would have to work forty hours after the price change in order to enjoy the same amounts of social-duty and leisure satisfactions.

Actually this type of case may be considered a special subset of a larger set of cases in which one can infer that price changes will have no impact on behavior in the egalitarian system because the price changes do not alter the percentage of capacity at which the individual is working. I have made clear that an individual's social-duty satisfactions depend upon the percentage of capacity at which he is working. Since both the wage rate of the job at which he is actually working and the wage rate of the highest-paid job he could obtain affect the percentage of capacity at which he is working, he must take both into account in determining how price changes have affected his social-duty satisfactions. If there is no change in percentage of capacity when both prices have been taken into account, the individual's effort will remain unchanged. We have already seen another example of this in the discussion of purely inflationary changes in the egalitarian system. To express the point more generally and more formally, so long as $W_1/\max W_1 = W_2/\max W_2$, then the number of hours worked (H) will remain constant (assuming that preferences remain constant).

*Summary and Comparison of Effects of
Price Changes on Both Systems*

Table 9 provides a summary and comparison of the possible effects of various price changes on effort in the PPM and egalitarian systems. The situation just considered is one in which the pluses and minuses of a wage increase (decrease) in the egalitarian system are exactly balanced by the pluses and minuses of an earning capacity increase (decrease). As we have seen before, it is also possible for the pluses and minuses of a wage increase (decrease) in the PPM system to be exactly balanced by the pluses and minuses of a cost of living increase (decrease).

Table 9: Effects of Price Changes on Effort

	PPM System	
	Income Effect	Substitution Effect
Wage increase	−	+
Wage decrease	+	−
Cost-of-living increase	+	−
Cost-of-living decrease	−	+

	Egalitarian System	
	Social-Duty Income Effect	Social-Duty Substitution Effect
Wage increase	−	+
Wage decrease	+	−
Earning capacity increase	+	−
Earning capacity decrease	−	+

What can one conclude from all this about the net effects of price changes on effort in the egalitarian system as compared with the PPM system? Unfortunately, one can conclude very little. The parallels suggested by the table make it tempting to conclude that price changes would affect effort in the same way in both systems. One can *not* use the "same relative value" assumption as a basis for inferring this, however, because the earning-capacity price which affects effort in the egalitarian system is different from the cost-of-living price which affects effort in the PPM system. Thus a price change which might affect effort in the egalitarian system might not affect it in the PPM system and vice versa. Given the indeterminacy of the effects of price changes on effort in both systems, there is no specific assumption we could adopt in order to create a mechanism which would ensure that price changes would not reduce effort in the egalitarian system more than in the PPM system (or increase effort in the PPM system more than in the egalitarian system). On the other hand, there is no a priori logical reason to assume that price changes would reduce effort more in the egalitarian system than in the PPM system or that they would increase effort more in the PPM system than in the egalitarian system. Therefore I shall simply have to consider in the next chapter whether there is any empirical evidence which suggests how price changes tend to affect effort in the PPM system and, if there is, I shall have to try to determine how this might affect the set of empirical conditions which would have to be satisfied in order for the egalitarian system to generate the same levels of effort as the PPM system.

One key difference. In this connection, there *is* one systematic difference between the ways price changes affect effort in the two systems which one can infer from a purely logical analysis of the two models and which may help to evaluate the empirical evidence which I shall consider in the next chapter. Because social-duty satisfactions depend upon the percentage of capacity at which individuals work and are not affected by changes in the cost of living, the motivational mechanism of the egalitarian system tends to filter out the effects of economic growth (or decline) in the same way that it filters out purely inflationary price changes. For example, suppose that increases in labor productivity lead to a 10 percent across-the-board increase in wages while the prices of consumer goods remain constant. In the PPM system, such an increase would affect the trade-off between income-consumption satisfactions and leisure satisfactions, as we have seen. In the egalitarian system, however, the trade-off between social-duty satisfactions and leisure satisfactions would remain unchanged. In other words, there would be no social-duty income effect or social-duty substitution effect since the 10 percent increase in wage rates would merely raise everyone's actual wage rate and everyone's highest possible wage rate by 10 percent and would leave everyone working at the same percentage of capacity. Effort would remain at the same level, despite the real change in productive output.

Of course, it is unlikely that productivity gains (or losses) would affect all wages at the same rate, but it is not so unlikely that in the long run and on the average economic growth (or decline) would tend to alter individuals' highest possible wage rates at the same rate that it would alter their actual wage rates. The effect of this supposition would be the same as the effect of the assumption I adopted. In other words, one can infer from the logic of the egalitarian system that economic growth (or decline) would tend neither to increase nor to decrease effort in the egalitarian system. Therefore if one can discover empirical evidence which indicates how economic growth (or decline) affects effort in PPM systems (if at all), one will have at least some basis for estimating how price changes would affect relative levels of effort in the two systems. For example, if one found that overall effort tended to increase over time with a rise in real wages, then one could infer that the egalitarian system would tend to generate less effort than the PPM system under conditions of economic growth. If one found that overall effort tended to decline over time with a rise in real wages, then one could infer that the egalitarian system would tend to generate *more* effort than the PPM system under conditions of economic growth.

Saving and Investing

I turn now to the question of how saving and investing are handled in the PPM and egalitarian systems. For the following discussion, I define "investment" as any expenditure on capital goods, "consumption" as any expenditure on goods and services except capital goods, and "savings" as the difference between income and consumption. (These definitions are in accord with conventional economic usage.) The problem is to determine both how the egalitarian system could generate at least the same level of savings as the PPM system and how it could ensure that these savings would be invested as efficiently as in the PPM system.

Saving in the PPM System

In the PPM system each individual decides whether to consume part, all, or more than all of his income (if he can borrow) on the basis of how much he values the satisfactions of present consumption over against the satisfactions to be gained by withholding income from consumption, including the satisfactions of future consumption. An individual may wish to save for a variety of reasons. For example, he may wish to have resources which will permit him to maintain his current standard of consumption in case his income is reduced by unemployment, illness, or old age. He may simply prefer to defer consumption to a later point in time. One important consideration may be that by withholding income from consumption the individual would be able to invest, that is, to allocate resources purchased through the withheld income to productive activity. Thus, by withholding income from present consumption, the individual would be able to acquire even more income available for consumption.[18]

Income-consumption satisfactions can be acquired through saving even if the individual saver does not wish to invest himself. Other individuals seeking to increase their incomes may wish to invest. They will therefore offer payment (interest) to the individual to induce him to let them use his savings for investment purposes. The same forces which govern the allocation of other resources will govern the allocation of savings to investment. If the market is functioning properly, the one who is able to make the most productive investment will offer the highest payment. Other things being equal, the individual would, of course, take the highest payment offered, but other things will often not be equal and the individual may take into account other factors.[19] Regardless of the original reason why the individual chooses to save—and it may have nothing to do with a desire to invest or even to increase future income—the individual will maximize his overall satisfactions by using his savings to generate the most additional income possible within the constraints of his original reason for saving and of his other preferences, assuming that he places some value on the satisfactions of acquiring income for consumption. At the same time, the amount which an individual is willing to save will be limited by the value he places on the satisfactions of current consumption. Given the principle of declining marginal utility, all individuals will find that the satisfactions to be obtained from further saving are outweighed by the satisfactions to be obtained by consumption at some point, although this point may vary from one individual to another.

In the PPM system the total amount of savings for the system as a whole is determined by the combined effect of separate individual decisions to save or borrow. The individuals who invest in a PPM system are frequently different from the individuals who save.[20] If an individual does use his own savings for investment, he is foregoing the interest which he could receive on the savings from some other investor. In effect, then, the individual as investor must be willing to pay himself as saver the going rate of interest and still regard the investment as worthwhile. Thus the decision to save is analytically distinct from the decision to invest.

Investing in the PPM System

What induces individuals in the PPM system to invest? I begin by defining profit as the (positive) difference between the income an individual can gain as a return from new capital goods and the interest he must pay to borrow someone's savings to purchase the capital goods. Profit thus represents a source of income-consumption satisfactions for the investor. It should not be assumed, however, that an individual will invest whenever he can make a profit from the investment.

As we saw earlier in the discussion of the widget factories owned by Arnold and Benedict, there may be other satisfactions affected by the allocation of property besides income-consumption satisfactions. It is easy to conceptualize the opportunity to transform the widget factory into a gadget factory as a profitable investment opportunity, assuming now that the transformation would require the purchase of new capital goods. Nevertheless, given the earlier assumptions about the relative values each of them attached to staying in the family business as over against income-consumption satisfactions, Arnold would make the investment and Benedict would not. I might also note that investments often require supervision and thus may reduce leisure satisfactions.[21] In short, an individual in the PPM system will make an investment whenever he places a higher relative value on the income-consumption satisfactions and other satisfactions to be gained from the investment than he does on the satisfactions which must be foregone because of the investment. Different individuals may make different trade-offs when faced with the same choice. Moreover, different individuals will have different talents, skills, knowledge, resources, and even luck, all of which may affect investment opportunities. Thus some individuals will invest, while others will not, and different individuals will make different investments.

Investing in the Egalitarian System

I turn now to the question of how saving and investing can be accomplished in the egalitarian system. I shall begin with the question of investing and I shall simply assume for the moment that there are savings available which can be borrowed for investment purposes in return for interest payments.

The key to understanding the motivation for investment in the egalitarian system is to see that investment opportunities affect an individual's earning capacity. Suppose that some individual knows that he could make a (pre-tax) profit from some investment (i.e., that the income he would gain from the investment would be greater than the interest costs he would have to bear to acquire the resources for the investment). This potential profit represents a part of his earning capacity. Thus if he fails to make the investment he receives fewer social-duty satisfactions than if he makes the investment. For this reason, social-duty satisfactions provide the same kind of incentives for investment in the egalitarian system that income-consumption satisfactions provide in the PPM system. Indeed the analysis of investment in the egalitarian system should be seen simply as an extension of the arguments in the first section of this chapter regarding the allocation of resources according to relative scarcity in the egalitarian system.

Investment in human capital. It should be noted that the arguments I am developing about investment in the egalitarian system apply fully as much to investment in "human capital" as to investment in other forms of capital. It is sometimes alleged that an equal distribution of income would deprive individuals of any incentive to develop their talents and skills. I shall leave to the next chapter the question of whether this negative judgment about human attitudes towards self-development is well-founded in empirical research. Here I wish simply to show that the logic of my egalitarian model contradicts this conclusion.

In most of the cases I have considered, I have focused on individuals making choices at particular points in time in which talents and skills were taken as given. I adopted this approach in order to simplify the exposition of the argument. The initial formulation of the social duty obligation, however, was not limited by any particular time constraint: "Individuals believe that they have an obligation to earn as much pre-tax income as they are capable of earning." To remove any ambiguity, I assert here that this obligation should be regarded as an obligation to earn as much pre-tax income as one can over one's life span. For long-term decisions it is long-term earning capacity that must be considered. If an investment in training or education would increase an individual's earnings over the long run beyond the cost of the investment and beyond the earnings foregone during the period of training, the individual would have an obligation to undertake that training. For example, if Jane Jones thought that she could earn more pre-tax income in the long run by becoming an engineer rather than a bricklayer, she would have a greater social obligation to study to become an engineer than to work as a bricklayer, even though in the short run she would acquire more pre-tax income as a bricklayer. The income foregone and the expenses of her study would be an investment. So long as the return on that investment in the form of future pre-tax income would exceed the cost (including the interest costs on both of these), she would be performing at a higher percentage of her capacity by studying than by working as a bricklayer. Consequently, she would receive more social-duty satisfactions for studying than for working as a bricklayer.

In the case of opportunities for investment in human capital, as in other kinds of investments, different individuals will have different talents, abilities, resources, knowledge, and luck. Moreover, as we have seen, different individuals will place different amounts of value on social-duty satisfactions and on alternative satisfactions. Thus different individuals will make different choices about how much to invest in education and training. What one can conclude, however, is that the egalitarian model does provide incentives for investment in human capital.

If one assumed for the moment that the same savings would be available to the same people at the same rate in the egalitarian system as in the PPM system, then it would follow from this and from the other assumptions of this chapter that the same investments would be made in the egalitarian system as in the PPM system. To take a familiar specific example, Arnold would make the investment required to transform the widget factory into a gadget factory because he would value the additional social-duty satisfactions to be gained from this investment more than the satisfactions to be gained from staying in the family business. Benedict would not make the investment because of his different relative values. Moreover, a price change which would make an investment more attractive in terms of income-consumption satisfactions in the PPM system would make that same investment more attractive in terms of social-duty satisfactions in the egalitarian system, for the reasons given above in the discussion of allocation according to relative scarcity. In short, the same arguments which I used earlier to show that resource allocation would be as efficient in the egalitarian system as in the PPM system can be applied to the analysis of investing in the egalitarian system. Thus the key question is whether the egalitarian system can generate the same level of savings as the PPM system and allocate the savings as efficiently. Therefore, I turn now to the question of how saving is to be achieved in the egalitarian system.

Saving in the Egalitarian System

I should begin discussion of the question of saving in the egalitarian system by recognizing that some mechanism for saving must be constructed which is radically different from the saving mechanism in the PPM system and which is not contained in the assumptions already adopted about the egalitarian system.

The existing assumptions of the egalitarian system create a serious dilemma with respect to saving, if left unchanged. In the PPM system saving is achieved as a result of individuals withholding income from consumption at least partly in order to acquire the additional income they can obtain by lending this income to investors in return for interest. In other words, their saving is partly motivated by a desire for additional income-consumption satisfactions. If the present arrangements of the egalitarian system were left intact, individuals would feel a social obligation to withhold some of their after-tax income from consumption, since the interest on this after-tax income would increase subsequent pre-tax income. Since I have been assuming that some individuals in the egalitarian system would place greater value on social-duty satisfactions than others, the consequence of this arrangement would be that some individuals in the "egalitarian" system would have lower standards of living than others and that the ones who placed the highest value on social duty would have the lowest standard of living. Even if such an arrangement would work (which seems doubtful in the long run),[22] it hardly seems consistent with any conceivable motive for distributing income equally.

A new prerequisite of the egalitarian system. The first task, then, is to modify the social-duty assumptions of the egalitarian system so as to separate the equal income share from the saving function. The following assumption accomplishes this.

Individuals in the egalitarian system believe that the obligation to earn as much pre-tax income as they are capable of earning does not extend to the use of their after-tax equal income shares, and, more specifically, they believe that they ought not to use savings from their equal income shares for the purpose of generating additional pre-tax income.

I leave open here the question of whether individuals who wish to save some of their equal income shares for other reasons may do so. If such savings were permitted though, it would be essential to provide some administrative mechanism to distinguish them from the savings generated for investment purposes.[23] I turn now to the question of how the egalitarian system might achieve saving for investment.

If the saving function is to be performed as efficiently in the egalitarian system as in the PPM system, there are two basic problems to be solved. First, the egalitarian system has to generate at least the same total amount of savings as the PPM system. Second, like the PPM system, the egalitarian system must create incentives for savers to lend their resources to those who can invest them most productively.

The prerequisites for efficient saving. These problems can be solved by modifying the egalitarian system through the adoption of the following three assumptions.

1. The tax laws of the egalitarian system permit pre-tax income above a certain level to be saved and such savings are tax-exempt (i.e., they do not count as part of an individual's equal income share).

2. The tax laws stipulate that such savings may not be kept in any form which provides personal consumption benefits.
3. The level above which income may be saved is set by the government.

These three assumptions create a mechanism which would provide very strong incentives for everyone earning a pre-tax income above the designated level to save the full amount of that pre-tax income above the designated level. The opportunity to save this income would increase an individual's earning capacity, since he could lend his savings in return for interest and thus increase his subsequent pre-tax income. If he failed to save, the income would simply be taxed away and he would acquire fewer social-duty satisfactions than if he saved the income in a form which would return interest. My assumptions leave open the option of holding the savings in any form which does not provide personal consumption benefits. (I shall discuss the need for this restriction later in the chapter when I analyze the role of income-consumption satisfactions in the egalitarian system.) An individual could hold savings in the form of bank deposits, bonds, stocks,[24] or he could use the savings directly for investment purposes. Whatever his decision in this respect, he would have almost no incentive *not* to save since some methods of saving (e.g., bank deposits) would require almost no effort and by failing to save he would lose social-duty satisfactions. Thus virtually all income above the designated level would be saved, and the government could increase or decrease the total amount of savings simply by raising or lowering the level above which pre-tax income could be saved. It follows that the egalitarian system could generate as much savings as the PPM system or more, if the government so chose.[25]

The second important feature of this mechanism is that savers would have incentives to lend their resources to those who could invest them most productively. I have noted before that those who are able to make the most productive investments will offer the highest payments for the use of savings, if the market is functioning properly. I have also noted that social-duty satisfactions depend upon the percentage of earning capacity at which indivdiuals perform. If savers were offered different interest rates, they would perform at a higher percentage of earning capacity and would thus acquire more social-duty satisfactions from lending to those offering higher interest rates. Therefore, while other factors may also affect lending decisions, as they do in the PPM system, one can conclude that these three assumptions do create incentives for savers in the egalitarian system to lend their resources to those who can invest them most productively.

Decentralization of saving. As a final comment on this mechanism for saving in the egalitarian system, I might note that the arrangement ensures that there is decentralized control over savings. Apart from setting the level above which pre-tax income may be saved and prohibiting the use of such savings for consumption purposes, the central government need exercise no more direction over what is done with savings in the egalitarian system than it does in the PPM system. In other words, even in the area of saving, the egalitarian system relies to a very large extent on the market mechanism.

The governmental involvement which is required in order to ensure both the equal distribution of after-tax income and an adequate level of saving operates through the market as much as possible rather than replacing the market with centralized direction of economic activity. Thus even here, most of the arguments which can be advanced about the advantages of decentralized control over economic activity apply as much to the egalitarian system as to the PPM system.[26]

Risk

Up to now I have conducted the analysis under the assumption that there were no risks entailed in allocating resources in the PPM and egalitarian models. I have framed alternatives in both systems as though the outcomes of choice were certain. For example, when I discussed the choice which Arnold and Benedict faced about whether to transform their widget factories into gadget factories, I assumed that they both knew (with certainty) that they could generate more income if they did transform their factories.

The assumption that there were no risks was a useful simplifying device but it is clearly unrealistic. The very mention of the word "investment" conjures up the idea of risk. An investment is the purchase of new capital goods in the expectation of future profit. But there are many possible factors which can prevent that expectation from being realized. Arnold and Benedict, for example, expect prices for gadgets to rise, but some new technological development could cause the bottom to fall out of the market. While all investments involve risk, some involve more risk than others, and, as we shall see, this affects both the willingness to invest and the return expected.

The element of risk affects all decisions regarding the allocation of resources, not merely decisions about investment. Some forms of saving are riskier than others. (Contrast the risks involved in U.S. Government bonds with those involved in New York City bonds, for example.) Even occupational choices are made in a context of risks. When I assumed that Jane Jones had to choose between working as a bricklayer at $5 an hour and working as a plumber at $6 an hour, I focused on a definite choice (and its subsequent specific modifications) at a moment in time. Choices of this kind frequently have long-term consequences, however. Once Jane has chosen to work in one field, it may be hard for her to find work years later in the other field. At the same time, it may be difficult to foresee whether the relative wage positions of the two occupations are likely to remain the same in the future.

All of this raises the question of how risk would affect economic activity in the PPM and egalitarian systems. I shall consider how risk would affect choices about income-consumption satisfactions in the PPM system and how it would affect choices about social-duty satisfactions in the egalitarian system.

Risk in the PPM System

I shall begin with a case in which the risks involved can be precisely calculated. Imagine that an individual named Monte can choose in the PPM system between one allocation of resources which offers a certain return of $50 and an alternative allocation which offers a 60 percent chance of returning $100 and a 40 percent chance of returning $0. How would Monte choose, given his desire for income-consumption satisfactions? The answer is that it depends on his preferences with respect to risk. Can one not infer that Monte would definitely choose the second allocation, since the odds are in his favor? Not necessarily. While the odds favor the better outcome, he still faces a 40 percent chance of coming up with nothing.

It is important to see that, from the perspective of the individual seeking income-consumption satisfactions in the PPM system, it is not the long-run tendency that counts but the actual outcome. Aversion to risk, even when the odds are in one's favor, may be quite rational in the PPM system. Many people might consider it far more important to know that they could count on at least $50 in income for consumption than to take a chance on a course of action which might leave them with no income. Perhaps they need the $50 for food, or their children's education, or their retirement. On the other hand, people who were willing to gamble would choose the second option. Indeed, even if the odds were reversed, some people might choose the second allocation, because they place such a high value on the possibility of a high return. (This might be called the "go-for-broke syndrome." It is illustrated by the couple in New Jersey who wagered all of their assets on the state lottery in 1977.) Again, given their values, such people are not making irrational choices. In short, even though these are cases of pure risk in which the probability of each outcome can be precisely determined, one cannot be sure what the choices of particular individuals would be in the PPM system unless one adopts specific assumptions about their attitudes towards risk.

Risk and inefficiency in the PPM system. One important consequence of these possible variations in individual attitudes towards risk is that the PPM system as a whole may tend to generate a lower total product than it would if all individuals were neither averse to risk nor attracted to it. In terms of systemic efficiency, it would be preferable if Monte and all other individuals took chances when the odds were in their favor and did not take chances when the odds were not in their favor. In the long run, that pattern of allocating resources would tend to generate a greater overall product than a pattern of allocating resources in which some do not take chances even when the odds are in their favor and others take chances even when the odds are against them. In short, what is rational and efficient from the individual's perspective in the PPM system, under conditions of risk, may not be rational and efficient from the systemic perspective.

Risk in the Egalitarian System

I turn now to the egalitarian system. My basic task is to determine how social-duty satisfactions are affected by the risks inherent in investments and other resource allocations and thus to determine how resource allocation is affected by risk in the egalitarian system. Since social-duty satisfactions depend upon the extent to which individuals fulfill their obligation to earn as much pre-tax income as they are capable of earning, the first step is to clarify what that obligation entails under conditions of risk.

Risk and social duty. Given the goal of efficiency for the egalitarian system, one must interpret that obligation as requiring each individual to allocate his resources (labor and property, savings and investments) in whatever way he perceives to be the most likely to generate the largest amount of pre-tax income (in the long run). For example, assume that Monte can choose between one allocation of resources in the egalitarian system which offers a certain return of $50 in pre-tax income and an alternative allocation which offers a 60 percent chance of returning $100 in pre-tax income and a 40 percent chance of returning $0. Under my interpretation, he would be obliged to choose the second allocation since that would be more likely to generate a larger amount of pre-tax income. Of course, in a given case an individual following such an obligation might acquire less pre-tax income than he would if he followed some alternative principle. For example, Monte could wind up with $0 in pre-tax income if he acted upon this obligation, whereas he had the alternative of a certain $50 in pre-tax income. Over the long run, however, if all individuals followed this obligation, the system as a whole would tend to maximize the total amount of pre-tax income. For every Monte and the three like him who gained $0 in pre-tax income, there would be six who gained $100 in pre-tax income.

Risk and social-duty satisfactions. Given this interpretation of the pre-tax income obligation in the egalitarian system under conditions of risk, it follows that social-duty satisfactions do not depend on the actual outcome of resource allocations. Since Monte would be fulfilling his social duty in choosing the second allocation, he would receive the same social-duty satisfactions in the case we have described, regardless of whether he acquired $100 or $0 in pre-tax income.[27]

This might seem to be a surprising assertion. In the PPM system Monte's income-consumption satisfactions clearly would depend on the actual outcome. If he chose the second allocation and acquired $0 he would receive no income-consumption satisfactions despite the fact that the odds had been in his favor. I have noted before, however, that social-duty satisfactions do not depend on the absolute amount of pre-tax income that one acquires but on the extent to which one fulfills one's social obligation to acquire as much pre-tax income as one is capable of acquiring. It would clearly be inconsistent to adopt a specific attitude toward risk as part of the definition of that social obligation and then to permit people to lose social-duty satisfactions because they adopted that attitude towards risk. After all, Monte could have been assured of $50 in pre-tax income. In choosing the second allocation, he was trying to perform his social duty more fully. Thus social-duty satisfactions cannot depend on fluctuations in pre-tax income which result from conditions of risk but rather they must depend on the extent to which individuals adopt a maximizing strategy in the face of risk. In effect, this transfers both the burdens and the gains of risk from the individual to society as a whole (with some qualifications, as we shall see).

Risk and efficiency in the egalitarian system. I noted at the beginning of the essay that one of the major objections to distributing income equally was the contention that equal distribution would reduce incentives to take risks in investments and other kinds of resource allocation. We have seen, however, that social-duty satisfactions depend on the willingness to take appropriate risks in allocating resources. Thus, far from reducing incentives to take risks, the egalitarian model actually increases the incentives for individuals to take risks which are rational from the perspective of systemic efficiency.

There are two important qualifications which should be added to this conclusion. First, if an individual in the egalitarian system were to face a choice between two alternative allocations and if it were impossible to determine which of the two allocations would be more likely to generate more pre-tax income, then he would have to choose on the basis of his subjective attitudes towards risk. For example, assume that Monte must choose between one allocation which offers a certain return of $50 in pre-tax income and an alternative allocation which offers a 50 percent chance of returning $0 and a 50 percent chance of returning $100 in pre-tax income. Obviously, the odds favor neither choice over the other. Thus, in terms of social-duty satisfactions, Monte has no incentive to adopt one allocation over the other. He will have to decide on the basis of his subjective preferences with regard to risk. If he is a cautious person, he will choose the first allocation. If he likes to gamble, he will choose the second.

This type of case is far more important than the example might seem to suggest. In realistic market situations, actual knowledge of the risks involved in alternative allocations is usually far less precise than the knowledge I have assumed in the cases discussed here. While it might be possible to distinguish a high-risk investment from a low-risk investment, it may be impossible to quantify what is meant by "high" and "low" with any precision. The greater the uncertainty the more difficult it becomes to determine which of the available alternatives is most likely to generate the most pre-tax income. Indeed attitudes towards risk are likely to influence the calculation of the risks themselves. One may be faced with "optimistic" estimates and "pessimistic" estimates and have no unassailable reason for choosing to rely on one rather than the other (or for choosing to "split the difference"). Thus, subjective attitudes towards risk can play an important role in the egalitarian system, even if individuals are intent upon fulfilling their social obligation to adopt a maximizing strategy in the face of risk.

Second, as I have observed before, there may be other satisfactions derived from allocating resources besides income-consumption satisfactions in the PPM system and social-duty satisfactions in the egalitarian system. For example, I suggested that a businessman might derive satisfaction from the power and reputation that accompany business success. And I noted that these satisfactions would be as available to individuals in the egalitarian system as they would be in the PPM system. Unlike social-duty satisfactions, these satisfactions would be as affected by the actual outcome of resource allocation in the egalitarian system as in the PPM system. A businessman who follows the odds in making an investment in the egalitarian system but whose investment turns sour in a particular case would not suffer any loss of social-duty satisfactions but he would lose the power and reputation which would have accompanied success.

Given the general assumption of identity between the two systems, one would have to assume that a given individual would have the same attitude towards risks involving these other satisfactions in the egalitarian system as he would have towards risks involving these other satisfactions in the PPM system.[28] Thus some might be averse to risks involving these other satisfactions. For example, an individual might not be willing to take a chance on losing an established economic position, even when the odds favored his taking a chance. Others might be attracted to risk. (The "go-for-broke" syndrome could emerge here too.)

Since a desire for these other satisfactions could influence decisions about the allocation of resources, one cannot conclude that *all* individuals in the egalitarian system would necessarily adopt a maximizing strategy in allocating resources under conditions of risk. Nevertheless, my earlier arguments about risk and social-duty satisfactions do permit one to conclude that, other things being equal, there would be a greater tendency for individuals in the egalitarian system to adopt a maximizing strategy under conditions of risk than for individuals in the PPM system to do so. Thus I can stand by my general conclusion that the egalitarian system would tend to increase the incentives for individuals to take risks which are rational from the perspective of systemic efficiency in the allocation of resources.

Risk and earning capacity. The introduction of risk into the egalitarian system raises one further question: How does the element of risk affect the role of earning capacity in the egalitarian system? The first consequence is that risk must now be taken into account in determining earning capacity and in determining the percentage of earning capacity at which an individual is working. Given the element of risk, calculations about long-term earning prospects have to be based on probability judgments about future prices. Thus, in estimating future pre-tax income, an individual must discount expected future pre-tax income in the light of foreseeable risk. For example, if Monte were to choose the allocation which offered a 60 percent chance of a $100 return and a 40 percent chance of a $0 return, this allocation would have an expected income value of $60. The principle of discounting for risk would apply *both* to the calculation of earning capacity (the maximum pre-tax income an individual could acquire) *and* to the calculation of the pre-tax income which an individual could expect to acquire from the actual allocation of resources which he adopts. Thus while the addition of risk complicates the calculations, it does not alter the process by which one determines the percentage of earning capacity at which an individual is performing. It is simply a question of the ratio between the long-term pre-tax income which an individual's current allocation of resources can be expected (in the light of risk) to produce and the maximum long-term pre-tax income which any allocation of the individual's resources could be expected (in the light of risk) to produce. The closer these two are to unity the higher is the percentage of capacity at which the individual is performing. The higher the percentage of capacity, the more social-duty satisfactions he receives. Thus the basic incentive structure of the egalitarian system is not altered by the introduction of risk.

A second consequence of the introduction of risk is that one must recognize that calculations about long-term earning capacity and about the expected long-term value of current allocations may change as actual and expected prices change. Under conditions of risk, some investments which were favored by the odds will not pay off. This will decrease an individual's earning capacity, but it will not necessarily decrease his social-duty satisfactions, because, as we have seen above, these satisfactions do not depend on the actual outcome of allocations under conditions of risk.

I can illustrate both of these points by reconsidering a case discussed earlier in the section on investment. There I observed that Jane Jones would be performing at a higher level of her earning capacity (and would be receiving more social-duty satisfactions) by studying to be an engineer than by working as a bricklayer, even though her pre-tax income at that moment would be lower as a student than as a bricklayer, so long as she could calculate that the pre-tax income she would eventually earn as an engineer would exceed the pre-tax income she could earn as a bricklayer by more than the cost of her studies, the pre-tax income foregone, and the interest on both. Now the first consequence of introducing risk is that it requires Jane to discount the expected earnings as an engineer in light of the risks associated with that career (including the risks created by foregoing any pre-tax income for her period of study) and also to discount her expected earnings as a bricklayer in light of the risks associated with that career. Assume that Jane makes these calculations and still judges that she is more likely to acquire more pre-tax income in the long run, all things considered, by becoming an engineer. Obviously she has a greater social obligation to become an engineer and will receive more social-duty satisfactions for doing so.

Now, assume that when Jane completes her studies she finds that the market value of her education has dropped. She is now forced to the conclusion that her investment will not pay off. In retrospect, she now judges that she would have earned more pre-tax income over the long run if she had become a bricklayer instead of going to school.

The first point to see is that this development cannot deprive Jane of the greater social-duty satisfactions she enjoyed while she was a student than she would have enjoyed had she been a bricklayer, because those satisfactions are in the past. Moreover, this is appropriate from a systemic perspective since she thought at the time that she was in school that studying would be more profitable than bricklaying in terms of long-term pre-tax income. As we noted above, it is one's attitude towards risk, not the actual outcome of an allocation, which determines social-duty satisfactions.

Second, the change in the market for engineers has reduced Jane's earning capacity. Does this mean that it has also reduced her present or future social-duty satisfactions? Not necessarily. These satisfactions depend on how she allocates her resources now and in the future, not on how she has allocated them in the past. Of course, in allocating resources now she must take into account the changed circumstances. She must make a new determination of what allocation of resources seems most likely at this moment to generate the largest amount of pre-tax income over the remaining long run. If she calculates that she could earn more pre-tax income over the long run by switching to bricklaying now, then she would acquire more social-duty satisfactions by switching fields. If she calculates that she would earn more pre-tax income over the long run by working as an engineer (despite the reduced prospects there and despite the fact that the investment might never be fully paid off), then she would acquire more social-duty satisfactions by continuing in the engineering field. Thus the mere fact that her earning capacity has been reduced, even when this results from a failed investment, does not mean that her social-duty satisfactions will be reduced. Her current social-duty satisfactions depend on the percentage of current earning capacity at which she is performing.

To summarize the conclusions of this section on risk: (1) An individual's social obligation is to allocate his resources in whatever way he judges at a given point in time to be the most likely to generate the largest amount of pre-tax income over the future long run. (2) The percentage of earning capacity at which an individual performs and thus the level of social-duty satisfactions which he enjoys at a given point in time depends on the extent to which he is allocating his resources in the way he judges at that point to be most likely to generate the largest amount of pre-tax income over the future long run.

Knowledge and efficiency in the egalitarian system. These formal conclusions may make it appear that people in an egalitarian system would have to be extremely sophisticated and that they would need access to a great deal of information about present and projected prices in order for the egalitarian system to function efficiently. In many important respects, this is a misleading impression created by the need to describe the logic of the egalitarian system clearly and unambiguously. The same kind of false impression is often created by rational-actor models of PPM systems.[29] Obviously, most real people are not the computerlike calculating machines which these models tend to suggest. Gathering information even in a decentralized market system can often be burdensome, and many people simply do not bother to do so in any conscious way. Nevertheless, PPM systems do function as a whole roughly in the ways suggested by the logic of PPM models, even though there may be relatively few individuals who would appear to satisfy the requirements of a rational actor. In the same way, I shall show in the next chapter (in the discussion of empirically necessary prerequisites) that the egalitarian system would function as a whole roughly in the ways suggested by the logic of the egalitarian model, even if relatively few individuals made the kind of conscious and detailed calculations which are characteristic of the individuals used as examples in discussing the model. While the egalitarian system would depend on people having greater knowledge of some prices than is required for the actual functioning of a PPM system, this knowledge would not be nearly so detailed, refined, and costly to them as might appear from the model.

Income-Consumption Satisfactions in the Egalitarian System

At the beginning of this chapter I assumed that income-consumption satisfactions played no role in the egalitarian system. I adopted that assumption in order to simplify the exposition of the major arguments concerning efficiency in the egalitarian system. I propose now to modify my earlier position by adopting the following assumption:

> Individuals in the egalitarian system place some value on income-consumption satisfactions.

The first and most obvious question to ask is why it is necessary to adopt this assumption at all. The answer is that the rationality of the system requires such an assumption. If it were not assumed that individuals had an interest in income-consumption satisfactions, then it would make no sense to assume that there was a social duty to earn as much pre-tax income as possible and there would be no point in requiring income to be equally distributed. Moreover, in the next chapter it will be shown that income for consumption will almost inevitably be highly valued in any politico-economic system which relies heavily on the market mechanism because of the instrumental relation which money has to many other goals.

I should perhaps note that this assumption in no way contradicts my earlier assumption that individuals place the same relative value on social-duty satisfactions in the egalitarian system that they placed on income-consumption satisfactions in the PPM system. As the discussion of work satisfactions and of leisure satisfactions has shown, it is quite possible for individuals to have many different sources of satisfaction. On the other hand, the introduction of income-consumption satisfactions does raise a question about whether this new assumption affects the earlier conclusions about the efficiency of the PPM system. In other words, does the assumption that individuals value income-consumption satisfactions in the egalitarian system alter any of my inferences about the ways in which individuals would allocate resources, about the amount of effort they would put forth, or about their willingness to save, invest, or take risks in the egalitarian system?

Why Income-Consumption Satisfactions Would Have No Impact on Efficiency under Ideal Conditions

Assume for a moment that the tax laws regarding equal distribution are perfectly efficient in arranging for equal distribution and are perfectly obeyed. If this were the case, individuals in the egalitarian system would have no motive to alter any of the behavior I have described (resource allocation, effort, saving, investment, risk), despite the fact that they would value income-consumption satisfactions. The reason is simple. No alteration of this behavior would increase or decrease one's income-consumption satisfactions. Given this assumption about the tax laws, an individual's income-consumption satisfactions would be determined entirely by the amount of his equal income share. No economic activity which he could undertake could noticeably affect the amount of his equal income share. For example, if an individual worked harder or took a higher-paying job this would not appreciably increase his own equal income share because the gain in pre-tax income would be spread out over the whole society in the distribution process. Similarly, if an individual slacked off or took a lower-paying job, this would not appreciably decrease his own equal income-share because the loss in pre-tax income would be spread out over so many equal income shares. Thus, no matter how great or how small an individual's desire for income-consumption satisfactions, he would have no incentives to alter the behavior which I inferred from the assumptions adopted earlier in the chapter. The efficiency of the egalitarian system would remain unchanged.

The Dangers of Loopholes

Unfortunately, no laws are perfectly efficient in achieving their ends nor are there many which are perfectly obeyed. It is important to see, therefore, that the assumption that individuals value income-consumption satisfactions would create incentives for inequalities and inefficiencies in the egalitarian system, in the absence of restraints. In this connection, it may be recalled that I assumed in the section on saving that individuals could not keep their savings in forms which provided personal consumption benefits.[30] In the absence of that constraint, individuals would have strong incentives to keep their savings in the form of (previously built) vacation houses, jewelry, expensive paintings, and so on. Since these are commodities which often appreciate in value, they could properly be considered a form of savings.[31] Nevertheless, they are forms of savings which may provide considerable consumption satisfactions to the people who possess them. To permit such savings would undermine the goal of equal distribution and would tend to draw income away from more profitable but less enjoyable forms of savings (e.g., stocks and bonds).

The desire for income-consumption satisfactions might lead individuals to look for tax loopholes which would enable them to include expenditures which provided them with personal consumption benefits under the heading of "business expenses" since, as we saw in the first chapter, business expenses do not count against one's equal income-share. If loopholes in the tax laws happened to permit some occupations which paid lower pre-tax incomes to provide more of such disguised consumption benefits than occupations which paid higher pre-tax incomes, some individuals might be induced to take lower-paying jobs than would otherwise be the case, and the efficiency of the egalitarian system would thereby be reduced. Even apart from this cost to efficiency, such disguised consumption benefits obtained through loopholes would clearly violate the income distribution requirements of the egalitarian system.

The Final Logically Necessary Prerequisite

Given these tendencies, it is essential to adopt the following assumption as a logically necessary prerequisite of the egalitarian system:

> There are no significant loopholes in the tax laws providing for equal distribution, and the tax laws are generally obeyed.[32]

In the next chapter I shall identify the empirically necessary prerequisites which would have to be met for the tax laws to be tightly drawn and widely obeyed. I wish simply to note here that this assumption avoids an unrealistic and unrealizable perfectionism. The assumption does leave room for small inefficiencies and inequalities. For one thing, there will always be borderline cases in rules about business expenses or permissible forms of saving, no matter where one draws the line. For another, it would no doubt be impossible to prohibit all forms of small-scale barter, home farming, and so on. The desire for additional income-consumption satisfactions beyond the equal income share would create incentives to engage in such activity to a greater degree than in the PPM system. However, social duty incentives would tend to counteract the effects of the income-consumption incentives. From this and from the assumption just adopted about the tax laws, one can infer that the inefficiencies and inequalities which would result from the desire for income-consumption satisfactions in the egalitarian system would be relatively small.

Freedom in the Egalitarian System

I must make one final point about the egalitarian model which I have constructed in this chapter. Individuals in the egalitarian system enjoy the same freedoms which individuals in the PPM system enjoy, except for the "freedom" to acquire more income for consumption than is provided by the equal income-share. In particular, individuals enjoy freedom of choice in occupation and in consumption.

Freedom of Choice in Occupation

Individuals in the egalitarian system are perfectly free to work as much or as little as they please and to work at whatever tasks they choose. Of course, as in the PPM system, choice is not always costless. Just as a choice not to work in the PPM system entails giving up income-consumption satisfactions, so a choice not to work in the egalitarian system would entail giving up social-duty satisfactions. Just as an individual in the PPM system can not always find an opening in the type of work he would like to do, so an individual in the egalitarian system might not always find an opening in his preferred field. Just as the PPM system offers no guarantee that every individual will be able to find a job which he enjoys and which provides him with a high income, so the egalitarian system offers no guarantee that every individual will be able to find a job which he enjoys and which provides him with a high level of social-duty satisfactions. On the other hand, it is not uncommon in PPM systems for individuals to take jobs which are both unpleasant and low-paying. At least in the egalitarian system, if an individual took a job which was both unpleasant and low in pre-tax income, it would seem likely that his earning capacity would be low and that the social duty-satisfactions from the job would be relatively high. In this respect, the egalitarian system offers a distinct advantage over the PPM system. I shall pursue this point further in Chapter 3. The fundamental point I wish to make here, however, is that the egalitarian system does not require any kind of restriction on freedom of choice in occupation beyond the restrictions inherent in any market system. I emphasize this point because it is sometimes argued that an equal distribution of income would require severe restrictions on freedom of occupation.

Freedom of Choice in Consumption

I have said very little about consumption in the egalitarian system up to this point, but, given the assumption of identity, individuals would be as free to spend their equal income shares in the egalitarian system as they are to spend their incomes in the PPM system. In other words, an individual could spend whatever proportion of his income he wished on food, clothing, shelter, entertainment, and so on. He could buy whatever quality of goods and services he chose within the constraints of his equal income share. Of course, this constraint is the same one imposed on individuals in a PPM system. That is, the income one has available for consumption limits one's expenditures in the PPM system as well as in the egalitarian system. Borrowing and saving for consumption purposes and the giving of gifts could create certain dilemmas for the maintenance of equality over time. I have discussed these dilemmas in the Appendix. Nevertheless, consumer choice would basically be as free and as effective in determining what was produced in the egalitarian system as it is in the PPM system. In the final chapter I shall discuss the possibility and desirability of determining production at least in part on some other basis than the marketplace choices of individual consumers. But here I wish to emphasize the scope which the system leaves for consumer choice, because some other models of highly egalitarian politico economic systems have placed drastic limits on freedom of choice in consumption, and, in the eyes of some, drastic limits on freedom of choice in consumption might be thought to be a prerequisite of a system which provided equal distribution.[33] As we have seen, such limits are not required by my egalitarian model.

The General Level of Freedom and of Satisfaction

The one restriction which clearly is required by the egalitarian system and is not required by the PPM system is a restriction on any individual's right to acquire more income for consumption than is provided by the equal income-share. Some people might feel this to be a serious restriction. For example, an individual might be dissatisfied with the level of consumption provided by his equal income share. He might be willing to work harder if he could receive more income for consumption. This option would simply not be open to him in the egalitarian system while it would be open to him in the PPM system.

On the other hand, it would be a mistake to conclude from this that the egalitarian system is either less free than the PPM system or less efficient in satisfying its participants. After all, an individual in the PPM system might work very hard and still be quite dissatisfied with the level of his consumption simply because he is paid at a very low rate. Such an individual would be far more satisfied with his level of consumption in the egalitarian system, assuming that it worked as efficiently as I have argued it would work. Moreover, an individual in the PPM system who is willing to work hard but can only earn a low wage may feel quite restricted by the property rules and market forces governing distribution in a PPM system. Such an individual would feel far more free in the egalitarian system given the higher level of income for consumption which he would enjoy and the new possibilities for choice in consumption which this created for him. Thus we must know what people's attitudes towards equal distribution are in order to determine whether the requirement that after-tax income should be equally distributed (and the corresponding prohibition on some acquiring more than an equal income share) is to be regarded as increasing overall freedom and satisfaction or decreasing them. We shall see in the next chapter that a widespread commitment to the value of equal distribution is one of the empirically necessary prerequisites of the egalitarian system. Anticipating this, I can conclude here that the egalitarian system would not be less free than a PPM system or less efficient in satisfying its participants.

Conclusion

In this chapter I have identified the ways in which an egalitarian system would have to differ from a PPM system in order to function efficiently. In all other ways, an egalitarian system could theoretically be the same as a PPM system and still function efficiently. In the context of the thought experiment, I have shown that, given only nine assumptions, one could infer that a politico-economic system which distributed income for consumption equally and relied on moral incentives could utilize the market mechanism as a major device for coordinating economic activity and could function as efficiently as a PPM system. Therefore one can conclude that these nine assumptions, together with the initial condition providing for equal distribution, constitute the logically necessary prerequisites of the egalitarian system.

Identifying these logically necessary prerequisites is only the first step of the investigation. I must now undertake the task of identifying the empirical conditions which would have to be satisfied in order for an egalitarian system to exist and to function in the real world, even in a utopian future. The task has been greatly simplified by the logical investigation which I have conducted so far, since I can focus in the next stage exclusively on the empirically necessary prerequisites of those features of the egalitarian system which *must* differ from PPM systems. In other words, I shall spell out now the conditions which would have to be satisfied in order for these logically necessary prerequisites to be realized in a real-world politico-economic system.

3 Empirically Necessary Prerequisites

Consideration of the empirically necessary prerequisites of the egalitarian system moves us to a different intellectual world from the one which we occupied in the previous chapter. There I used a rational-choice model to analyze the ways in which individuals would behave if I assumed them to have certain preferences. That chapter can be seen as an exercise in economic theory because it is in economics that this type of rational-choice analysis has been most fully developed. In this chapter, by contrast, the task is to explain how people might come to have the basic preferences which I assumed them to have in the previous chapter. In other words, I am seeking to identify the sociocultural preconditions which would lead people to develop the kind of motivation needed to make the egalitarian system work. Thus this chapter is much closer to sociology than to economics. Individuals are viewed more as social products molded by their environment than as rational actors. While the chapter does not abandon all consideration of the logic of the egalitarian system, it draws primarily on evidence from empirical social theory.

Although the types of argument used in the two chapters are quite different, the chapters are bound together in the overall structure of the work, because the discussion of empirically necessary prerequisites presupposes the earlier analysis of logically necessary prerequisites. From that earlier analysis, it should be clear that not all of the logically necessary prerequisites are of equal importance. The first three are the most important. To recall, they are:

1. Individuals in the egalitarian system believe they have

a social duty to earn as much pre-tax net income as they are capable of earning.
2. Individuals in the egalitarian system derive satisfaction from performing this social duty to earn as much pre-tax income as they can.
3. Individuals in the egalitarian system place the same relative value on the satisfactions derived from performing their social duty to acquire pre-tax income . . . as individuals in the PPM system place on the satisfactions derived from acquiring income for consumption.

The question that must now be answered is, What empirical conditions would necessarily have to be fulfilled in order for these assumptions to be realized in a real-world politico-economic system?

Before addressing this question directly, I offer one preliminary clarification about the nature of my inquiry with respect to the third prerequisite. I am not asking what empirical conditions would have to be satisfied in order to take some real person (some real Jane Jones) and to transform her values so that she would place as much value on social-duty satisfactions as she formerly placed on income-consumption satisfactions. This would entail questions about the prerequisites for transition to the egalitarian system, and I have ruled such questions out of the inquiry. What I am asking instead is, What are the empirical prerequisites for getting any given person to place a given amount of value on social-duty satisfactions and how do these prerequisites compare with the prerequisites for getting that same person to place an equivalent amount of value on income-consumption satisfactions, assuming in both cases that the person had no prior established values? The point is to see both that this is a purely theoretical question and that I am concerned primarily with the comparability between the empirical prerequisites of the egalitarian system and the empirical prerequisites of the PPM system on matters of motivation. This point will become clearer as the investigation proceeds, but it seemed useful to draw attention to it in advance.

Socialization and Social Duty

The fundamental answer to the initial question can be expressed in one word: socialization. The basic position I shall adopt (with some modifications and refinements) is that all human motivation is the result of socialization and that it is theoretically possible to socialize people in the egalitarian system into placing as much value on the satisfactions associated with performing their social duty to earn pre-tax income as individuals in the PPM system place on the satisfactions derived from acquiring income for consumption.

Let us look first at the general relationship between socialization and motivation in order to understand why someone might be willing to earn as much pre-tax income as he could, even if he knew his earnings would not affect the actual amount of money he had to spend on consumption. According to Robert Merton, all societies have

> culturally defined goals, purposes, and interests, held out as legitimate for all or for diversely located members of the society. The goals are more or less integrated—the degree is a question of empirical fact—and roughly ordered in some hierarchy of value. Involving various degrees of sentiment and significance, the prevailing goals comprise a frame of aspirational reference. They are the things "worth striving for".... Though some, not all, of these cultural goals are directly related to the biological drives of man, they are not determined by them.[1]

Merton's view that people's goals and values are determined by the prevailing culture is echoed by other sociologists. Inkeles writes, for example:

> If it does not quite treat him as a *"tabula rasa,"* modern sociology nonetheless regards man as a flexible form which can be given all manner of content....
> *Socialization,* the process of learning one's culture while growing out of infant and childhood dependency, leads to internalization of society's values and goals. People come to want to do what from the point of view of society they must do.[2]

Inkeles observes elsewhere that

> Late childhood and early adolescence are the prime periods for the formal inculcation of social values. In good part the indoctrination is specific, explicit, and didactic.³

The basic empirically necessary prerequisite for the egalitarian system, therefore, is simply that individuals be taught during late childhood and early adolescence that they have a social obligation to earn as much pre-tax income as they can. This obligation would have to be a "culturally defined goal" in the egalitarian system. Since my logically necessary assumption requires that the same value be placed on social-duty satisfactions in the egalitarian system as is placed on income-consumption satisfactions in the PPM system, the place of this culturally defined goal in the "hierarchy of value" Merton refers to would depend on the place of income-consumption satisfactions in the hierarchy of value of the PPM system. That is, if one assumed a high value was generally placed on income-consumption satisfactions in a PPM system, then the goal of fulfilling one's social obligation to earn as much pre-tax income as one can would have to occupy a high place in the hierarchy of value of the egalitarian system.

Would the teaching stick? Why would people actually believe they had a social obligation to earn as much pre-tax income as they could? Why would they care if they did have such an obligation, that is, why would they accept it as a goal for themselves? The answers to these questions are the same as the answers which would be given similar questions asked about why people accepted any other culturally defined goals. As Miller describes the process:

> At each stage of development the self is identified in accordance with the meanings and values of some group, such as the family or peers or teachers. At first the group is important because it can enforce conformity to its standards by punishments and rewards. Later it is incorporated as part of one's internal society, at which time

conformity depends on internal pressures of shame and guilt in addition to the fear of discovery. Level of self-esteem fluctuates with the discrepancies between behavior and the norms of one's external and internal groups.[4]

The groups to which Miller refers are the bearers of the prevailing culture and are the agents through which the "culturally defined goals" which Merton describes are inculcated in the individual. (Not all groups inculcate the same goals, however, nor are all equally efficacious. I shall pursue these points further in my discussion of deviance later in this chapter.) Other psychologists and sociologists might object to particular details of Miller's description, but all are agreed on the basic elements of the process.[5] All agree that individuals have a basic need for the approval of others both as something which is of instrumental value to the satisfaction of other needs and as something which is valued in itself. Thus individuals will do those things which will win them the approval or esteem of others and will avoid doing those things which bring disapproval. Moreover, most social scientists would agree that most individuals in a social system will not only conform their behavior to the expectations of others but will internalize these expectations as norms for themselves. As Moore puts it,

> It is important to note that there are both empirical and logical limits to the extension of a kind of external, reactive, hedonic view of behavior. One individual's actions may be accounted for by reference to the sanctioned expectations of others. But one cannot account for the expectations or the sanctions in these terms. Some portions of the collectivity, and influential portions at that, must believe in the goals and rules, for the system could not otherwise survive the discovery of its mythical character.[6]

Consider how these principles would apply to the egalitarian system. What the arguments of Merton, Inkeles, Miller, and Moore suggest is that, if children were taught while growing up that they had a social obligation to maximize pre-tax income and if they found that the social approval (esteem) they received from others depended on the extent to which they achieved this goal, they would, for the most part, strive to achieve it. Most of them would also internalize the goal so that their own feelings of self-esteem would depend on whether they achieved this goal. Moreover, having internalized the goal, they would grant approval to others (or withhold it from them) on the basis of how much those others strove to achieve this goal of fulfilling *their* social obligation to earn as much pre-tax income as they could. Thus they would help to socialize others into striving for this goal and the process would perpetuate itself.

From this outline it can be seen that the "satisfactions derived from performing one's social duty" would include both the satisfactions of self-esteem and the satisfactions of social approval (esteem), and the sanctions for failing to perform one's social duty would include both guilt and social disapproval.

Developmental models. So far I have deliberately expressed the argument in such a way as to make it as independent as possible of any *particular* theory within the fields of sociology, psychology, and social psychology. In other words, my basic argument about socialization is compatible with all of the major schools of thought within these disciplines. I have adopted this approach in order to make my findings as persuasive as possible to as wide an audience as possible. It may be useful to note, however, that the argument can be strengthened further if one adopts the cognitive-development model of Jean Piaget and the moral-development model of Lawrence Kohlberg.

In Piaget's cognitive-development model, children go through various stages of social learning.[7] At the highest stage, which they reach at a fairly young age, they acquire a capacity for abstraction which enables them to gain a conceptual understanding of the social order in which they find themselves. In the egalitarian system, this capacity for abstraction would enable people to see that the obligation to acquire pre-tax income was not an arbitrary and irrational rule but rather an expectation that served an important social function. In other words, people would understand that the more pre-tax income they acquired, the more they would have contributed to the total productive output of society and therefore (given equal distribution) the more they would have contributed to the material well-being of their fellow citizens.[8] Presumably, this understanding would make people more inclined to accept their obligation to acquire pre-tax income than they would if they thought it a purely arbitrary expectation.

In Kohlberg's moral-development model, which builds upon Piaget's work, people go through stages of cognitive development.[9] At the highest stage, people judge specific questions of right and wrong in the light of general moral principles which have a high degree of logical comprehensibility. These universal principles can be expressed in various forms but they all entail some concept of justice in which the rights claimed and the duties put forward are grounded on the principles of equality and reciprocity. The principles upon which the egalitarian system is based would clearly satisfy these requirements, since each individual has an obligation to contribute to society what he is able to contribute (reciprocity) and each individual is entitled to an equal share of the goods and services produced in society (equality of rights). Thus those who reached the final stage of moral development would have additional reasons for accepting the moral legitimacy of the egalitarian arrangements, including the obligation to acquire pre-tax income.

As we saw in my original, more general statements about socialization, neither the cognitive development model nor the moral-development model is indispensable for the general argument about socialization. Moreover, if one did accept these models, it would not be necessary to assume that, in order for the egalitarian system to function, every individual would have to reach the highest stage of development. As long as people believed they had an obligation to earn as much pre-tax income as they could and as long as they placed sufficient value on the satisfactions derived from fulfilling this obligation, the egalitarian system would work, whether or not people understood the underlying rationality of the system or the broad moral principles on which it was based.

Nevertheless, for those who acquired these capacities, abstract reasoning and moral judging could help to reinforce the feelings of social duty which had been acquired in other ways in the socialization process in the egalitarian system.

Eight Sets of Questions

This tidy little scenario of perpetual socialization is apt to provoke a host of questions in the reader. For the sake of convenience, I shall divide the ones that occur to me into eight categories.

First, are there no limitations on the kinds of "culturally defined goals" which may be adopted in a social system? Are there any obstacles to the inculcation of this particular "culturally defined goal" of the egalitarian system? Are there any prior conditions which would have to be satisfied before people could be socialized into accepting this as an important goal?

Second, why are people motivated by income-consumption satisfactions? Are they not more the result of nature and less the result of nurture (socialization)? Would it not be easier to teach people to adopt the acquisition of income for consumption as a goal, at least if the opportunity for acquiring consumer goods existed, than to teach them to adopt the social duty to earn as much income as they can as a goal? Are not income-consumption satisfactions intrinsically related to economic activities in a way that social duty satisfactions are not?

Third, would people need a more extensive knowledge of relative prices in the egalitarian system than in the PPM system? If so, would this not make it more difficult to socialize people to respond to social-duty incentives than to respond to income-consumption incentives?

Fourth, is not the model a bit too tidy? What kinds of deviance might arise in the egalitarian system and how could they be controlled? Are not strains built into the egalitarian system as a result of the assumption that people seek income-consumption satisfactions as well as social-duty satisfactions? Does not the egalitarian system demand an especially high level of virtue of its members and would not the control of deviance require especially repressive measures?

Fifth, is it necessary for the egalitarian system to eliminate elites in order to survive? If not, why would elites tolerate it? Would not elites be the ones who derived the least advantage from such a system? Would they not try to change the rules of the system or the basic values or both? If they did try, how could they be prevented?

Sixth, are there not good empirical reasons for believing that the PPM system would spontaneously tend to adjust levels of effort upwards in response to economic decline while the egalitarian system would not? Would not the egalitarian system be dependent on elite intervention to increase the importance of social-duty satisfactions in a situation of economic decline?

Seventh, would not the elimination of income inequality just give rise to new forms of inequality? Indeed are not the satisfactions of esteem and self-esteem new sources of inequality which simply replace the inequality of income? Would not other inequalities, such as those of prestige and power, become more important if inequalities of income were eliminated?

Finally, how would this self-perpetuating system of socialization get started in the first place? Where would the first people come from who would feel a social obligation to earn as much pre-tax income as they could, even though this would not affect the amount of income available for consumption? Does not the experience of Communist countries in fact show that the inculcation of "moral incentives" requires an extensive and repressive bureaucracy, and that, in the long run, moral incentives are inevitably wasteful, inefficient, and unreliable as sources of motivation, at least in any industrial politico-economic system?

In the rest of this chapter, I shall attempt to answer these questions. Not all of them will be answered negatively. Through the process of answering these questions, I shall identify the remaining empirically necessary prerequisites of the egalitarian system. I think that the procedure of answering these questions will bring the controversial aspects of this work into sharper focus than would a mechanical listing of the logically necessary prerequisites and an identification of their empirically necessary prerequisites. At the end of the chapter I shall briefly review the logically necessary prerequisites and show that the discussion has in fact identified the most important empirical conditions which would have to be fulfilled in order for all of these logically necessary prerequisites to be met in a real-world system.

The Plasticity of Human Nature

The General Argument

I contended above that the fundamental empirically necessary prerequisite for the motivational hypothesis of the egalitarian system was simply an effective socialization process which would inculcate in people the belief that they had a social obligation to earn as much pre-tax income as they could. I ask now whether there is any reason to believe that people could be socialized into adopting this particular belief or whether my argument rests on a more general argument about the possibilities of socialization. In fact, there is a widespread social norm in the modern world which is analogous in important ways to the social duty of the egalitarian system. Moore observes that in most or all urban and industrial societies, "For at least the male who has completed his formal education, there is a clear obligation to seek work, presumably commensurate with his abilities."[10] And Moore suggests at another point that this norm applies even to those whose economic position would enable them to live comfortably without working.[11] The primary basis for my argument, however, is not this specific analogy but rather the general proposition that the range of culturally defined goals which have been discovered to exist in actual societies is so great that the contention that people could, in principle, be socialized into adopting this particular goal must be considered highly plausible in the absence of some specific argument or evidence to the contrary.

What I am saying here is stronger than simply asserting

that there is no reason not to believe that people could be socialized into adopting this goal. The latter statement could be made in the absence of any evidence whatsoever about theoretical limits and possibilities. For example, someone might argue that there is no reason not to believe that intelligent life exists in some other solar system because we do not have enough evidence to make any intelligent judgment about the probabilities in the matter. But, on the same grounds, one could argue that there is no reason to believe that intelligent life exists in other solar systems. There are no good grounds for making a judgment one way or the other. In the case I am discussing, however, the argument is different. I am claiming that there is sufficient evidence based on our empirical knowledge of the range of human cultural values to conclude that human nature is so flexible that, given the proper conditions of socialization, almost any goals could be adopted on a widespread basis in a society. If almost any goal could be adopted, there is good reason to believe that the goal of maximizing pre-tax income could be adopted unless there is some specific reason to believe it falls into that group of goals excluded by the qualifier "almost." Of course, positive proof that such a goal could be adopted could only be provided by empirical evidence showing that it actually had been adopted in an egalitarian system. I have made clear from the beginning, however, that the egalitarian system which I am discussing is only a theoretical system, and so I am necessarily obliged to rely upon evidence from empirical theory about the limits and possibilities of social systems.

The general proposition I am advancing here is stated clearly by Kuhn:

> important errors have been made in the past by psychologists and social scientists in assuming that there exists some clear, inborn, unchangeable, universal "human nature" which we can ignore only at our peril. The weight of current evidence, whether from psychology, comparative anthropology, or elsewhere is overwhelmingly to the contrary. Whatever may be the urges all men share by birth they are flexible in the extreme and can be accom-

modated to any social structure compatible with biological survival.[12]

The view expressed by Kuhn is certainly the dominant view in modern sociology,[13] but it has not been accepted without criticism. Some psychologists and sociologists have charged that the prevailing sociological view is built upon an "oversocialized" view of man and neglects the physical aspect of man.[14] Psychologists studying motivation have certainly paid much more attention to the physical causes of behavior than have sociologists.[15] Some psychologists and sociologists have attempted to identify drives, instincts, or needs which are prior to socialization and innate in all human beings.[16] These attempts have not been very successful on the whole. As Cohen puts it,

> nobody has ever been able to formulate an inventory of original or unsocialized tendencies that has commanded more than scattered and temporary agreement.... The very meaning of "original human nature" in any sense other than a range of possibilities, each of them dependent upon specific experiences for its development or maturation, has always proved exceedingly elusive and obscure.[17]

Some clarifications. Despite the difficulty, indeed apparent impossibility, of trying to identify any determinate human nature, the objections to the "plasticity" view of human nature which I have espoused require some further response. First, as Slater has pointed out, the general view that society molds and even creates desires in people does not commit one to the position that these desires are compatible with the society that creates them nor does it commit one to the position that the desires can be sated without conflict.[18] People may be socialized into antisocial attitudes or two people may be socialized into wanting something which only one of them can have.[19] In principle, neither of these observations applies directly to the particular goal of the egalitarian system with which I am concerned, since the desire to earn as much pre tax income as one can is not inherently antisocial and since the desire is defined in terms of people's capacities and therefore all individuals would theoretically be capable of satisfying this desire.

Second (and this is related to Slater's first point), there must be a reasonable degree of consistency among the goals and values which are inculcated in individuals through the socialization process, or the individuals and/or the society will be unable to function.[20] On these grounds, we might say that one empirically necessary prerequisite of the egalitarian system is that there must be a "reasonable degree of consistency" between this goal of earning as much pre-tax income as possible and other goals of the egalitarian system. There are unfortunately no precise guidelines for determining how much inconsistency is too much, but this clarification of the limits on the plasticity of human nature requires us to pay close attention to any sources of conflict or strain which may be built into the goals of the egalitarian system and to specify how these conflicts or strains can be controlled. I shall do this in my discussion of the possible sources of deviance later in the chapter.

Third, Homans has argued that the enormous variability in the things which people value does not entitle us to conclude that "men are equally likely to learn anything in the way of behavior provided only that they encounter in the social and physical environment the appropriate stimuli."[21] Homans insists that the differing physical characteristics which people possess play a role in determining the kinds of goals they will adopt:

> They do not start life, so to speak, as blank sheets of paper on which the environment can readily write whatever it occurs to it to write in the way of learning. Not only their experience but their genetic endowment—not only nurture, but nature, to use the neat antithesis— determines what they learn.[22]

Homan's focus here is on differences among individuals within the same cultural environment. In other words, the same socialization process may be more effective in inculcating a given goal in one person than in another because of differences in their genetic endowments. This is quite compatible with the position I am adopting and indeed I shall discuss in the section on deviance the consequences of the variability in socialization which results from this and from other factors. For the moment, however, it is important also to see that Homans is not arguing that there are generally shared genetic endowments which impose general limits on the kinds of values which people can be taught to adopt. In fact, earlier in the same book, Homans asserts that people's values are "infinitely varied."[23]

The fundamental position that I am advocating, therefore, is not one which denies that there are any basic human urges, needs, instincts, or drives, but rather one that asserts that whatever basic urges, drives, instincts, or needs there are, they are always mediated by the socialization process, that there is no apparent limit to the forms this mediation can take, and that it is futile to try to sort out what elements in any particular motivational pattern are due to nature and what to nurture.[24] The goal of trying to earn as much pre-tax income as one can might seem a good example of a goal which is entirely the product of nurture or culture, yet many people identify the need for social approval as a basic human drive, instinct, or need, and if achieving this goal brings social approval the desire to achieve the goal may be seen as the result of a basic drive or instinct and/or as a way of satisfying a basic need.

Biological survival as a limit on plasticity. There is one qualification which should be added to the position I have put forward here. Some authors who adopt an extremely "plastic" view of human nature nevertheless insist that the values or goals which people adopt must be "compatible with biological survival" (as Kuhn puts it).[25] It is not entirely clear whether these authors are saying that people cannot be socialized into adopting goals which are incompatible with biological survival (i.e., that they will resist such socialization) or merely that if they are socialized into adopting such values, they will not survive. The latter proposition is tautologous and the former seems empirically doubtful given the history of human warfare. Nevertheless, if there were any basic drive or need which people could agree was innate in man, it would probably be the drive or need for physical survival.[26] Studies of the effects of starvation on human values (conducted through research on concentration camp survivors and in experiments on volunteers) strongly suggest that the long-term absence of adequate amounts of food and drink leads to a dramatic reduction in the salience of all other values besides those of acquiring food and drink.[27] In the light of such studies, it would be prudent to add as an empirically necessary (or, at least, empirically probable) prerequisite of the egalitarian system, the condition that the system possess sufficient physical resources to provide for the physical subsistence of its members. If access to sufficient food, clothing, and shelter for survival were not provided by the equal income-share of the egalitarian system, it seems likely that many or most would fail (or cease) to be motivated by the goal of maximizing pre-tax income, regardless of how extensive the socialization process was, and would turn if possible to the task of providing directly for their physical needs. I state the requirement in this minimal way in order to make clear that I am *not* claiming here that prosperity or affluence is a prerequisite of the egalitarian system.[28] The ability to maintain the physical existence of its members is all that is necessary. Nevertheless, this is not a trivial prerequisite, since there are a number of nations in the world today where that capacity does not exist.

The Intensity of the Socialization Process

In the preceding section I argued that the enormous variation in the kinds of goals which have become important in different societies provided a reasonable basis for inferring that the social obligation to earn as much pre-tax income as one can could become a culturally defined goal and one which individuals would internalize under proper conditions of socialization. This argument, however, does not prove that all goals are *equally* easy to inculcate. Since the logically necessary motivational assumptions of the egalitarian system require that individuals place the same value on social-duty satisfactions as on income-consumption satisfactions, one must ask whether it would require the same amount and intensity of socialization to place the goal of maximizing pre-tax income at a given level in the hierarchy of value of the egalitarian system as it would take to place the goal of acquiring income for consumption at that same level in the hierarchy of value of the PPM system.

The real importance of this question stems from the fact that it is widely believed that acquiring income for consumption is a "naturally" powerful source of motivation, or, if not "naturally powerful," then at least inevitably powerful in a monetarized, industrial politico-economic system which permits freedom of choice in consumption. It is also believed by some that the provision of differential amounts of income for consumption is the most effective way of motivating people to perform productive tasks, at least in the long run and in any system where productive roles are filled on the basis of achievement and not ascription.[29] In this section, I shall examine these conventional beliefs in some detail.

*Income-Consumption Satisfactions as a
Product of Socialization*

The first and most obvious point to be noted is that the desire to acquire income for consumption is socially learned. Even those theorists who argue that certain basic drives exist which are not socially learned and who consider the desire for money to be an important "drive" in human motivation agree that it is acquired as a result of socialization.[30] At one level, this means only that the very concept of "income" presupposes a social structure in the way that the concept of "food" does not. Animals acquire food. They do not acquire income. Or, as Parsons put it, "money and social approval are generalized symbolic media of interaction whereas technical help and food objects are not."[31]

The anthropological evidence. At a second level one can argue that the fact that the desire for income is acquired through socialization means that the extent to which people will seek to acquire income will depend upon the extent to which income is a culturally defined goal and on the way it is related to other culturally defined goals. This assertion is apt to be more controversial but there is considerable support for it in the literature of comparative anthropology. For example, Barth observes in a study of Dafur, "By Mountain Fur conventions, it is shameful to work for wages in the local community."[32] On the other hand he notes that it is quite permissible to work for beer and that there is a relatively open labor market in which people exchange labor for beer. Do people simply buy beer, then, and use it to recruit labor? No, because it is also considered morally reprehensible to sell beer for cash.[33] One consequence of all this is that there is considerable difficulty in recruiting labor to work for wages despite the fact that the wages offered are much higher than the value[34] of the beer obtained for comparable work.

In the Mountain Fur case, it might be possible to argue that the people are economically motivated, as is demonstrated by their willingness to exchange labor for beer, and that beer is really their form of income for consumption, since money has no effective exchange value for the good they most wish to consume (beer). Such an argument would overlook both the fact that there are other consumption goods which the Mountain Fur people can acquire with money and the fact that the only reason beer and labor are not exchanged for money is because people have been taught (socialized into believing) that it is shameful to make such exchanges. Thus this case would seem to support the claim that the role of socialization is crucial in determining the extent to which income will become a source of motivation.

A number of anthropologists have advanced an even broader claim than the one just put forward. Polanyi and his followers, especially Dalton, have emphasized the variety of motives which have led people in different societies to work and to produce.[35] They have argued that the desire for personal economic gain is not a "natural" motive for economic activity and is not even a common one outside of modern, industrial, market-based economies. The anthropological methods of Polanyi, Dalton, and the others of this school have been sharply criticized by some other anthropologists.[36] And cases of primitive economies have been discovered in which personal economic gain does seem to be a crucial source of motivation.[37] Nevertheless, most anthropologists would probably accept Nash's general observation that "people engage in economic activities for rewards often extrinsic to the economy itself. From this point of view there are no economic motives but only motives appropriate to the economic sphere."[38]

If Nash's view were held to apply to all societies, it would support the contention that social-duty satisfactions could be as effective a source of motivation for economic activity as income-consumption satisfactions, given equally effective conditions of socialization. That is, income-consumption satisfactions could not be considered to be a more logical or more natural source of motivation for productive activity than social-duty satisfactions.

Someone might argue, however, that it would be a mistake to extrapolate from findings about primitive societies to judgments about modern, industrial ones. Modern industrial societies, it might be said, are characterized by a high degree of structural differentiation. Economic functions are more sharply distinguished from other social functions in industrial societies than in primitive ones. Therefore, it is likely to be more effective and it may even be essential to rely on pecuniary incentives (income-consumption satisfactions) as the basic source of motivation for economic activities.[39]

Alternative Motives for Economic Activity in Industrial Societies

Without denying the general contention that modern industrial societies are more highly differentiated than primitive ones, I intend to argue that there are good empirical reasons for believing that "noneconomic" motives (motives other than those of acquiring income for consumption) can be as effective as and sometimes more effective than income-consumption satisfactions in motivating economic activity.

The Protestant ethic. The most famous argument in support of my position is the one developed by Max Weber in *The Protestant Ethic and the Spirit of Capitalism.* Weber argued that it was precisely the fact that some Protestant capitalists were *not* motivated by the desire to acquire income for consumption but rather by the desire to acquire this-worldly proof of their eternal salvation that enabled the modern capitalist economic system to emerge. According to Weber, the conventional capitalist was inclined to behave in a very traditional way, producing by traditional methods, receiving a traditional amount of profit, and consuming most of his income. It was the Protestant ascetic by contrast who felt compelled for religious reasons to maximize production through innovation and the reinvestment of his earnings. As Weber puts it, "He gets nothing out of his wealth for himself, except the irrational sense of having done his job well."[40] Weber's thesis has been the subject of considerable controversy, but there are a number of other studies which indicate as well that religious values can have an important impact on economic activity in the process of industrialization.[41] In a related vein, Kingsley Davis has suggested that nationalism may be a much more important force in the process of economic development than a personal concern for the acquisition of income for consumption.[42]

The need for achievement. The most important contemporary evidence in support of my argument, however, comes from the research of David McClelland and his associates on achievement motivation. The research on the need for achievement indicates that this "need" is essentially made up of values about work and change and effort acquired through the socialization process. These values are conceptually and empirically distinct from the desire to acquire income for consumption, and yet they are key factors in motivating individuals to engage in entrepreneurial activity in the economic system. As McClelland and Winter put it, what interest or desires for return are characteristic of men with high n Achievement? The evidence seems clear that these men are interested in excellence for its own sake rather than for the rewards of money, prestige, or power. *Men high in n Achievement will not work harder at a task when money is offered as a reward.... Their achievement concern is not affected by having to work for the group rather than only for themselves.* Over time they tend to become successful entrepreneurs rather than equally wealthy men in other roles. ... it seems clear that n Achievement leads to an interest in entrepreneurial excellence in its most general sense, and not to interests which may be superficially associated with it or confused with it in Western industrial culture such as wealth, prestige, or individual prominence and influence.[43]

The importance of these findings for my argument seems clear. Even in PPM systems, the desire for income-consumption satisfactions is not the key source of motivation for those who are most dynamic and entrepreneurial. Rather the source of motivation is the need for achievement which is connected to the acquisition of income only because income is an indicator of success. The need for achievement would continue even if the personal economic rewards were eliminated.

Thus, if McClelland is correct, we could infer that in the egalitarian system those with a high n Achievement would respond just as vigorously to price cues as they do in the PPM system since success would be defined in terms of their ability to earn as much pre-tax income as they could. More generally, McClelland's findings indicate that the source of motivation for economic activities, even in industrial societies, may be values other than the desire to acquire income for consumption. Thus the earlier objection that pecuniary rewards may be uniquely appropriate as motivators in industrial societies seems to be without foundation. There is no reason, therefore, to assume that the social-duty satisfactions of the egalitarian system could not be an effective source of motivation, even in an industrial society, given the proper conditions of socialization.

Income-Consumption Satisfactions in Industrial Societies

Even if it is granted that goals other than those of acquiring income for consumption may be effective sources of motivation for economic activities in modern industrial societies, it may be argued that the desire to acquire income for consumption will also be an important goal and necessarily so. As Homans says,

> there are some values that men in particular kinds of society would have difficulty in *not* acquiring. These are so-called *generalized values* . . . good examples of which are money and social approval . . . money and social approval can serve as rewards for a wide variety of actions and not just for some single kind.[44]

Homans fails to specify what the characteristics are of the particular kind of society in which men would have difficulty in not acquiring the value of money. Presumably, he means a society with a widespread and relatively unrestricted market in goods and services for consumption (unlike the Mountain Fur case). I do not wish to quarrel with this position too strongly. After all, I am assuming that people in the egalitarian system will value income-consumption satisfactions, and Homans's observation that money has enormous instrumental value would obviously apply to the egalitarian system as well as to PPM systems. Besides, if money were not valued fairly highly, we would have no reason to be concerned about how it was distributed. Nevertheless, it is important to qualify somewhat the contention that money will inevitably be highly valued, and it is even more important to analyze the reasons why money is valued in PPM systems in order to see how this might affect the analysis of the prerequisites of the egalitarian system.

Since the time of the Hawthorne studies there has been considerable debate among social scientists about the relative importance of income incentives and other incentives such as peer-group approval, work satisfaction, and the like in motivating economic behavior in PPM systems. Although there are a great many conflicting arguments, there seems to be a considerable amount of evidence to suggest that, at the very least, income-consumption satisfactions are not the only important source of motivation for economic activity in advanced industrial societies and that, in many cases, they are not as important as other motives.[45] Some people are much more responsive to income incentives than others, and some are not very responsive at all, even in PPM systems. This is perhaps an obvious point but it is one which should not be lost from sight.

The role of socialization. More important, it is essential to recognize that the value placed on income-consumption satisfactions does not depend only on the structure of the politico-economic system (on the existence of a market for consumer goods or even, in the PPM system, on the existence of the possibility of acquiring differential amounts of income for consumption). Rather the value placed on income-consumption satisfactions still depends heavily on the socialization process. As Parsons and Smelser put it, "economic values which form the basis of the meaning of wealth and income to the individual, are internalized in the process of socialization. They are social values...."[46] More specifically, Merton contends that the relatively high value placed on money by Americans is the result of an intensive socialization process in which people are taught to value the acquisition of income for consumption:

> To say that the goal of monetary success is entrenched in American culture is only to say that Americans are bombarded on every side by precepts which affirm the right, or often, the duty of retaining the goal even in the face of repeated frustration. Prestigeful representatives of the society reinforce the cultural emphasis. The family, the school, the workplace—the major agencies shaping the personality structure and goal formation of Americans —join to provide the intensive disciplining required if an individual is to retain intact a goal that remains elusively beyond reach....[47]

Later he observes: "striving for monetary success is not a matter of individuals *happening* to have aquisitive impulses rooted in human nature, but is a socially-defined expectation."[48] Thus, the goal of acquiring income is, like all goals, culturally defined and acquired by the individual through the process of socialization.

There is a further important point which follows from Merton's analysis. Because acquiring money is a "socially defined expectation," the forces of social approval and disapproval help to inculcate this value in the individual and lead him to internalize the value. Thus when individuals seek to acquire income available for consumption, they are motivated to do so not only by the desire for the money as an instrument for the gratification of other desires but also by the desire for the social approval (esteem) they will receive and the self-esteem they will feel as a result of acquiring the income.[49] In other words, the same forces of social approval and self-esteem which would induce individuals to fulfill their obligations to earn as much pre-tax income as they could in the egalitarian system operate in the PPM system to induce individuals to acquire income available for consumption.

This has two important consequences for my analysis. First, it shows that the satisfactions derived from acquiring income for consumption are more like the satisfactions derived from fulfilling one's social obligation to earn as much pre-tax income as possible than might appear to be the case on the surface, since both of them involve the satisfactions of social approval and self-esteem. In that respect it makes the socialization task of the egalitarian system seem easier since it would be parallel to what is being done in the PPM system. Second, however, it shows that the egalitarian system would have to rely more heavily on the satisfactions of esteem and self-esteem since the instrumental satisfactions associated with the acquisition of income for consumption are not available in the egalitarian system.

In order to understand this second point more clearly, let us assume the existence of a society with a widespread market for consumer goods and with a given set of culturally defined goals, abstracting from that set the goal of acquiring income available for consumption. In order for the acquisition of income for consumption to become a culturally defined goal having a given place in the hierarchy of values of this society, people must undergo a socialization process. The socialization process involves two analytically distinct factors which will induce individuals to place a given amount of value on this goal. The first factor is the one common to the adoption of all culturally defined goals—the social approval which is granted by others for achieving this goal and the self-esteem which becomes associated with achieving the goal once the goal has been internalized. The second factor is the fact that, given the market for consumer goods, income available for consumption can be an important instrument for achieving other culturally defined goals (those things which the culture had defined as desirable to consume). Thus some value will be placed on the acquisition of income for consumption simply because of its instrumental relation to other culturally defined goals.

In the egalitarian system, by contrast, this instrumental factor is removed. Let us assume the same society with the same widespread market for consumer goods and the same set of culturally defined goals, abstracting from that set this time both the goal of acquiring income for consumption and the goal (unique to the egalitarian system) of fulfilling one's social duty to earn as much pre-tax income as one can. In order for this goal of fulfilling one's social obligation to maximize pre-tax income to become a culturally defined goal having a given place in the hierarchy of values of the society, people would have to undergo a certain socialization process, as we saw in the beginning of the chapter. In contrast to the task of inculcating the goal of acquiring income available for consumption, however, there would be only one factor available here to induce individuals to place a certain amount of value on the goal of fulfilling their social obligation to earn as much pre-tax income as they can. That would be the factor of the social approval granted by others for achieving the goal and the self-esteem which becomes associated with achieving the goal once it has been internalized. The instrumental factor would not be available since the amount of income available for consumption that a person would acquire in the egalitarian system would not depend on how much he conformed to the goal of earning as much pre-tax income as he could. Therefore, if the goal of fulfilling one's social obligation to earn as much pre-tax income as possible were to have the same place in the hierarchy of values of the egalitarian system as the goal of acquiring income available for consumption has in the PPM system, this instrumental factor would have to be replaced by an increase in the social importance attached to this social-duty goal as compared with the *social* importance attached to the income-consumption goal. In other words, there would have to be more social approval granted for conformity to the goal of maximizing pre-tax income in the egalitarian system than would have to be granted in the PPM system for conforming to the goal of acquiring income for consumption, in order for the two goals to occupy the same place in the hierarchy of values of their respective systems.

(The acquisition of income for consumption would be valued in the egalitarian system because of its instrumental relation to other culturally defined goals, but its place in the hierarchy of values would be determined entirely by this instrumental value. It would not be reinforced by the factors of social approval and self-esteem since all would receive the equal income-share regardless of their economic performance or their conformity to other social goals.)

More Intense Socialization an Empirically Necessary Prerequisite

Should one conclude from the preceding analysis that the socialization process of the egalitarian system must be more intensive than that of the PPM system? If one defines greater reliance on the factor of social approval (and the derived self-esteem) as a more intense socialization process—and such a definition does not seem unreasonable—then the answer is yes. The inculcation of the goal of fulfilling one's social duty to earn as much pre-tax income as possible would require a more intense socialization process than would the inculcation of the goal of acquiring income for consumption in the PPM system. This more intense socialization process is an empirically necessary prerequisite of the egalitarian system.

It is essential, however, not to read too much into this requirement. The fact that a more intense socialization process would be required in the egalitarian system does not mean that it could not be achieved. It should be recalled that social approval is generally considered to be one of the most powerful sources of control over human behavior, both because of its intrinsic value and because it too (like money) has enormous instrumental value for the achievement of a wide variety of other culturally defined goals.

The possibility of decentralization. One should not infer from the requirement for a more intense socialization process that the socialization process would have to be consciously planned and managed by a highly centralized bureaucracy. The intensity with which different goals are inculcated through socialization varies considerably from one society to another. As we have seen, Merton contends that among Americans the socialization process which inculcates the goal of acquiring income is very intensive in terms of the social approval which is attached to this goal. Nevertheless, Merton nowhere suggests that this intensity is the result of centralized direction or bureaucratic control over the process of socialization. Rather he indicates that it is relatively decentralized agencies—family, school, and work-place—which are primarily responsible for this intense socialization, presumably for the most part because they share a consensus on the considerable importance they attach to this goal and not because they are being directed to inculcate this goal by some ruling elite, although he does indicate that "prestigeful representatives of the society reinforce the cultural emphasis." The point is that it is quite possible to have a highly intensive socialization process which attaches great social importance to some particular goal and yet which is decentralized, informal, and even, for many of the agents of socialization, unconscious and unintended. It might be difficult or impossible for a goal to be a major source of social approval if the elites of the society did not accept the goal,[50] but the fact that elites may accept the goal does not mean that they consciously direct the socialization process. In the egalitarian system, therefore, if the goal of fulfilling one's social duty to earn as much pre-tax income as possible were regarded by most adults as an important goal, there would be no need for the socialization process to be centrally directed or bureaucratically controlled. The only difference from the socialization process required for a PPM system is that more social approval would have to be granted for conformity to the goal of earning pre-tax income in the egalitarian system than needs to be granted in the PPM system for conformity to the goal of acquiring income for consumption. A more intense socialization process does not necessarily entail a different *system* of socialization.

Altruism and Self-Interest

The term "moral incentives" may suggest a type of motivation which is essentially altruistic. By contrast, the income incentives of a PPM system are often regarded as the archetype of motivation through appeal to self-interest. The comparison of the socialization requirements in the PPM and the egalitarian systems should show how misleading this dichotomy is. The dichotomy assumes a fixed and limited view of human nature, but this is precisely what we have argued is not warranted by the available evidence.

A concept of self-interest which applies to all individuals presupposes that all individuals have the same interests. Thus it neglects the crucial role of socialization in developing and shaping interests. What an individual considers his self-interest to be will depend on what values he holds. This can vary from one individual to another. Within a given culture, it may be reasonable to assume that individuals share broadly similar notions of self-interest because people within that culture will have been inculcated in broadly similar values. But one should not try to elevate a culturally specific view of self-interest, such as that characteristic of modern PPM systems, into an eternal principle. Moreover, even if a value is widely accepted as a constituent element of self-interest, the ways in which that value may be realized will be limited by social norms and structures. For example, even in a society which places great value on material acquisition, there will be socially prescribed limits on the methods of acquisition. If these social norms are widely shared, those who seek material goods will find it to be in their self-interest, even in terms of acquisition, to conform to these norms. In other words, if they violate widely shared norms they are less likely to be successful in attaining the goal of material acquisition.[51]

A similar point can be made with respect to the concept of altruism. At least when used in contrast to self-interest, the term seems to imply an element of self-sacrifice, of foregoing something which is in one's own interest (or doing something against one's interests) for the sake of other people. But whether an action is altruistic or not depends partly on how one defines self-interest. Indeed some people would claim that all human action, even action which is apparently altruistic, is ultimately self-interested.[52] Certainly we are all familiar with examples of this type of behavior, such as charitable giving which is used as an expression of social superiority or as a way of exercising control. But this line of argument can be pushed too far. If one defines whatever a person does as being in his self-interest simply because he does it, one adopts a formalistic approach which destroys the utility of both self-interest and altruism as concepts. We use the term "altruism" to distinguish certain kinds of motivation and behavior from other kinds. The distinctions are meaningful and important even if we do not always agree about the applicability of the term to a particular case, or even if we disagree, in some cases, about the criteria to be used in deciding whether or not to apply the term.[53] (The existence of border disputes does not show that there are no boundaries. Rather it presupposes them.)[54] To define away the possibility of altruism is to obscure the distinctiveness of those motivations and actions for which we wish to use the term. In the same vein, if we use the concept of self-interest to describe all motivated behavior, we can no longer use it to distinguish one kind of motivated behavior from another.

Perhaps the most important point to note about the concepts of self-interest and altruism is that much human motivation does not fit readily into either category. As Alasdair MacIntyre puts it:

> in most of my dealings with others of a cooperative kind, questions of benevolence or altruism simply do not arise, any more than questions of self-interest do.... if I want to lead a certain kind of life, with relationships of trust, friendship, and cooperation with others, then my wanting their good and my wanting my good are not two independent, discriminable desires. It is not even that I have two separate motives, self-interest and benevolence, for doing the same action. I have one motive, a desire to live in a certain way, which cannot be characterized as a desire for my good rather than that of others. For the good that I recognize and pursue is not mine particularly, except in the sense that I recognize and pursue it.[55]

In the light of this discussion, it should be clear why it would be misleading to describe the moral incentives of the egalitarian system as altruistic. Begin from the perspective of self-interest. People in the egalitarian system would have a different notion of self-interest from those in PPM systems. Because of the differences in the socialization process, they would value social approval more and income less. Moreover, the structure of the egalitarian system reinforces the emphasis on social approval as an element in self-interest. Individuals cannot significantly affect their levels of after-tax income in the egalitarian system by their own behavior. This element of their self-interest is fixed. By contrast, individuals can affect the amount of social approval they receive by their behavior. From this perspective, positive responses to price signals in the egalitarian system could be seen as purely self-interested behavior by individuals seeking to attain higher levels of social approval. Fulfillment of social duty to acquire pre-tax income should not be regarded as altruism because the individual is not acting against his own interests for the sake of others. At the most, he is choosing among different and conflicting elements in his own self-interest, (e.g., social approval vs. leisure) just as people do in PPM systems (e.g., income vs. leisure). In this light, the benefit to others resulting from the pursuit of social duty would be as incidental to the individual's motivation in the egalitarian system as it is in the PPM system.

Treating social-duty incentives as fundamentally egoistic, as I have done in the preceding paragraph, provides a necessary corrective to the tendency to classify all moral incentives as "altruistic," but it creates another kind of distortion in the process. We saw above that the egalitarian system required a more intense socialization process than the PPM system because the instrumental attractions of income acquisition in the PPM system were not duplicated by social-duty incentives in the egalitarian system, even though social approval offers important instrumental attractions. The counterpart to this greater intensity of socialization is a greater internalization of the values being pursued. Thus MacIntyre's point about the motivation for cooperative interactions would apply to the egalitarian system.[56] People would fulfill their social duty to acquire pre-tax income because they would regard it as a good thing to do, that is, they would have internalized the value of fulfilling this social duty. They would not distinguish sharply between the benefit to themselves (social approval) and the benefit to others (material well-being) which would result from their behavior. They would not regard the good to others and the good to themselves as distinct and independent motives. Moreover, the internal coherence of the motivation to fulfill one's social duty reflects the internal coherence of the egalitarian system. It is appropriate to define the acquisition of pre-tax income as a social duty and to grant social approval for fulfilling this duty because acquiring as much pre-tax income as one can is a course of behavior which benefits everyone in the system. It is not just an arbitrarily defined form of social duty. Too much emphasis on the self-interested pursuit of social approval would obscure the underlying rationality of the egalitarian system.

Knowledge of Relative Prices

We have seen that the egalitarian system requires a more intense socialization process than the PPM system. There is a second factor besides that of intensity which would make it somewhat more difficult to socialize people to respond to social-duty incentives than to socialize them to respond to income-consumption incentives: In order for social-duty incentives to work in the egalitarian system, people would have to have a somewhat greater knowledge of relative prices than would be necessary for income-consumption incentives to work in the PPM system.

Social Approval and Relative Prices

The difference between the two systems becomes more apparent when one considers the role of social approval in the egalitarian system. I stated earlier that individuals who had internalized the goals of the egalitarian system would grant approval to others (or withhold it from them) on the basis of how much those others strove to achieve this goal of fulfilling their social obligation to earn as much pre-tax income as they could. And I noted that this granting or withholding of social approval played a crucial role in the ongoing process of socialization within the egalitarian system. Now the problem is this: In order for the process to work, individuals in the egalitarian system must be able to perceive the extent to which others are fulfilling their social duty. In other words, an individual not only has to know what percentage of capacity he himself is working at, but he has to know what percentage of capacity others are working at as well, so that he can withhold or grant his approval accordingly.

Social approval does play a role in the PPM system, too, but there is no necessary connection in the PPM system between actual income and potential income. Thus, in theory, individuals in the PPM system need only know what others are actually earning, not what they are capable of earning, in order to grant or withhold social approval. Moreover, an individual's consumption life-style can be used as one important indicator of his income level in a PPM system, while it would obviously be irrelevant to his pre-tax income level in an egalitarian system. We should also recall that the role played by social approval in the PPM system is less important than that played by social approval in the egalitarian system because of the utilitarian value of income in the PPM system.

Would it be possible for real people to acquire the knowledge which would be required for social approval to play its role in the egalitarian system, and, if so, under what conditions could this knowledge be acquired?

The first point to note is that the social approval which I have asserted to be such a powerful motivating force is neither the generalized approval of society as a whole nor the approval of any member of society taken at random but rather the concrete approval of specific actors whose judgments the individual regards as significant. Both the initial socialization and the ongoing reinforcement of that socialization are performed not by society as a whole but by decentralized and specific social units such as family, school, and workplace. Indeed these functions are performed by specific people— family members, teachers, friends, fellow workers, superiors, subordinates—who act, consciously or unconsciously, as the agents of society. Thus one can see that the egalitarian system would not require everyone to know about everyone else's pre-tax incomes and earning capacities. Only the limited number of people whose approval was actually valued by the individual would have to know about that individual's earning capacity and about his performance, in order for the egalitarian system to function. (I am assuming here, of course, that these people themselves would have internalized the goals of the egalitarian system and would grant their approval on the basis of how much this individual was fulfilling his social duty with regard to pre-tax income.) Now it is precisely these significant others whose approval was sought who would be the most likely to be able to judge what an individual's capacities were and to be able to judge the extent to which he was utilizing these capacities, since they would be the most likely to know the individual well. Thus the knowledge required for the egalitarian system to function is not so grandiose as might first have appeared to be the case.

Even on this more limited basis, it still seems difficult to imagine that real people would be able to acquire detailed information about the actual and projected prices, relative risks, and the like associated with the allocation of someone else's resources. Fortunately, people could make rough judgments about the extent to which another individual was utilizing his earning capacity without knowing such details. Indeed, in PPM systems, individuals rarely attempt to acquire such finely detailed information about relative prices even when they are allocating their own resources and seeking income-consumption satisfactions. Gathering information about actual prices and making complicated calculations about projected prices and relative risks can be costly in time, effort, and money. To reduce these costs, people use the experience of others, the impressions of friends and acquaintances, and other such devices to form judgments about alternatives. (E.g., the local factory-work is steady though low-paying. Carpentry pays better but is very seasonal. It would not be wise to spend time as an apprentice learning to set hot type. Computers are a good field to get into.) These rough popular impressions are an important source of informal information about relative prices, projected prices, relative risks, and so on.

It is precisely this kind of popular, readily available information which people could use to make judgments in the egalitarian system. While consumption life-styles could not be used as a source of information about pre-tax incomes, there are many other mechanisms which communicate information about labor prices in a market system (job advertisements, employment agencies, guidance counselors). People would have to pay somewhat more attention to informal sources of information about relative prices than they might in a PPM system since they would be concerned with others as well as themselves. Moreover, they would have to make some judgment about the earning capacities as well as the actual performances of those individuals with whom they interacted. Nevertheless, given these informal sources of information, these tasks would not be difficult. Assuming that they knew an individual reasonably well, they would be able to make some judgment about whether he had pursued schooling or other training as far as he should, whether he had looked reasonably hard for a job that paid well (given his skills), whether he was working hard, taking advantage of opportunities as they presented themselves, and so on. And they could bestow or withhold their approval on the basis of these judgments.

In sum, greater knowledge of prices would be an empirically necessary prerequisite of the egalitarian system. However, it would be possible for people to acquire the additional knowledge that would be required for social approval to play its role in the egalitarian system because a relatively limited number of people would be involved in any given case, and these people could simply take greater advantage of informal sources of information which would also be available in a PPM system.

Self-Esteem and Relative Prices

As we have seen, social-duty satisfactions involve not only the satisfactions of social approval but also those of self-esteem. In order for self-esteem to play its role in the egalitarian system, individuals again must have a somewhat greater knowledge of prices than in the PPM system, though the additional knowledge required for self-esteem is less than was required for social approval.

If one abstracts from effort, the knowledge required for self-esteem to play its role in the egalitarian system is exactly the same as the knowledge required in the PPM system. In making choices about resource allocation, the individual in the PPM system would theoretically take into account all alternative allocations of his labor and property. As we saw in the last chapter, he might ultimately decide to choose some allocation which would yield less than the maximum return in income in order to acquire some alternative satisfaction (e.g., a more enjoyable job). Nevertheless, in theory, he would consider all his alternatives. In other words, he would take his earning capacity into account in making decisions about the allocation of his resources. In practice, he would undoubtedly use informal sources of information to determine that earning capacity, as we have just seen, but even in practice the individual in the PPM system would take alternatives (i.e., earning capacity) into account in deciding how to allocate his resources.

In the egalitarian system, the desire for self-esteem would also lead the individual to take into account all available alternative allocations, as we saw in Chapter 2. Since the only knowledge he would need would be knowledge about available alternatives (i.e., earning capacity), he would need no more knowledge than in the PPM system. As in the PPM system, he could take advantage in practice of informal sources of information, but again he would need no more knowledge than would be available to him in the PPM system.

When we considered decisions about effort, we saw that the individual in the PPM system need consider only the relation between his income and the cost of living, in order to decide how to respond to a price change in one or the other or both. He could ignore his earning capacity at that point. By contrast, in the egalitarian system, the individual would still have to take into account his earning capacity in making any decisions about effort, since his self-esteem would be dependent on the percentage of capacity at which he worked. (He would not have to know how price changes affected his standard of living, but that is no particular advantage since he could be assumed to know that as a consumer anyway.) In sum, in order for self-esteem to play its role in the egalitarian system, an individual must pay closer attention to the effects of price changes on his earning capacity than he does in the PPM system. This constitutes a second factor in the empirically necessary prerequisite that individuals have greater knowledge of prices in the egalitarian system than in the PPM system.

As we have just seen, an individual would be able to utilize informal sources of information about the effects of price changes on his earning capacity. Thus this need for additional knowledge would not place a great burden on individuals in the egalitarian system, especially since it is only a question of paying closer attention to a price which the individual would already take into account in making any decisions in the PPM system.

Deviance in the Egalitarian System

I turn now to the question of what kinds of deviance might arise in the egalitarian system and what kinds of measures would be needed to control it. There are two possible kinds of deviance that must be considered. The first is deviance from the social goal of fulfilling one's social obligation to earn as much pre-tax income as one can. The second is deviance from the social rule that income available for consumption will be distributed equally. The two kinds pose quite different kinds of problems for my analysis.

Variability of Socialization and Variability of Relative Value Placed on Social-Duty Satisfactions

I have generally described the socialization process as a fairly uniform process. This practice was adopted purely for convenience of exposition. The assertion that goals are "culturally defined" certainly does not commit one to the position that every individual in a given society will place the same relative value on a given culturally defined goal. I explicitly noted at one point that the same socialization process might be more effective in inculcating a given goal in one person than in another because of differences in their genetic endowments, and I have implied elsewhere (in the discussion of achievement motivation and of the Hawthorne studies) that one could expect to find considerable variation in the extent to which different individuals in the same society would seek to achieve any given goal. The reasons for this variability are obvious. As Moore puts it,

> the infant is scarcely born into society in the full meaning of the term but into a decentralized concrete structure—normally a family—which represents society only imperfectly. In childhood, the individual's encounter with society is virtually always with such decentralized and sometimes rather specialized social units. His care, custody, socialization and social participation are the functions of the family, the playgroup, the neighborhood, and occasionally such specific organizations or their representatives as the clinic and the police. These units of the great society are not only structurally differentiated, but are also subject to chance variability....[57]

One would expect therefore to find as much variation in the relative value placed by different individuals on given culturally defined goals in the egalitarian system as one would find in the PPM system. Indeed this variation is required by my assumptions about the relative values placed on sources of satisfaction. It follows therefore that some individuals in the egalitarian system would place the culturally defined goal of fulfilling one's social duty to maximize pre-tax income at a lower rank in their personal hierarchies of value than most of the other individuals in the egalitarian system. Others would place it higher than most. Would this variability pose any problem for the functioning of the egalitarian system?

In principle, the answer is no, if the conditions, which I have previously identified as empirically necessary prerequisites of the egalitarian system have been met. I have acknowledged that a more intensive socialization process would be required in the egalitarian system than in the PPM system for the egalitarian goal of earning pre-tax income to occupy the same place in a hierarchy of value as the PPM goal of acquiring income for consumption. Given that more intensive socialization process, however, the egalitarian social-duty goal would occupy the same place in the hierarchy of value as the PPM income-consumption goal. Since there would be variability in the hierarchy of value from one individual to another, some individuals in the egalitarian system might choose, for example, to accept a low-paying job which was personally satisfying instead of accepting a high-paying job which they found alienating. If my empirically necessary prerequisites have been met, however, the same individuals in the PPM system would make exactly the same choices. That is, in the egalitarian system, individuals would trade off social-duty satisfactions against work satisfactions and in the PPM system individuals would trade off income-consumption satisfactions against work satisfactions. This kind of trade-off poses no problems for the analysis so long as the same allocation of resources would result in the egalitarian system as in the PPM system. I have established this point in earlier chapters. At this level, then, variability in the value which different individuals might place on social-duty satisfactions would pose no problem for the egalitarian system.

Extreme deviance from social duty. It might be asked, however, whether the difference between social-duty satisfactions and income-consumption satisfactions together with the equal distribution requirement of the egalitarian system might not create special problems for the egalitarian system in cases of extreme deviance from the goal of earning pre-tax income. Suppose, for example, that some individuals placed such little value on the goal of fulfilling their social duty to earn pre-tax income that they earned no pre-tax income at all.[58] Given the requirements of the egalitarian system, they would still receive their equal income shares. Would not such cases have an enormous negative impact on the willingness to work of the rest of the population in the egalitarian system?

Again, the answer is that this situation would cause no greater problem for the egalitarian than the comparable situation of failure to earn income would for the PPM system, if the empirically necessary prerequisites of the egalitarian system have been met. Suppose, for example, that individuals in the PPM system placed such a low value on the acquisition of income for consumption that they refused to work to acquire an income. Suppose further that to display their distaste for the acquisition of income they burned money. Would this have an enormous negative effect on the willingness to acquire income of the rest of the population in the PPM system? I mention the burning of money, of course, because some of those who "dropped out" in the sixties actually did this. Many others refused to acquire an income in any conventional manner. Some may note the qualification "in any conventional manner" and say, "but they did have to acquire some income simply in order to survive." Perhaps, but the acquisition of a minimal survival income through grants from relatives, strangers, or state agencies can scarcely be considered a significant sign of conformity to the goal of acquiring income for consumption.

The sanctions for not seeking the culturally defined goals are built into both the egalitarian and the PPM systems. In both cases, these sanctions are apt to be ineffective if people do not desire the rewards which are withheld or fear the penalties which are imposed for nonconformity. In the case of the egalitarian system, individuals who would refuse to earn any pre-tax income would have to be indifferent to the extreme social disapproval which would be visited upon them for their behavior. In the case of the PPM system, individuals who would refuse to earn income for consumption in any conventional way would have to be indifferent both to the instrumental value of money and to the social disapproval which they would incur for their behavior (though this social disapproval would be less severe than that incurred in the egalitarian system, given my assumptions). It does not seem to me to be reasonable to assert that there is a fundamental difference between the two cases because in the PPM case the individuals do have to acquire sufficient income for survival. Neither the individuals themselves nor others in the system would be likely to view the acquisition of a minimal income (especially if it were acquired as grant) as a sign of acceptance of the basic goal of acquiring income for consumption. One can conclude, therefore, that whatever negative impact such extreme deviant behavior would have on the willingness to earn pre-tax income in the egalitarian system, it would be no greater than the negative impact which comparably extreme deviant behavior would have on the willingness to work in the PPM system. To judge otherwise would be to assume implicitly or explicitly that income is, at bottom, a more effective motivator than social approval and that the desire to acquire income for consumption is not itself a product of socialization subject to the same extreme ranges of variability among individuals as any other culturally defined goal.

Factors tending to reduce deviance from social duty. Let us return briefly to the initial question. Would the refusal to earn pre-tax income by some members of the egalitarian system have a severe negative impact on the willingness to work of other members? This question cannot be answered categorically on an a priori basis (except in terms of a comparison with the PPM system). Nevertheless, it seems reasonable to assert that the probability of such deviant behavior having a serious impact would be extremely low if the egalitarian system had a reasonably effective socialization process. The central reason for this is that most people are extremely reluctant to be considered deviant.[59] People do not wish to incur social disapproval. Thus they usually conform to social values even when they have not themselves internalized these values as personal goals. Presumably, the stronger the social disapproval associated with nonconformity, the more likely individuals are to conform. In the egalitarian system, the social disapproval for refusing to earn any pre-tax income would be extreme. Thus while deviance might occur as a result of variability in socialization, it would not be likely to spread.

As a secondary and supporting reason for this conclusion, we may note that it is by no means clear that leisure is generally preferable to work even apart from all considerations of social approval or disapproval. The value placed on work or on leisure would be determined by the process of socialization. If work itself were valued in the egalitarian system (even apart from the social duty to earn pre-tax income), then the likelihood of a negative impact from the kind of deviance I have been describing would be further reduced. This general theoretical point receives considerable empirical support from studies which have been conducted in the United States on the attitudes of the unemployed towards work and on the effects of income maintenance programs on incentives to work. For the most part those who do not have jobs want to find them even if they are receiving income from government programs and even if working would not significantly increase the actual income available to them for consumption.[60] Moreover, those who have actually received income supplements apparently are not more likely than those who do not receive such supplements to cease working, despite the fact that the income supplements greatly reduce the financial advantages of work.[61]

Deviance from Equal Distribution

The second kind of deviance which we must consider is deviance from the social rule requiring equal distribution of income available for consumption. For the moment let us assume that the tax laws which would provide for equal distribution are not themselves deviant, that is, do not contain loopholes which permit some to acquire more income for consumption than others. In the next section I shall consider possible sources of pressure for the creation of such loopholes and the prerequisites which would have to be met to contain these pressures. The question here, however, is whether individuals in the egalitarian system would evade the requirements of the tax laws. Obviously this kind of deviance would pose a critical problem for the egalitarian system since equal distribution is an essential requirement of the system. In terms of my original framework, I am asking here what the empirically necessary prerequisites are for the assumption that individuals obey social rules, including the rules regarding distribution.

What makes this question particularly salient is that we have already seen that the acquisition of income for consumption would be a goal for individuals in the egalitarian system because of its instrumental relation to other culturally defined goals. In this sense there is some pressure for deviance from the equal distribution rule built into the egalitarian system. Why would the tax laws not give rise to widespread corruption of law enforcement officials and widespread violation by the population? Why would they not become unenforceable, like prohibition and laws against gambling? Or, more precisely, what empirical conditions would have to be satisfied to prevent the tax laws from being widely violated?

The norm of equal distribution. In the beginning of this chapter I cited Robert Merton's analysis of how people in a given society come to acquire goals. Later in that same discussion, Merton observes,

> A second element of the cultural structure defines, regulates, and controls the acceptable modes of reaching out for these goals. Every social group invariably couples its cultural objectives with regulations, rooted in the mores or institutions, of allowable procedures for moving towards these objectives.... In all instances, the choice of expedients for striving towards cultural goals is limited by institutionalized norms.[62]

In the egalitarian system, the rule requiring equal distribution of income may be considered, in Merton's terms, an "institutionalized norm" limiting the acceptable modes of acquiring income available for consumption. The norm excludes as illegitimate any methods of acquiring income for consumption which would provide one individual with more income available for consumption than another. What would be required then, if the tax laws were to be enforceable, would be a widespread commitment to the norm of equal income distribution.

What would create a widespread commitment to the norm of equal income distribution? Again the answer is socialization. For the reasons discussed at the beginning of the chapter, one can conclude that, given an effective socialization process, most people would internalize the norm that income available for consumption ought to be distributed equally[63] and would conform to that norm voluntarily. One would, of course, expect some variation in the degree to which different individuals would actually accept the norm. Some might not accept it at all. Nevertheless, if most of the people accepted the norm, one could expect that even those who did not accept it would conform to it. That is, they would not try to acquire more income available for consumption than that provided by the equal income share, since such a violation of the norm, if discovered, would bring severe institutional sanctions upon them and would deprive them of precisely what they sought to gain—additional income for consumption.

It may be useful to note that the range of tolerable behavior and the kinds of sanctions invoked for deviance would be quite different with respect to the norm of equal distribution from what they would be with respect to the goal of earning pre-tax income. Both the norm of equal distribution and the goal of earning pre-tax income might be said to fit under the general heading of "social expectations of the egalitarian system." All societies have a variety of social expectations, including both goals and norms as I have defined them, and there are considerable variations in the degrees of control which may be exercised over behavior in attempts to assure conformity to a given social expectation. In inducing people to earn pre-tax income, the egalitarian system would be able to tolerate a fairly wide range of behavior and would rely primarily on the informal sanctions of social disapproval to control deviants. This flexibility exists because the effective functioning of the egalitarian system in terms of production would not require that everyone earn as much pre-tax income as he possibly could, any more than the effective functioning of a PPM system would require that everyone acquire as much income for consumption as possible. By contrast, with regard to the equal distribution of income, the egalitarian system could not afford to tolerate any significant range in behavior, because this would compromise the basic nature of the system. This is why the norm regarding equal distribution would have to be expressed through formal laws (the tax laws) and why the informal sanctions of social disapproval for deviance would have to be reinforced by the formal sanctions of criminal procedure.

Honest officials. A second empirically necessary prerequisite for conformity with the rules requiring equal distribution would be that the officials responsible for enforcing the law would have to be honest. This seems so obvious that it almost need not be stated. Honest officials are needed for the enforcement of any law. In fact, someone might argue that honest enforcement officials and the tax laws themselves are all that would really be needed to prevent deviance from equal distribution. It is important, however, to see that the possibility of getting honest officials would in fact be highly dependent upon the first prerequisite, the widespread commitment to the norm of equal income distribution. As McMullen notes in an analysis of the causes of corruption, laws differ in the extent to which they are supported by public opinion.[64] Laws which do not enjoy wide public support are likely to invite the corruption of officials. Thus a widespread commitment to equality would also seem to be a prerequisite for the existence of officials willing to enforce the egalitarian tax laws honestly.

We might also note here, following McMullen, that laws can differ in the ease with which their violation can be detected.[65] Small violations of the strict laws of the egalitarian system would probably be difficult to detect and for that reason might be likely to occur. On the other hand, individuals engaging in unusually expensive life-styles would stand out in an egalitarian system, so that large violations would presumably be much easier to detect and thus much less likely to occur. I am not asserting therefore that the existence of a widespread commitment to equal income distribution and of a body of honest law enforcement officials would end all deviance from the tax laws of the egalitarian system. There is never perfect compliance with any social expectation in any social system. Nevertheless, it does seem reasonable to assert that the satisfaction of these two conditions would minimize deviance and would keep it within the boundaries specified by the requirement that income be equally distributed "for the most part."

The Problem of Elites in the Egalitarian System

In discussing the problem of deviance from equal income distribution, I have been assuming up to now that the tax laws themselves contained no major loopholes. While recognizing that there might always be disputes about borderline cases in the definition of business expenses, permissible forms of savings, and so on, I have assumed that those who made the laws sought as best they could to formulate rules which would achieve the distributional goals of the egalitarian system as I have defined them. The question now is: Under what conditions would this assumption about the lawmakers in the egalitarian system be correct?

Incentives for Elites to Change the Laws and Norms Requiring Equal Distribution

The problem is this: It is generally regarded as inevitable in any large society that a relatively few people will exercise more power than most others in determining public policy. If nothing else, this is seen as an inevitable consequence of the need for organizational efficiency in decision-making.[66] For my purposes, the key point is that only a small number of people could be directly involved in formulating the tax laws of any system, including the egalitarian system. Now suppose that the lawmakers in the egalitarian system earned pre-tax incomes which were well above the average pre-tax income. (This would seem to be a reasonable supposition since it would presumably be desirable to recruit highly talented people for these positions and it would be necessary to compete for talented people.) Moreover, assume that most of their personal contacts were with other people who were earning pre-tax incomes well above the average (lawyers, high-level administrators, business executives, and the like).

The lawmakers and their friends and associates would all value income-consumption satisfactions for the same reasons that people in the egalitarian system generally would value income-consumption satisfactions. If inequality were permitted in the distribution of after-tax income, the lawmakers and their friends and associates would all enjoy more income-consumption satisfactions. Therefore, even if one began with a set of laws that fulfilled the goals of the egalitarian system, why would the lawmakers not change the rules to permit inequality in distribution? They could do this covertly by relaxing the definitions of business expenses and permissible forms of saving or overtly by directly and explicitly modifying the redistributive goals of the tax laws.

I have focused on the lawmakers since they would be the ones who would directly determine the formulation of the rules about income distribution, but there might well be other strategically placed elites in the egalitarian system who would also enjoy more income-consumption satisfactions if inequality were permitted. For example, why would not those who occupied key positions in the mass media try to change public opinion about the desirability of equality? In short, would there not be a built-in tendency for elites in the egalitarian system to try to change both the rules and the basic values of the system? Would not a reintroduction of inequality of distribution be inevitable in the long run, even if equal distribution were achieved for a while?

General Limits on Elites

The first point to make in responding to these questions is that elites are never entirely autonomous in any society. As Merton puts it, "To be continuously effective, authority must be exercised within the constraining limits provided by the norms of the group."[67] Merton argues that a failure to recognize these limits tends to lead to a loss of authority. Prewitt and Stone, who emphasize the power which elites exercise in all societies, nevertheless concede that "elites are limited... by the policy priorities... already established by the society especially where these priorities... are widely accepted."[68] And Lane and Sears observe that elites who advocate views which are strongly at variance with deeply held convictions of their audience are more likely to find their influence as opinion leaders reduced than to change the opinions of their listeners: "Public opinion places considerable restraint upon the ability of a leader successfully to advocate important measures which do not accord in some degree with public opinion. Even the most prestigious public figures cannot achieve general opinion change in the face of significant opposition."[69]

I have already shown that a widespread commitment to the norm of equal distribution would be an empirically necessary prerequisite if the tax laws of the egalitarian system were to be obeyed. This discussion of the potential incentives for elites to alter the rules and values of the egalitarian system does not change the nature of that prerequisite but it does show just how fundamental and widespread that commitment to equal distribution would have to be. It would have to be one of the most deeply held and widely shared values in the social system. It would have to be a major focal point of the socialization process (though, again, this does not imply that the socialization process need be centrally directed or bureaucratically controlled). Under these conditions it would be difficult for elites to introduce major inequalities in distribution even if they wanted to, at least in the short run.

Despite the importance of mass commitment to the norm of equal distribution as a constraint upon elites, this factor alone might not be sufficient to prevent a gradual increase in inequality of distribution, if elites saw that as desirable. For one thing, while elites must adhere to existing norms to a large degree, they are often able to change those norms over the long run.[70] For another, the inevitable complexities of the tax laws might make it possible for elites to introduce a significant amount of inequality merely by liberalizing definitions of business expenses and permissible forms of savings, while continuing to pay lip service to the norm of equality. Covert changes of this kind would be more difficult to detect and less likely to attract intense opposition than would a direct attack upon the norm of equality, but they could lead to a serious erosion of the egalitarian goals of the system.

Elite Commitment to the Norm of Equal Distribution

In the final analysis, therefore, the only thing which could prevent the elites from changing the rules and values of the egalitarian system would be the elites' *own* commitment to the norm of equal distribution. In order for the egalitarian system to be preserved, the elites themselves would have to share the consensus that equal distribution of after-tax income was the right, proper, and just way to distribute income for consumption. If they believed this, they would not try to change the rules or values of the egalitarian system because they would regard such a change as undesirable.

Why would elites be likely to believe this? They would be likely to believe it for the same reason that everyone else in the egalitarian system would be likely to believe it. That is, they would have been socialized to accept the norm of equal distribution. Any person growing up in an egalitarian system would have to be a child before he or she could become an adult and an elite. (We can leave open for the moment the question of how individuals would become elites.) Given the widespread, deeply rooted commitment to the norm of equal distribution which has already been identified as an empirically necessary prerequisite of the egalitarian system, most elites-to-be would have internalized the norm of equal distribution long before they became elites. It is not likely that they would change such long held and deeply rooted beliefs, even if they came to perceive that inequality of distribution would offer them certain consumption benefits.

The underlying argument here is an extension of the earlier argument about the need for most individuals to accept the legitimacy of the legal restraints on their behavior, if the legal restraints are to be effective in controlling behavior. As Merton puts it, "Many procedures which from the standpoint of particular individuals would be most efficient in securing desired values—the exercise of force, fraud, power—are ruled out of the institutional area of permitted conduct."[71]

The principle applies to elites as well as to ordinary individuals. There are many examples of restrictions on elite conduct which are accepted by the elites themselves, even when such restrictions deprive them of desired values. Perhaps the most obvious and striking example in modern Western societies is the acceptance by public officials of the norm that they should relinquish office if defeated in an election. It seems clear that in stable polyarchies the overwhelming majority of defeated officials do not relinquish power because they are afraid that they could not hold on to power even if they tried, but because they believe that they have an obligation to relinquish power and they accept that obligation. The possibility of trying to hold on to power despite an electoral defeat probably does not even occur to most of them.[72] Similarly, given effective socialization, elites in the egalitarian system could be deeply commited to the norm of equal distribution even though unequal distribution would provide them with additional consumption benefits.

If the elites themselves were deeply commited to equal distribution, they would use their power to make sure that the tax laws actually provided for equal distribution and they would reinforce this norm of equal distribution to the extent that they could influence public opinion. Moreover, assuming that the elites themselves controlled access to elite positions, their commitment to the norm of equal distribution could make acceptance of this norm a prerequisite for admission to an elite position and for the maintenance of an elite position. Attempts to change either the rules or the norms regarding distribution could be regarded as an abuse of power and a betrayal of public responsibility. Again, a comparison with polyarchies seems appropriate. Those who attain positions of leadership are expected to be even more committed to the procedural principles of a polyarchy than ordinary citizens.[73] Thus the elite recruitment procedures in the egalitarian system could entail a process of secondary socialization which reinforced the commitment of new elites to the norm of equal distribution. This would in turn support the commitment to equal distribution in the system as a whole over the long run.

Polyarchy and the Egalitarian System

Thus far, in discussing the conditions which would have to be satisfied in order to prevent elites from transforming the egalitarian system, I have deliberately avoided making any assertions about the specific political arrangements of the egalitarian system. I have done this for three reasons. First, I wished to emphasize that a widespread, deeply held commitment to the norm of equal distribution, shared by both elites and masses, would be the most important prerequisite for preserving the egalitarian character of the system. Second, I wished to take into account the possibility that some influential elites (e.g., intellectuals and members of the media) might not be part of the formal political process and might not be subject to formal political controls. It would be important to secure their support of the principle of equal distribution, too. The assumption of a general value consensus achieved through socialization ensures this support. Third, I wished to suggest by implication that no particular political arrangement could be considered an *indispensable* precondition of the egalitarian system. In theory, the egalitarian system could function under any type of regime, given only this widely shared commitment to equal distribution.

While no particular political arrangement would be an indispensable precondition of the egalitarian system, some arrangements would seem more likely than others to help preserve and support an egalitarian system. In particular, polyarchal arrangements[74] seem particularly well suited to the egalitarian system.

Polyarchy provides greater popular control over elites than less democratic alternatives. This would be useful in an egalitarian system because, as I have observed before, no system of socialization is ever perfect. Thus, despite my emphasis on the consensus among elites about the desirability of equal income distribution, it would be possible that some of those involved in formulating the tax laws might not share this general consensus about equality. Polyarchal arrangements would reduce in two ways the likelihood that such deviant individuals would implement their beliefs.

First, polyarchies require periodic elections in which those elites most directly involved in formulating public policies must compete openly with others. If nonelites are dissatisfied with the performance of a particular elected official they can replace him. In the egalitarian system, one can assume from what has been said about the value placed on the norm of equal distribution that any question having to do with distribution would be a highly salient issue to the voters. Thus, if a legislator attempted to introduce a loophole in the tax laws, his political opponents would undoubtedly try to exploit the issue and the voters would be likely to vote against the legislator.[75] Anticipating this, an elected official who desired to remain in office would take care not to offend the electorate on questions of distribution, even if he did not share the general view on this matter.

Second, in polyarchies, elected officials may feel obliged not to support policies which they think their constituents strongly oppose even if they have no reason to believe that their constituents would become aware of their actions or would vote against them if they did.[76] In other words, such individuals adopt the view that the legislator's role is to be a delegate, not a trustee. Again, this type of legislator would not support inegalitarian changes in the tax laws, even if he personally approved of them, so long as he believed that his constituents would disapprove of such changes.

Finally, note that polyarchal arrangements and the arrangements of our egalitarian system would tend to be mutually reinforcing. It has long been argued by political theorists that relatively egalitarian distributions of income and wealth were more favorable to democratic arrangements than highly unequal distributions. While most theorists have not argued that a completely equal distribution of income was a prerequisite for democracy (or polyarchy), it seems clear that equal distribution would favor the greater equality of political power which is one of the fundamental goals of polyarchal arrangements. By the same token, the egalitarian ethos characteristic of arrangements which seek to democratize political power would tend to reinforce the commitment to the economic equality provided by the equal distribution of income in the egalitarian system.

In some ways, the egalitarian system is to economic arrangements what polyarchy is to political arrangements. The goal of polyarchal arrangements is not to provide every citizen with equal influence on every issue but to ensure, as far as possible, that each citizen has equal weight in the "final say."[77] The goal of the egalitarian system is not to provide each citizen with equal control over all economic resources but simply to ensure that, in the end, each person has access to an equal amount of consumable goods and services.

The Effects of Growth and Decline on Effort

When I introduced the discussion of elites several pages ago, it was in the context of questions about the threats which elites might pose to the egalitarian system. It is also important to point out, however, that under certain conditions elites would have to play an especially important role in preserving the efficiency of the egalitarian system. I am concerned now not with the question of distribution but with the question of the levels of effort in the egalitarian system.

When I discussed the question of effort and price changes in the second chapter, I observed that there was no a priori reason to assume any particular pattern to the conflicting income and substitution effects which price changes would create in different ways in both systems. I did note, however, that the logic of the egalitarian system differed from the logic of the PPM system in one key respect: In the egalitarian system a general increase or decline in labor productivity or in the cost of living would tend not to affect effort (assuming that preferences regarding the trade-off between leisure and social-duty satisfactions did not change) since social-duty satisfactions were tied to earning capacities and to pre-tax incomes. An increase or decline in labor productivity would be likely to affect earning capacities at the same rate as actual pre-tax incomes over the long run, so that the effects of a change in pre-tax income would simply be counteracted by the effects of a change in earning capacity and vice versa. An increase or decline in the cost of living would simply have no effect on social-duty satisfactions. By contrast, in the PPM system, income-consumption satisfactions were tied both to actual incomes and to the cost of living. An increase or decline in labor productivity would affect incomes and would thus create income and substitution effects. Similarly, an increase or decline in the cost of living would create income and substitution effects. The question asked at that point and deferred to this chapter was what empirical evidence there was about the relative force of income and substitution effects in response to changes in labor productivity or in the cost of living.

Empirical Evidence about PPM Systems

As far as I can determine, the only clear empirical evidence about these income and substitution effects is that there is a tendency for workers in PPM systems to increase leisure (and thus decrease effort) over the long run if their wages increase at a faster rate than the cost of living.[78] It is more difficult to find empirical evidence which bears on the question of how workers respond to a situation in which the cost of living increases faster than their wages (or decreases at a slower rate than their wages), since in all the cases of which I am aware this phenomenon has been accompanied by substantial involuntary unemployment. In other words, the overall level of effort in the system (as measured by hours worked) has decreased, but this is a result of the general underutilization of resources rather than of a voluntary choice to substitute leisure for income. Moreover, if an individual works longer hours simply because the choice is to work those hours or not to work at all, this can hardly be considered evidence that the income effect (as conventionally described) is more powerful. There is some evidence to suggest that the increase in working hours at the beginning of the industrial revolution was due to this kind of coercive situation rather than to voluntary choices about the trade-off between income and leisure.[79]

Growth and Effort in the Egalitarian System

How does all this bear on our judgments about the relative levels of effort in the PPM and egalitarian systems? First, it suggests that the egalitarian system would tend to generate higher levels of effort than the PPM system under conditions of economic growth, since there would be no mechanism by which people could use their increased income to "buy" leisure. While this means that the egalitarian system would be more efficient than the PPM system by our definition of efficiency, it could be argued that the system would be *too* efficient. Leisure, too, is an important value, and the egalitarian system runs the risk of overvaluing material consumption.

This is both a simple and a profound problem. (It is also a pleasant problem because so much effort has been expended arguing that equal distribution would reduce incentives to work that anyone who would seriously worry about excessive effort in the egalitarian system may presumably be considered a convert to my views on the major issues at stake in this essay.) At one level the solution to the problem of excessive effort in the egalitarian system would seem simple. In the analysis in Chapter 2, I explicitly assumed that preferences would remain constant. In fact, however, it seems unlikely that preferences would remain constant in the face of economic growth. As people gradually become more satisfied with their levels of consumption, they would gradually and spontaneously tend to reduce the importance placed on the social duty to acquire pre-tax income.

Socialization processes are not static. People adjust their views of what values are important in response to changes in the environment. It can be argued, for example, that people of a certain level of affluence in Western societies have begun to deemphasize the value of income-consumption satisfactions. This is not simply a question of trading income for leisure but of a decentralized and spontaneous change in the socialization process which has made income-consumption satisfactions so important in PPM systems.

In the egalitarian system, it would make sense to believe that one had a social duty to earn as much pre-tax income as one could only to the extent that consumption was something which was highly valued by one's fellow members in society. If consumption became less important to most people in society, the obligation to acquire pre-tax income should become less important as well. Attentive elites could play an important role in helping people to make this connection and to reduce the importance placed on the social duty to acquire pre-tax income. It is important to remember, however, that the social approval which plays such a key role in the egalitarian system is primarily approval by others whom one knows reasonably well. If an individual could perceive that he and his "significant others" were satisfied with existing levels of consumption, and if he and they assumed that others in the system felt the same way, they would be likely to reduce effort spontaneously, without the direction of elites.

Decline and Effort in the Egalitarian System

What can one say about levels of effort in the egalitarian system as compared with those in a PPM system in the face of economic decline (a situation in which wages are increasing more slowly or decreasing more rapidly than the cost of living)? If the decline was accompanied by significant involuntary unemployment, then there would seem to be no reason to believe that effort would be lower (or higher) in the egalitarian system than in the PPM system. As I noted before, involuntary unemployment implies that some people who are not putting forward any effort would be quite willing to work if they could find opportunities. Assuming that social-duty satisfactions are generally effective for the reasons discussed earlier in this chapter, unemployed people in the egalitarian system would work if they could find jobs.

Therefore, there is no reason to believe that a PPM system would generate a higher level of overall effort under these conditions than the egalitarian system. This leaves the hypothetical possibility of a situation in which there is economic decline despite full employment. Although this is only a hypothetical case for modern PPM systems (so far as I am aware), it is nevertheless one worth considering. The growing scarcity of natural resources could actually lead to such a situation in some conceivable future.

The problem is this: In PPM systems, if any individual sees his level of consumption declining below a level which is satisfactory to him, he can increase his effort in order to increase his consumption (assuming that work is available). As we have seen, there is no guarantee that individuals will respond to a decline in consumption by increasing effort, because of the contradictory income and substitution effects. Nevertheless, if the decline is severe enough, it seems plausible to suppose that an individual would increase his effort. Therefore in the face of a general decline and under conditions of full employment, the PPM system might have a mechanism which would cause the overall level of effort to be increased.

The need for elites. By contrast, in the egalitarian system, there is no mechanism by which an individual who is dissatisfied with his own personal level of consumption can increase that consumption by increasing his effort. The effects of any increased effort on his part are spread over the entire system and affect his own consumption very little. Why not suppose that there would be a spontaneous and gradual increase in the importance placed on social duty and thus an increase in effort in response to the general economic decline and general dissatisfaction with the level of consumption, just as I argued that there would be a spontaneous and gradual decrease in effort in response to economic growth and increasing satisfaction with the level of consumption? Such a spontaneous increase in effort might occur but it seems less likely than the spontaneous decrease in the face of improved consumption described earlier. The reason is this: If one assumes effort to be a cost, an individual receives an immediate benefit from reducing effort. Thus people would have an incentive to make the connection between a general increase in satisfaction with consumption and the reasonableness of decreasing the importance attached to the obligation to acquire pre-tax income. By contrast, people would have an incentive not to make the connection between a general decrease in satisfaction with consumption and the need to increase the importance attached to the obligation to acquire pre-tax income, since they would feel obliged to increase effort once they made that connection. Therefore, the elites in the system would have to play a greater role in drawing attention to the need to increase the importance attached to one's social duty than they would in drawing attention to the possibility of decreasing that importance. In other words, in order for the egalitarian system to increase the level of overall effort in response to economic decline, the elites would have to play a significant role in mobilizing people to place greater importance on social-duty satisfactions.

It is important not to exaggerate the differences between the cases of economic growth and economic decline. In both cases it is a question of changing the socialization process in response to changes in the environment. Spontaneous forces would have to play a large role in both cases. In the second case, people would have to be responsive to mobilization efforts by elites. They would have to accept the reality of the changed situation once it had been pointed out to them. The essential difference between the two cases is simply that one is a case of good news and the other is a case of bad news. Most people are more reluctant to draw unpleasant conclusions than pleasant ones. Thus it would be more important for elites to play a role in pointing out the unpleasant realities than in pointing out the pleasant ones. Of course, the same argument suggests that elites would be less likely to draw attention to the changed situation in the second case than in the first. This is the classic dilemma of political leadership. In sum, a high quality of political leadership would be needed in the egalitarian system in the face of this kind of economic decline in order to generate an increased level of overall effort, while such increased effort might be spontaneously generated in a PPM system in the same situation through individual efforts to increase personal consumption levels.

New and Old Inequalities in the Egalitarian System

Inequalities in Social Approval and Self-Esteem

The seventh set of questions introduced earlier in the chapter raised the issue of whether the egalitarian system would tend to create new inequalities which would replace the income inequality of the egalitarian system. There are several forms in which this question can be raised.[80] First, would not inequalities in pre-tax income create inequalities in social approval and self-esteem in the egalitarian system? Moreover, since it is a logically necessary prerequisite of the egalitarian system that individuals place the same relative value on these social-duty satisfactions that individuals in the PPM system place on income-consumption satisfactions, would not the inequalities in the egalitarian system be felt as keenly as the inequalities in the PPM system? These are important questions. If answered positively, they would suggest that the egalitarian system was basically an elaborate shell game and that the differences between the PPM and egalitarian system would be more apparent than real from the perspective of participants in the systems.

The role of earning capacity. Fortunately, one does not have to answer the questions positively. In the egalitarian system, as we have seen before, social approval and self-esteem do not depend simply on the absolute amount of pre-tax income that one acquires, but rather on the relationship between one's pre-tax income and one's earning capacity. The higher the percentage of earning capacity at which a person performs, the more social approval he receives and the more self-esteem he enjoys. This means that an individual who earned a low amount of pre-tax income but who also had a low earning capacity should receive more social approval and should enjoy more self-esteem than an individual who earned a slightly higher amount of pre-tax income but who had a much higher earning capacity. For example, an ordinary laborer working forty hours a week for the highest wage he could obtain should receive more social approval and enjoy more self-esteem than an executive who also works forty hours a week but who passes up opportunities for promotions and higher salaries, despite the fact that the executive would have a higher pre-tax income than the laborer.

The contrast with the PPM system is clear. In the PPM system, the more income a person acquires, the more goods and services he can consume.[81] His earning power is irrelevant. In the PPM system, the executive would simply enjoy more goods and services than the laborer, even if he were working at a lower percentage of capacity. In theory, and to a large extent in practice, the social approval and self-esteem which the executive would enjoy would also be greater than the social approval and self-esteem enjoyed by the laborer, because in the PPM system social approval and self-esteem are based simply on the absolute amount of income one acquires.[82] Thus, if the egalitarian system worked according to design, it would not replicate the inequalities of the PPM system, since differences in social approval and self-esteem would not depend simply on the absolute amount of pre-tax income acquired.

The crucial importance of the link between social duty and earning capacity should now be apparent. It may therefore be useful to recall here a point made earlier in the chapter in the discussion of the knowledge of relative prices required by the egalitarian system. It would not be necessary for any central governmental body to state or even to know what the earning capacities of different individuals were. It would only be necessary for the individual himself and the relatively limited number of people whose approval he valued highly to know what his earning capacity was, and even a rough, approximate knowledge would be sufficient to make the system function effectively. This kind of knowledge should be readily available through decentralized and informal networks of communication. Thus the link to earning capacity seems epistemologically feasible.

But other, more fundamental questions can be raised about the effectiveness of this device in preventing the rise of new inequalities. Would there not be an inevitable tendency for individuals to pay more attention to actual amounts of pre-tax income and less attention to earning capacity than the model suggests? After all, those with higher pre-tax incomes could point out that these pre-tax incomes measured the value of their economic contributions to the community. If they were contributing more (as measured by pre-tax income) would they not inevitably receive more social approval and enjoy more self-esteem?

Egalitarian attitudes towards contribution. The answer to these questions is that it depends entirely on what attitudes people in the egalitarian system take towards the relationship between contribution and social approval. The attitudes implied in the questions are by no means the only natural or inevitable attitudes one can adopt. Bellamy suggests an alternative perspective in his novel *Looking Backward:*

> Desert is a moral question, and the amount of the product a material quantity. It would be an extraordinary sort of logic which should try to determine a moral question by a material standard. The amount of effort alone is pertinent to the question of desert. All men who do their best, do the same. *A man's endowments, however godlike, merely fix the measure of his duty.* The man of great endowments who does not do all he might, though he may do more than a man of small endowments who does his best, is deemed a less deserving worker than the latter and dies a debtor to his fellows. The Creator sets men's tasks for them by the faculties he gives them; we simply exact their fulfillment.[83]

In an amusing exchange, Bellamy goes on to consider and reject the argument that this attitude is excessively idealistic.

"No doubt that is a very fine philosophy," I said.

"Nevertheless it seems hard that the man who produces twice as much as another, even if both do their best, should have only the same share."
"Does it, indeed, seem so to you?" responded Doctor Leete. "Now do you know that seems very curious to me. The way it strikes people nowadays is that a man who can produce twice as much as another with the same effort, instead of being rewarded for doing so, ought to be punished if he does not do so. In the nineteenth century, when a horse pulled a heavier load than a goat, I suppose you rewarded him. Now we should have whipped him soundly if he had not, on the ground that, being much stronger, he ought to. It is singular how ethical standards change."[84]

Clearly what the egalitarian system requires if it is to function according to design is that people generally adopt an attitude towards the relationship between contribution and reward rather similar to that described by Bellamy. *Noblesse oblige,* if you will.

Would it be possible to develop such attitudes rather than the ones implied in the questions? Melvin Tumin's answer to this is a clear "yes."

Skill has to be valued in a special way before it can become a determinant of differential evaluation and rewards. There is nothing demonstrably "natural" about reacting to differential skills in the ways generally found in modern industrial societies. A number of additional factors such as a very particular learned motivational scheme and social goals, arrayed in very particular hierarchies are required to be present.... Clearly, numerous alternatives could be devised, involving alternative motivational schemes and alternative systems of belief as to social obligations and rights. They may not be able to be invoked tomorrow.... But we are not talking about what is possible tomorrow. Rather we are considering what is possible in human affairs, assuming the availability of a population with a fresh slate on which no major cultural themes have yet been written.[85]

I should note again that the context of my investigation is the same as Tumin's. I am concerned not with identifying the prerequisites for a transition from some existing system to the egalitarian system but only with the prerequisites for an egalitarian system which I concede to be only a theoretical possibility. Tumin remarks later that "Tasks may be highly unequal in many regards without invoking judgments of unequal social worth and unequal entitlement to rewards, *if people are socialized to view matters in this way.*"[86]

Thus, even if people recognize that those with higher pre-tax incomes are contributing more to the total social product, it does not follow that they will think that those with higher pre-tax incomes should be entitled to greater social approval, just as it does not follow that they will think those with higher pre-tax incomes should be entitled to more income for consumption.[87] What people will believe about these matters will be determined by what they have been socialized to believe. Once again, I return to socialization. An effective socialization process is what is needed to get people to adopt the attitude that "a man's endowments... merely fix the measure of his duty." Lest this should make the egalitarian system seem too coercive, one should recall that an effective socialization process would also be required to get people to adopt the attitude that a greater contribution to the economic process entitles a person to a greater social reward.

This discussion does not add a new requirement to the egalitarian system. The attitudes towards the relationship between contribution and reward which I have identified as necessary to the egalitarian system are already implicit in the definition of social duty in the egalitarian system. What I have done here is simply to highlight an important feature of the empirically necessary prerequisite which I identified at the beginning of this chapter, namely, the prerequisite of effective socialization with regard to social duty.[88]

Equal opportunity and unequal rewards. I have just shown why inequalities in pre-tax income in the egalitarian system would not create inequalities in social approval and self-esteem replicating the inequalities in income distribution in the PPM system. Nevertheless, there would be inequalities in social approval and self-esteem in the egalitarian system if different individuals performed at different levels of capacity, as my comparison of the laborer and the executive suggested. The egalitarian system cannot avoid such inequalities because it permits individuals to make their own trade-offs between social-duty satisfactions and other satisfactions.

Are these inequalities of social approval and self-esteem in the egalitarian system less offensive to general egalitarian principles than the comparable inequalities of income, social approval, and self-esteem in the PPM system? At first blush, the answer would appear to be yes. In principle, in the egalitarian system every individual would have the opportunity to acquire as much social approval and self-esteem as every other individual, because these rewards would depend only on the percentage of capacity at which one worked. If one individual received less social approval and enjoyed less self-esteem than another, it would be because he had chosen to work at a lower percentage of capacity for the sake of some other satisfaction. By contrast, in the PPM system, some individuals might never be able to acquire as much income as others, no matter how hard they tried (and no matter how much they wanted the income), because they simply would not possess the property or talents or skills which would bring high rewards in the market.

Compensatory Inequalities in the PPM and Egalitarian Systems

Someone might object that this line of argument overlooks the compensatory role played by income inequalities in the PPM system.[89] Since the time of Adam Smith economists have observed that some occupations pay higher wages than others because they involve greater disadvantages, such as the costs of training or the unpleasantness of the work. The higher income compensates for the disadvantages. Would not this compensating function of unequal distribution be eliminated by the egalitarian system? If so, would not the "egalitarian" system actually increase the net inequality of satisfactions over that of the PPM system?

In answering these questions, one must begin by understanding what disadvantages (if any) occupations in the egalitarian system might have for which unequal distribution could theoretically compensate and which are not compensated in the egalitarian system. In a PPM system, unequal distribution may compensate for the financial costs of an occupation such as the costs of training and the financial risk. In the egalitarian system, however, these financial costs would be borne by the society as a whole. Individuals would receive equal income shares throughout any periods of occupational training so that they would not be foregoing any income-consumption satisfactions by taking up one occupation rather than another. Moreover, I have stipulated that individuals would be expected not to use their equal income shares for saving or investment purposes. Thus, no occupational choice could impose any financial cost on an individual in the egalitarian system, so there would be no need to compensate anyone for this.

In a PPM system, some individuals earn more than others by working longer hours than others. In an egalitarian system, however, an individual who worked longer hours than another would receive more social approval, other things (including the availability of work) being equal. Thus, the egalitarian system does provide compensation for differences in effort, at least to a large extent.[90]

Other disadvantages for which unequal income-distribution may theoretically compensate in a PPM system can be lumped under the heading "work satisfactions" (or "work dissatisfactions").[91] Some jobs are more pleasant or unpleasant than others, for a variety of reasons. Jobs may be boring, tiring, or dangerous. Of course, not all people react to any given kind of work in the same way. What one person finds stimulating, another may find dull. Some people like routines. Others detest them. Tastes differ. One of the potential virtues of a market mechanism, however, is that it could provide compensation for the relative pleasantness or unpleasantness of a job, without having to impose a uniform standard of judgment about what is pleasant or unpleasant. For example, suppose all individuals had equal abilities and all jobs had the same financial costs. Under conditions of perfect competition, all income differences in a PPM system would simply be compensating for the differences in work satisfactions provided by a job, as determined by the workers themselves. If most people preferred carpentry to bricklaying, for example, and if there were an equal demand for carpenters and bricklayers, bricklayers would have to be paid more than carpenters to compensate them for the unpleasantness of their work relative to carpentry. Otherwise, it would be impossible to attract enough carpenters.

Once again, however, this kind of compensation is provided by the egalitarian system in the form of greater social-duty satisfactions. Under the conditions I have assumed, all individuals would have equal earning capacities because of their equal abilities. To attract sufficient bricklayers it would be necessary to offer higher wages, as in the PPM system. Those who chose to be bricklayers would be working at a higher percentage of capacity than the carpenters and they would enjoy more social approval and more self-esteem than the carpenters. They would be compensated for the relative unpleasantness of their work.

Compensatory versus additive effects of unequal distribution. There is one type of situation, however, where the egalitarian system would not provide compensation for differences in work satisfactions, and the PPM system would. Suppose that there are two representative individuals, Jim Jones and Sandra Smith. Suppose that Jim enjoys working as a secretary and also that he does not have the ability to do anything at which he could earn more income than he does as a secretary. Suppose further that Sandra also enjoys working as a secretary but that she has the ability to be an executive even though she does not like that kind of work.[92] Finally, assume that Sandra can earn more as an executive than as a secretary and that she decides to work as an executive. In the PPM system the larger income which Sandra acquires in comparison to Jim's income compensates her for the greater unpleasantness of her job in comparison with Jim's job. By contrast, in the egalitarian system, Sandra's ability to do executive work would have raised her earning capacity relative to Jim's. If one assumes for the sake of simplicity that she would be working at the same percentage of capacity as an executive as the percentage of capacity at which Jim would be working as a secretary, one can see that she would not receive any compensation in the form of greater social approval or self-esteem despite the fact that her work would be more unpleasant than Jim's. Thus it could be argued that the net inequality of satisfactions between Sandra and Jim would actually be greater in the egalitarian system than in the PPM system since the income difference in the PPM system only compensates for the difference in work satisfactions.[93]

This kind of situation could occur in the egalitarian system, as the critics suggest. On the other hand, there is a second type of situation which could also occur. Suppose that Sandra enjoyed working as an executive more than working as a secretary and that she enjoyed her work as an executive even more than Jim enjoyed his work as a secrtary. Further assume that her executive job still paid more than Jim's secretarial job simply because the supply of executive talents was very limited and the demand for executive talents was very high. Under these conditions the income difference between Sandra and Jim in the PPM system would not compensate Sandra for the greater unpleasantness of her work but would add to the advantage she already enjoyed over Jim in terms of work satisfactions. By contrast, in the egalitarian system, if one assumes again that Sandra and Jim both worked at the same percentage of capacity, they would both enjoy the same levels of social approval and self-esteem derived from performing social duty. Thus, there would be no difference in social-duty satisfactions to add to Sandra's advantage in work satisfactions. The net inequality of satisfactions would therefore be lower in the egalitarian system than in the PPM system.

Obviously, if one is to evaluate the criticism that the egalitarian system eliminates the compensatory function of unequal distribution, it would be useful to know whether the first type of situation would be more likely to occur than the second or whether the second would be more likely to occur than the first. If the first were more common, then the compensatory effect of income inequality in the PPM system would be stronger than what I shall call the additive effect (the tendency for income inequalities to add to inequalities of work satisfactions). In this case the criticism of the egalitarian system would be justified. On the other hand, if the second type of situation were more common, then the additive effect of income inequality would be stronger than the compensatory effect. In this case, the egalitarian system would decrease the net inequality of satisfactions over that of the PPM system. Assuming that the compensatory effect could not be separated from the additive effect, the criticism of the egalitarian system would not be justified.

The key question then is whether higher-paying jobs would provide more work satisfactions (or fewer work dissatisfactions) on the average than lower-paying jobs. In principle, this is an empirical question which could be answered in different ways in different societies. The empirical evidence from existing PPM systems indicates quite strongly that higher-paying jobs tend to provide more work satisfactions than lower-paying jobs.[94] However, it is rather difficult to separate the variable of work satisfactions from the variable of income-consumption satisfactions in PPM systems.[95] Moreover, the issue is complicated by the fact that individuals' feelings of satisfaction or dissatisfaction are strongly influenced by their use of comparative standards and these standards themselves are influenced by a variety of historical, cultural, institutional, and personal factors.[96] Still, on the basis of the available evidence, it seems clear that the additive effect of income inequality is greater than the compensatory effect in existing PPM systems. Thus one can reject the criticism that the egalitarian system would eliminate the compensatory function of income inequality and would thus increase net inequality of satisfactions over that of PPM systems.

Other Social Inequalities

One further question might be raised about the potentially inegalitarian consequences of the egalitarian system. Would not other social inequalities such as those of power and prestige become more important in a society in which income inequalities had been eliminated? In answering this question one must distinguish between two possible interpretations. First there is the question of an actual increase in inequalities. Here the question is whether measurements used to determine differences in power, prestige, and so on would indicate that there were greater differences on the average and on the whole in the egalitarian system than would be found in PPM systems.[97] Second, there is the question of subjective attitudes towards inequalities. Assuming that actual, measured inequalities of power and prestige were no greater in the egalitarian system than in PPM systems, would people nevertheless be more aware of the inequalities that did exist and would they place more importance on them?

Objective inequalities. In response to the first question, let me recall that I assumed in the second chapter that the same inequalities in power and prestige would exist in the egalitarian system as in the PPM system unless those inequalities were directly connected to the possession of different amounts of income for consumption. I made this assumption, it will be recalled, in order to isolate the role of moral incentives in the egalitarian system. Of course, to some degree differences in power and prestige are connected to differences in the amounts of income for consumption that people possess and to that extent the egalitarian system would require the elimination of these inequalities. On the basis of a logical analysis of the egalitarian model, therefore, one can assume that actual inequalities in power and prestige,[98] in the egalitarian system would be the same as or less than actual inequalities in PPM systems.

There is no logical reason for believing that these other inequalities would tend to increase in the egalitarian system. I have shown that social-duty satisfactions would serve the need for incentives as efficiently as income-consumption satisfactions, and there is no logical reason to believe that this incentive system would break down. Furthermore, there are no good empirical reasons for believing that under conditions of equal distribution of after-tax income, actual differences in power and prestige would tend to grow. There is certainly no evidence that social inequality is some kind of fixed quantity in every (or any) society, so that if one inequality is eliminated another must be put in its place. Indeed, all historical and sociological evidence is to the contrary. Although all societies have some inequalities, the range of inequalities is enormous.[99] Even within societies of a given type (e.g., modern Western industrial capitalist societies), there is clearly no fixed amount of inequality.[100] There is certainly no good evidence that such reductions in economic inequalities as have occurred in these states through progressive taxation and welfare measures have led to increases in inequalities of power and prestige. Indeed there is some evidence to suggest that the opposite is actually the case, that reductions in inequalities of income have tended to reduce inequalities in power and prestige.[101] Thus, if anything, the empirical evidence would suggest instability in the direction of less actual inequality, rather than more, in areas other than income where social inequalities might exist.

Subjective attitudes towards inequalities. This leads to the question of how people would feel about these other inequalities. The first point to make again is that the heuristic assumption of identity in the second chapter simply assumes that people would have the same feelings about these other inequalities in the egalitarian system that they had in the PPM system. The real question, however, is whether there are any empirical reasons for thinking that feelings about other inequalities would change under conditions of equal income distribution.

The ways in which different people in different societies respond to different kinds of inequalities and to different combinations of inequalities are enormously varied and complex. W. G. Runciman has argued persuasively that people's feelings about particular inequalities have to be studied in a particular historical and cultural context.[102] There is no general rule by which one can predict in advance what attitudes people will take towards a given kind of inequality. Different people will adopt different attitudes under different circumstances. This agnostic conclusion is all the more compelling when one recalls that this discussion of the egalitarian system deliberately abstracts from the question of transition, so that one cannot presuppose any particular cultural or historical context for the discussion. Thus the fundamental answer to this question of how people would feel about inequalities of prestige and power in the egalitarian system has to be, simply, that one cannot tell.

Despite this general argument for agnosticism, one should not ignore the fact that the egalitarian system does presuppose a specific cultural norm of equality in income distribution and a widespread sense of social obligation in the area of economic activity. It would seem plausible to argue that this egalitarian ethos and community orientation in the economic sphere would be likely to spill over into other spheres as well. I previously observed that the egalitarian political ideology implicit in polyarchal arrangements would tend to reinforce the egalitarian economic ethos and vice versa. Moreover, it is known that one critical variable affecting the attitudes which people adopt towards social inequalities is their perception of the inevitability or non-inevitability of these inequalities.[103] Thus, it would seem reasonable to suppose that most people in the egalitarian system would bring an increasingly critical focus to bear on any remaining social inequalities which were not perceived as inevitable.

Some inequalities might still be perceived as inevitable (correctly or incorrectly) and thus might arouse little criticism. Moreover, the mere fact that most people might be critical of some social inequality would by no means guarantee its removal. For one thing, the people could be mistaken and the inequality could be inevitable.[104] For another, those who benefit from the inequality might successfully resist its elimination, at least for a time. Thus, under some conceivable circumstances, popular dissatisfaction with the degree of social inequality could be greater in the egalitarian system than in a PPM system with much greater objective inequalities.[105]

What this hypothetical situation raises once again is the question of the costs of transition. This time, however, it is a question not of the costs of a transition from a PPM system to the egalitarian system but of a transition from the egalitarian system in my narrow sense to an egalitarian society in a much fuller sense. This question of the costs of transition is one of the most fundamental problems facing any proponent of social change. In this essay, however, I am not advocating change but simply analyzing the prerequisites for the egalitarian system. I have studiously avoided discussing the costs of transition to the egalitarian system and I shall exercise that same restraint here. Therefore, I shall simply note that this hypothetical situation of discontent would be irrelevant to judgments about the justice of the egalitarian system,[106] and, even more important for our purposes, that it would not alter the reality of the reduction in objective social inequalities which the egalitarian system would achieve when compared with PPM systems.

Cuba, China, and the Creation of Egalitarian Values

It may seem strange that I have made no reference thus far to either China or Cuba in my discussion of the empirically necessary prerequisites of the egalitarian system. All Communist nations are formally committed both to the goal of creating a new type of human being who will be motivated to work by a desire to serve others and to the goal of replacing the inegalitarian principle of distribution according to work with the egalitarian principle of distribution according to need.[107] But most Communist countries adopt the view that these goals can be directly pursued only after the existing economy of scarcity has been transformed into an economy of abundance. In the interim period of socialist construction, reliance on material incentives and inequality of distribution are inevitable.[108] By contrast, Cuban and Chinese leaders have argued that it is essential to build the new man at the same time as the new economy. Both countries have attempted to reduce reliance on income differentials and on monetary incentives such as bonuses, overtime pay, and piecework, and to replace these with moral incentives.[109] What happened in these cases and how does it affect the arguments about the empirically necessary prerequisites of the egalitarian system?

Moral Incentives in China and Cuba

In China moral incentives and egalitarianism were particularly stressed from 1958 to 1960 during the Great Leap Forward and from 1966 to 1970 during and after the Cultural Revolution. Dissatisfaction with the performance of the economy during the Great Leap Forward led to a sharp change in policy from 1961 to 1965. The principle of "distribution according to work" was emphasized and material incentives became much more prominent. Moral incentives and egalitarianism were also deemphasized after 1970 but the shift was much less pronounced. Since 1976, China seems to have moved further in the direction of reliance on material incentives.[110]

In Cuba the experiment with moral incentives and egalitarianism was even more radical at its height. Between 1966 and 1970 the Cubans conducted a "Revolutionary Offensive" which was designed to transform the Cuban economy and the Cuban population simultaneously. Moral incentives were central to the campaign. Most commodities were produced in limited amounts and were tightly rationed in order to generate savings for investment. Moreover, the prices of these commodoties were fixed at relatively low levels. Thus, a high percentage of the population earned more money than could be spent on available consumer goods. This had two important consequences. First, it greatly reduced inequalities in the standard of living despite the fact that formal inequalities in wages were not greatly affected. Second, it greatly reduced the material incentives for people to work. Thus for many Cubans the only real source of motivation to work was some sort of moral incentive. In 1970, Castro conceded that the Revolutionary Offensive had not succeeded. Since that time, Cuba has placed greater emphasis on material incentives, including the systematic use of income differentials. The production of consumer goods has been increased and the prices of a few items have been raised so as to increase the effectiveness of these incentives.[111]

Lessons about outcomes. Some observers have argued that the Cuban and Chinese experiences should be taken as proof that moral incentives and egalitarianism in distribution will inevitably create major economic inefficiencies.[112] This view is obviously in direct conflict with the argument advanced in this essay. There are three major reasons why I think that this interpretation of the "lessons" of the Cuban and Chinese experiences is mistaken and that these experiments with moral incentives are far less crucial for this investigation than they might appear at first glance.

First, I am attempting to explore theoretical possibilities in this essay. The failure of a few preliminary attempts to rely on moral incentives could no more be decisive for the question of whether such incentives could ever be effective than the failure of a few preliminary attempts to fly could be decisive for the question of whether air travel was possible. The point is not that anything can happen. That kind of vague generalization would destroy the whole purpose of the inquiry. The point is rather that there is a significant body of theoretical literature in the social sciences which is based on empirical investigations but which attempts to draw general lessons not limited to particular cases. This literature provides the best evidence currently available about the possibilities and requirements of human social organization. I have attempted to build my arguments upon evidence drawn from this literature. The Cuban and Chinese experiences clearly provide evidence about what social arrangements are possible in Cuba and China at this moment in history, but this evidence does not modify the theoretical literature in any significant way, and thus it is not decisive for our analysis.

Second, I have stipulated from the beginning that I would not be concerned in this essay with questions about the transition from some existing politico-economic system to my ideal one. But a central feature of both the Cuban and Chinese experiments is that they have attempted a rapid and fundamental transformation of preexisting cultural values and motivational patterns. Under these circumstances, it is hardly surprising that they did not succeed entirely. Indeed, what is remarkable is the extent to which the experiments did succeed. In both countries a significant number of people were motivated to work primarily by moral incentives.[113] Moreover, some observers have detected signs of fundamental change in basic cultural values in both countries.[114] Thus it is not even clear that the experiments with moral incentives should be considered a failure. The renewed emphasis on material incentives may be a tactical retreat rather than a permanent withdrawal. (The Chinese pattern certainly suggests this, although it is not clear whether the pattern of renewed experimentation will continue now that Mao is dead.) And if the underlying values have been transformed, the next attempt to rely on moral incentives may prove more successful.[115]

Severe economic pressures made it difficult for Cuba and China to continue the policy of relying on moral incentives in the face of serious short-run economic costs. It is possible that moral incentives would have proven effective over the long run if these short-run costs could have been borne. And one cannot simply infer from the fact that a policy has changed that the policy was a complete failure. Policy shifts often reflect the outcome of internal political struggles or external political pressures which are only partially related to the success or failure of any given policy. Internal politics have clearly played an important role in China's policy shifts and Cuba has had to take Soviet pressures into account in its policies. But the fundamental point is that failure to get people with an established set of values to respond to moral incentives cannot be taken as proof that people could never be induced to respond to moral incentives. As Lindblom says,

> Neither Cuba's difficulties nor China's caution with moral incentives constitute anything approaching proof that they cannot be made effective. In both systems they were introduced concomitant with an attempt to create a new man rather than after. If in Cuba contemporary man will not respond sufficiently to moral incentives, it still remains a possibility that new men might.[116]

There is a third, more specific point which is important to take into account in assessing the relevance of the Chinese and Cuban experiences for my investigation. Cuba and China regard reliance on moral incentives as both a motivational and an administrative alternative to the market.[117] By contrast, a central assumption of the egalitarian system is that the market has many administrative advantages, so that the task is to combine those administrative advantages with the distributional advantages to be gained from reliance on moral incentives.[118] Thus, in studying the Cuban and Chinese experiences it is crucial, for my purposes, to try to distinguish problems created by inadequate motivation from problems created by incompetent administration.

Given my concept of moral incentives, the key question is whether the Cubans and Chinese were willing to work hard and consistently, to accept training and responsibility when offered, to use initiative, and so on. If productivity dropped because willing workers were given nothing to do, because supplies were misallocated, because managers were selected on the basis of political ideology rather than expertise, this should not be regarded as an indictment of moral incentives but rather as an indictment of the system of administrative planning. From my perspective, therefore, it would be misleading to conclude that moral incentives proved inefficient simply because economic productivity declined during the Cultural Revolution in China or during the Revolutionary Offensive in Cuba. Unfortunately, given the scarcity of data, it is very difficult to distinguish between economic problems caused by inadequate motivation and economic problems caused by mismanagement. There is abundant evidence that mismanagement has been a serious problem, but there is no way to determine how much weight should be given to this as over against motivational problems. I do not mean to suggest that reliance on moral incentives caused no motivational problems. That is much too extreme a position. The best available indicator of motivational problems is probably the rate of absenteeism, and fragmentary data from Cuba suggest that absenteeism was high during the period of the Revolutionary Offensive. In June 1969, for example, absenteeism for permanent farm laborers in Camaguey Province was above 35 percent. In 1968 the rate in the construction industry was 17 percent.[119] Even these kinds of measures must be treated with caution, however, because poor working conditions, the waste of available manpower, and the need to spend time in line to acquire rationed consumer goods created disincentives to work quite apart from the absence of material compensation.[120] The fundamental point again is simply that the failures of performance in the Chinese and Cuban economies during the periods when they relied most heavily on moral incentives cannot be taken as conclusive evidence that the moral incentives (in my sense of the term) were the sole, or even the primary, cause of these failures.

Lessons about methods. Thus far I have focused on the claim that the Cuban and Chinese experiments with moral incentives prove that such incentives are inevitably ineffective. I have tried to show why this claim is unwarranted. But there is a second alleged lesson of the Chinese and Cuban cases which should also be considered. Many observers have been struck by the intensive ideological campaigns which accompanied the emphasis on moral incentives in Cuba and China. The political leaders of both countries attempted to use all available social organizations as vehicles for the creation of the new man. Much of the schooling in both countries was devoted to overt political and moral education in the new socialist morality. The Communist party, trade unions, farmers' organizations, neighborhood groups—all were used as agents of socialization and mobilization. Moral incentives were the subject of political speeches and of mass-media campaigns.[121]

Some have concluded from this that the constant intrusion of overt political direction into all areas of human activity is a necessary feature of any system which seeks to rely on moral incentives. But the methods employed can be explained far more easily as a consequence of the attempt to bring about a rapid and massive change in basic values than as a consequence of the particular character of the new values being introduced.[122] Studies on adult resocialization indicate that it is extremely difficult to alter fundamental values after childhood and adolescence. Some studies suggest that adults can be effectively resocialized only if they are placed in conditions of absolute dependency comparable to those of early childhood.[123] Thus the intensity of the ideological campaigns and the scope of the organizational pressures reflect the difficulty of transforming any well-established values. Similarly, careful and explicit attention to the formal socialization of children was essential for the creation of new values precisely because the children live in a society in which all of the adults have been socialized into old, prerevolutionary values. It is impossible, however, to control all socializing agents (especially the family), many of whom retain old values; even those chosen to conduct the overt socialization processes (e.g., teachers) may retain old values subconsciously and transmit them unwittingly. Thus it was necessary to exercise as much scrutiny as possible over the socialization process and to find new vehicles for the conscious and explicit transmission of new values.

This essay has deliberately avoided any discussion of the problems of transition from some other politico-economic system to the egalitarian system. Thus the problems identified above are not applicable to this case and the solutions cannot be considered empirically necessary prerequisites. As I argued earlier in this chapter, the social duty to maximize pre-tax income could be inculcated through the same set of informal, routine, and often unintended agencies of socialization that now transmit materialist values so effectively in PPM systems. It is not moral incentives but deliberate change that makes overt political control of socialization necessary.

The Origins of Egalitarian Values

The final set of questions introduced at the beginning of the chapter asked about the origins of the egalitarian system and about the relevance of the Communist experience with moral incentives to judgments about the empirically necessary prerequisites of the egalitarian system. I have already discussed the relevance of the Communist experience, and to a large extent intend simply to duck the question about origins. I stipulated at the beginning that I did not intend to discuss the question of how a transition might occur from some other politico-economic system to the egalitarian one. I still think this procedure was justified. It would be an exceedingly complex task to try to identify the conditions under which the American or Swedish or Soviet or Chinese politico-economic system might evolve into something like the egalitarian system of this essay. The historical, cultural, political, economic, and social variables which would have to be considered are overwhelming. The task I have undertaken here is quite different. It has been an explicitly theoretical task concerned only with specifying the prerequisites for a particular hypothetical system on the basis of what is known about the prerequisites for any human social system and in abstraction from any particular historical system. I have simply assumed a population with the values that I have identified as necessary to the egalitarian system and have tried to show only that these values were not incompatible with human nature as we know it and that these values could be passed on to others, with the system thereby being maintained.

Despite all this, the socialization process has been so central to this analysis of how the system would be maintained that it seems only reasonable to provide some general observations about the way in which changes in values do occur and to indicate hypothetically some ways in which the values of the egalitarian system might emerge.

Values change and develop for all kinds of reasons. For one thing, the goals of a culture may be more or less integrated. All cultures contain values which are conflicting and even contradictory, partly because social systems contain contradictory requirements such as the need for both change and stability.[124] Any particular cultural resolution of these conflicts is always partial and temporary. Moreover, the socialization process itself is always imperfect and frequently inconsistent. It is not society with a capital "S" which socializes but rather particular agents such as families and schools, which only imperfectly impart the prevailing cultural values and which frequently modify them in particularistic ways.[125] Individuals themselves frequently hold internally inconsistent values and are motivated by one set or another according to particular circumstances.[126] These are some of the factors internal to a given social system and its processes of transmitting values which may lead to challenges to and modification of the prevailing values of that social system. In addition, there are a variety of external factors which can lead to value-conflict and change. Changes in the physical environment, technological development, the impact of another culture are only three of the many possible factors which may impinge upon a given system of values from without.[127]

These general sources of value-change could be integrated into many possible scenarios by which people could first come to believe they had a social obligation to earn as much pre-tax income as they could even though the pre-tax income would not affect the size of the income available to them for consumption. Revolutionary change such as that attempted by Cuba and China is one possible scenario. But such a belief might also emerge as a result of a gradual, largely unconscious evolution of attitudes in a politico-economic system with a highly progressive tax structure and extensive welfare arrangements. It is a commonplace since Tocqueville to see the growth of egalitarian attitudes and a decline in the legitimacy of social inequality as a fundamental trend of the modern age.[128] It has never been clear to me why this decline in the legitimacy of inequality (including income inequality) should stop at the current point. I am not asserting here that this belief *would* emerge from such a system or even that it necessarily *could* emerge from such a system. I am simply pointing out that there are other theoretical scenarios to describe the emergence of this belief besides the one provided by the Chinese and Cuban experiences. What scenario might be most plausible to explain the emergence of this belief and the institutionalization of the tax rules of the egalitarian system in a particular society would depend on the political and economic conditions of the society, on its history, on its culture, and on a myriad of other factors. This is precisely the question of transition which I have excluded from the investigation.

Change in the Egalitarian System

Let me add one final point about the egalitarian system and social change. I have noted that there are many possible scenarios for the emergence of the values of the egalitarian system. It would be equally easy to construct possible scenarios for the decline of the egalitarian system after it had been institutionalized. All of the general sources of value-change mentioned a few pages ago represent possible sources of such change for an existing egalitarian system. Indeed, I assumed at the beginning of this work that there was no interaction between the egalitarian system and other politico-economic systems precisely because I recognized that interaction with other systems could be a major source of potential change, and I wished to avoid adding this complication to the analysis. In identifying the logically and empirically necessary prerequisites of the egalitarian system I have tried to design the theoretical system in such a way that the internal tensions and contradictions would be minimal, given the goals of the system. Even so, it is clear that the system is not without internal strains, as the discussions of deviance and of the role of elites made clear. I do think that if the prerequisites I have identified were met, it is reasonable to conclude in a theoretical discussion that the strains would not undermine the system. But the real world is obviously far more complex than the simple theoretical model I have constructed, and in the real world such strains could be more important than I have calculated. Moreover, I have considered only a very limited number of variables. While I have tried not to ignore any variables of clear systematic, theoretical relevance, I have inevitably been forced to ignore a whole host of variables which could tend to undermine (or stabilize) an egalitarian system in the real world. Thus I make no claim that an egalitarian system would last forever if only one were built according to my blueprints. I will be more than satisfied if the reader is persuaded that an egalitarian system could exist and could function efficiently if the logical and empirical prerequisites which I have identified were met and that such a system would not necessarily fall apart.

Summary

In the second chapter of this essay I identified the following ten logically necessary prerequisites of the egalitarian system.

1. Individuals in the egalitarian system believe they have a social duty to earn as much pre-tax net income as they are capable of earning.
2. Individuals in the egalitarian system derive satisfaction from performing this social duty to earn as much pre-tax net income as they can.
3. Individuals in the egalitarian system place the same relative value on the satisfactions derived from performing their social duty to acquire pre-tax income ... as individuals in the PPM system place on the satisfactions derived from acquiring income for consumption.
4. Individuals in the egalitarian system believe that the obligation to earn as much pre-tax income as they are capable of earning does not extend to the use of their after-tax equal income shares, and, more specifically, they believe that they ought not to use savings from

their equal income shares for the purpose of generating additional pre-tax income.
5. The tax laws of the egalitarian system permit pre-tax income above a certain level to be saved and such savings are tax-exempt (they do not count as part of an individual's equal income share).
6. The tax laws stipulate that such savings may not be kept in any form which provides personal consumption benefits.
7. The level above which income may be saved is set by the government.
8. Individuals in the egalitarian system place some value on income-consumption satisfactions.
9. There are no significant loopholes in the tax laws providing for equal distribution, and the tax laws are generally obeyed.
10. Incomes will be taxed and money redistributed so that after taxes each adult individual enjoys an equal amount of income for consumption. (This tenth prerequisite is merely a formal statement of the equal-distribution requirement.)

In this chapter I have identified the following empirically necessary prerequisites of the egalitarian system.

1. There must be an effective socialization process which causes people in the egalitarian system to value the social approval and self-esteem gained from performing one's social duty to acquire pre-tax income.
2. The egalitarian system must possess sufficient physical resources to provide for the physical subsistence of members of the egalitarian system.
3. The socialization process in the egalitarian system must be more intense than the socialization process in the PPM system if people in the egalitarian system are to place as much value on social-duty satisfactions as people in the PPM system place on income-consumption satisfactions. The socialization process need not be centrally directed or bureaucratically controlled, however.

4. People in the egalitarian system must have a greater knowledge of relative prices than people in the PPM system. This knowledge is needed to bestow or withhold social approval upon others and to acquire appropriate amounts of self-esteem. Only one's "significant others" need to know one's earning capacity, and they can utilize informal sources of information about prices.
5. There must be a widespread commitment to the norm of equal income-distribution in order for the tax laws to be generally obeyed. This widespread commitment would have to be created through socialization to the norm of income equality.
6. The officials enforcing the tax laws must be generally honest in order for the tax laws to be generally obeyed.
7. Elites in the egalitarian system must share the general consensus on the desirability of equal distribution, if the tax laws are not to have loopholes and if the elites are not to attempt to change the prevailing values on distribution.
8. If economic decline were combined with conditions of full employment, elites would have to play a greater role in mobilizing people to increase effort in the egalitarian system than they would have to play in the PPM system.

Polyarchal political arrangements would tend to reinforce long-term commitment to equal distribution in the egalitarian system, although polyarchal arrangements cannot be considered an empirically necessary prerequisite of the egalitarian system.

How are these empirically necessary prerequisites connected to the logically necessary prerequisites identified earlier? The first, second, third, fourth and eighth empirically necessary prerequisites spell out the basic conditions which would have to be met in order for the first three logically necessary prerequisites to be met in the real world. The fifth, sixth, and seventh empirically necessary prerequisites spell out the basic conditions which would have to be met in order for the sixth, ninth, and tenth logically necessary prerequisites to be met in the real world.

This leaves four logically necessary prerequisites (4, 5, 7 and 8) for which I have not identified explicit empirically necessary prerequisites. In the course of this chapter, however, I did explain that the instrumental value of money in a market economy would inevitably lead people to place some value on income-consumption satisfactions in the egalitarian system. This covers the eighth logically necessary prerequisite.

I did not explicitly identify empirically necessary prerequisites for the remaining three logically necessary prerequisites because all three are technical requirements that would pose no particular problems, if the other empirically necessary prerequisites were met. The fourth logically necessary prerequisite merely provides a slight modification of the nature of social duty. It constitutes a detail which would have to be taught during the basic socialization process. The fifth and seventh logically necessary prerequisites call for particular modifications of the tax laws in order to provide adequate savings for investment. Given lawmakers committed to the norm of equal distribution, these two prerequisites become merely a problem of administration. Thus I have identified the major empirically necessary prerequisites of the egalitarian system.

It is almost as important to see what the egalitarian system does not require as to see what it does require. Much of the space in these two chapters has been devoted to showing how relatively limited and simple the prerequisites of the egalitarian system are. The differences from what is required for a PPM system are not nearly so great as one might have first thought. Essentially it is a question of providing strong moral incentives and an effective tax system, both of which depend primarily upon an effective socialization process. This socialization process could be highly decentralized and informal. In theory at least, the conflicts between efficiency and equality and between freedom and equality are not as inevitable as is commonly believed.

4 Implications

In this final chapter I want to explain how the analysis offered thus far advances our understanding of ideal politico-economic arrangements. How this happens is by no means obvious. In the traditional egalitarian socialist vision, for example, the ideal society would distribute goods according to need rather than on the basis of a mechanical equality, would reduce inequalities of power and opportunity, would enable people to participate directly in decisions affecting their lives, would make productive work an end in itself rather than a means to a livelihood, and would replace the alienation and competition of the capitalist order with the cooperation and social solidarity of a true community. Next to this, my egalitarian model may seem a pale and desiccated utopia at best.

The problem goes still deeper, however. It can be argued that the egalitarian system not only fails to offer a comprehensive utopian vision but also that it cannot even provide the foundation for such a vision because of its link to the market. The argument goes like this.[1] Market systems create inequalities of power and opportunity even apart from the distribution of income. Moreover, in market systems decisions about production and allocation are ultimately based on consumer demand. Thus such systems necessarily rest upon an individualistic and utilitarian calculus of value. Market systems have no standards of good and bad beyond those expressed through individual preferences. "Pushpin is as good as poetry," so long as people want it.[2] The public interest is defined simply in terms of the production of more and more goods demanded by consumers. Market systems satisfy wants rather than needs. Because such systems place a price on everything, they subvert any sense of community and alienate people from one another. And by exalting consumption over production, they repress inner direction about the goals of labor. Thus, the failure of the egalitarian model to present a complete utopian vision comparable to the vision of egalitarian socialism is the result of a structural defect in the model itself, namely, its link to the market. Moreover, the flaws of the market are magnified in the egalitarian system because the system makes it a moral obligation to maximize pre-tax income. In effect, the egalitarian system seems to treat commodity fetishism and alienation as morally desirable goals. Moreover, these objections to the egalitarian system do not depend on any direct disagreement with the discussion of prerequisites in the preceding chapters, because the objections focus on the implications of the egalitarian system and on its desirability. Thus even someone persuaded by my earlier arguments might wonder whether the essay is more an exercise in logic than a contribution to our understanding of ideal politico-economic systems.

In my view, these criticisms greatly overstate the limitations of the egalitarian system. The egalitarian model is not a complete utopia because it has been designed primarily to solve one fundamental problem: how to combine economic efficiency with just distribution. To accomplish this task it was essential to show that the productive functions of the market could be separated from the distribution of income. Despite this narrow focus and in part because of it, the egalitarian model is far more useful than the criticisms suggest, because it is much more flexible than it appears to be at first glance. In identifying the prerequisites of the egalitarian system, I focused only on certain features of the model and adopted certain limiting assumptions for purposes of exposition. I shall attempt in this chapter to spell out the broader implications of the system. I shall consider the objections raised in the preceding paragraphs in order to clarify both the limitations and the potential of the model, and I shall try to indicate what kind of normative justification is presupposed by the egalitarian system. Among other things, I shall show how the egalitarian system could function with a relatively egalitarian distribution of power and opportunity, how the system could distribute income on the basis of need rather than simple equality, and how it could go beyond the individualistic, utilitarian values expressed through consumer preferences to take account of intellectual, aesthetic, ecological, and communal goals established through collective decision-making. The ultimate purpose of the chapter is not merely to show how the egalitarian system might work but to show why it would make sense as part of a utopian ideal.

Inequalities of Power and Opportunity

I shall begin with the question of how the egalitarian system could function with a relatively egalitarian distribution of power and opportunity. The thought experiment developed in Chapter 2 required one to imagine a PPM system with a given set of resources, property rules, and distribution of ownership, and then to imagine a second system with identical conditions except for the rules governing distribution. The assumption of identity between the egalitarian and PPM systems was designed to provide the egalitarian system with considerable organizational flexibility.

In the particular PPM system I chose to imagine, I assumed that an individual could own a factory and that he could pass on the rights of ownership to his children. This obviously would entail inequalities of power and opportunity. I then showed that the same kind of ownership (apart from the right to after-tax income) would exist in the hypothetically identical egalitarian system and thus that the resulting inequalities of power and opportunity would exist in the egalitarian system as well. I adopted the specific assumption about ownership in the PPM system in order to illustrate the point that the egalitarian system could be as efficient as a PPM system, regardless of the particular institutional arrangements or cultural features that might be deemed essential to efficiency in a PPM system. The moral incentives in the egalitarian system would replace the income incentives in the PPM system. But if other inequalities of power or opportunity were somehow crucial to the efficiency of a PPM system, the egalitarian system could provide the same level of efficiency at the cost of the same types of inequalities. Only the inequality of incomes (and any other inequalities created directly by inequality of incomes) would necessarily be altered by the egalitarian system.

I never argued, however, that inequalities of power and opportunity were in fact essential to the efficiency of PPM systems. The organizational flexibility created for the egalitarian system by the assumption of identity applies just as much to more egalitarian versions of PPM systems as to less egalitarian ones. Imagine, for example, a PPM system in which ownership of productive property is widely dispersed among individuals or among groups (e.g., workers' collectives) and in which inequalities of opportunity are greatly limited by legal and cultural norms which restrict inheritance and prohibit discrimination.[3] Although such a system would be more egalitarian than existing PPM systems, the system would still distribute income unequally so long as there was an effective labor market. If one adopts the assumptions of the egalitarian model, however, the system could keep all its other relatively egalitarian features *and* distribute income equally as well, without any reduction in efficiency. In other words, the arguments in Chapter 2 which show the compatibility of equal distribution with otherwise inegalitarian arrangements can just as easily be used to show the compatibility of equal distribution with otherwise egalitarian arrangements.

Open Character of the Egalitarian System

This line of argument may appear to take away with the left hand what had previously been given with the right. In fact, it merely illustrates the open-ended character of the egalitarian system. I have offered no judgment on the question of whether inequalities of power and opportunity contribute to the efficiency of PPM systems. The analysis has deliberately left this question open. If it can be shown that certain inequalities of power and opportunity do contribute to the efficiency of PPM systems, the egalitarian model does not alter this. The egalitarian model merely shows that it is possible to use these same inequalities of power and opportunity to attain the same level of efficiency without distributing income unequally. On the other hand, if it can be shown that inequalities of power and opportunity do not contribute to the efficiency of PPM systems (or at least that they need not under certain circumstances), then the egalitarian model does not require these inequalities. In other words, the assumption of identity adopted in Chapter 2 enables the egalitarian model to show that arguments about the relationship between efficiency and inequalities of power and opportunity can be kept logically distinct from arguments about the relationship between efficiency and inequality of income. The egalitarian model was deliberately constructed so as to keep these issues distinct because I wished to focus on the question of whether equal distribution would necessarily reduce efficiency. Claims about the inevitable costs of equal distribution are at the heart of most critiques of utopian egalitarianism, and so it seemed worthwhile to isolate this issue and to confront it directly. Nevertheless, this approach does give the egalitarian system an open-ended character with respect to inequalities other than income, and this limits its usefulness as an ideal.

Any coherent egalitarian philosophy would presumably seek a system which would minimize inequalities of power and opportunity as well as those of income. Because my egalitarian model only eliminates inequalities of income, it must be regarded as only a partial utopia from an egalitarian perspective. Nevertheless, the model makes an essential contribution to the construction of a more complete egalitarian utopia. By removing the issue of income distribution from the agenda, the model permits one to concentrate on the task of devising supplementary institutional arrangements which would minimize inequalities of power and opportunity. It may be possible to show that these inequalities, too, can be reduced or eliminated, at least in theory, with little or no cost to efficiency. For example, there seems to be good theoretical and empirical evidence to support the claim that extensive participation by workers in industrial decision-making would enhance rather than harm efficiency.[4] If this is not the case in some areas, it should be possible to become clearer about what trade-offs are required. One should not infer from the emphasis I have placed on the efficiency of the egalitarian system that it would not be worthwhile to sacrifice some efficiency in order to reduce inequality. On the other hand, there is no point in sacrificing efficiency when this is not necessary to achieve equality (or some other important goal). One great virtue of the egalitarian model is that it specifies conditions in which it is not necessary to sacrifice any efficiency in order to achieve equal distribution. Thus the model makes it easier to justify reductions in efficiency required by other institutional arrangements, if these should prove necessary in the construction of a more complete egalitarian utopia.

Distributional Flexibility

A second objection to the model focuses on the distributional principle of equality. There are a number of possible reasons why people might find a strictly equal distribution of incomes to be unsatisfactory. For example, it may be objected that equal distribution fails to take account of differences in needs. Given the emphasis this essay has placed on equality, it may seem strange to suggest that the egalitarian model could provide the basis for an ideal politicoeconomic system which incorporated some principle of distribution other than equality. But, in one sense, the selection of equality as the distributional principle was somewhat arbitrary. The arguments that contend that equal distribution would reduce efficiency would apply just as fully to any other distributional principle which separated production from distribution. The major contribution of the egalitarian model is to show that it is theoretically possible to separate the productive functions of the market from the distribution of income without reducing efficiency. Moral incentives play the key role in maintaining the efficiency of the system, once production is separated from distribution. Given effective moral incentives, it would be theoretically possible to utilize any distributional principle that was regarded as ideal by people in the society, provided that there were ways of implementing the ideal without reestablishing the link between production and distribution in some form.[5]

Distribution According to Need

One can understand this point by considering the principle of distribution according to needs as an alternative to equal incomes. Assume for the moment that the classic problems of deciding what is to count as a need, what priorities are to be established among needs, and so on are all solved. Simply assume that the government knows what consumption goods are required to meet people's needs and that it will distribute these goods directly to the people to satisfy their needs.

The planner sovereignty model. How will the government get the goods it wants to distribute? One alternative is to create what Charles E. Lindblom has called a "planner sovereignty market system."[6] In all PPM systems, governmental authorities purchase some final outputs (education, highways, missiles). The government leaves to the market the problem of determining *how* these outputs will be produced. Lindblom argues that governmental authorities could purchase *all* of the final outputs of the system.[7] This would make it possible for the preferences of governmental authorities (in this case, their preferences for those things defined as needs) to determine what would be produced instead of having this determined by the preferences of individual consumers, but it would spare the authorities the task of trying to specify how the final outputs should be produced (what kinds of raw materials, labor, and so on should be used). This chore would be left to the interactions of enterprises and individuals in the market. The moral incentives which have been explored in this essay would be crucial to the scheme, however, if distribution is to be based on need. In order for the market to work effectively, workers must be paid pre-tax wages which reflect the relative scarcities of different types of labor. But if the government is to distribute all goods directly on the basis of need, workers cannot be permitted to keep any of their wages. Why will they work, and if they do work, what incentives do they have to work at those tasks where they will contribute the most? The answer is to be found precisely in the moral incentives discussed here. Individuals must feel that they have a social duty to maximize pre-tax income, even though they cannot keep any of the income for themselves. All of the arguments showing how moral incentives would work in the egalitarian system could also be used to show how moral incentives would work in this planner sovereignty market system in which goods were distributed according to need. The only difference would be that commitment to the principle of distribution according to need would have to replace commitment to the principle of equal distribution. Market prices would then indicate to individuals where the productive resources they control (including their labor) would contribute the most to the task of providing for the needs of the community.

The planner sovereignty market model discussed above treats the principle of distribution according to needs as a radical alternative to the principle of equal income-distribution. This illustrates the point that the possibility of using moral incentives in a market system is not strictly tied to one narrow distributional ideal. This is important, because even people who object to capitalist principles of distribution do not always agree on the specifics of an alternative ideal distributional principle. The egalitarian model may therefore have much to contribute to utopian politico-economic systems which adopt some distributional ideal other than equality of incomes.

Need and equality. The selection of equal incomes as the distributional principle for the basic model was not simply arbitrary, however. The goal of this essay was to identify some of the prerequisites of a *realistic* utopia. I have been concerned only with arrangements which I could show were at least theoretically plausible given what we know about the possibilities of human social organization. From this perspective, one of the fundamental problems with the ideal of distribution according to needs is that there is no theoretically plausible social mechanism for directly implementing the ideal. In the model just discussed I assumed away the problems of how society would determine what would count as needs, what priorities would be established among alternative needs, and so on. In a politico-economic system of any complexity these tasks appear to pose insoluble difficulties for collective decision-making unless one is simply satisfied with an imposed definition of needs.

Equal distribution is a way of allowing people to identify their own needs and to establish their own priorities among those needs. As such it seems to offer a much more satisfactory approximation of the ideal of distribution according to needs than any device for implementing that ideal directly, so long as one assumes either that people have roughly the same needs or that there is no adequate basis for distinguishing among the relative merits of different needs. This assumption seems justifiable for many purposes. People have roughly the same basic needs for food, clothing, and shelter, and there seems to be no adequate basis for distinguishing among the relative merits of different needs in secondary areas such as entertainment or for distinguishing among the relative merits of different tastes for various kinds of food, clothing, and shelter.

On the other hand, there are some kinds of needs which almost everyone in a given society would regard as basic, which are fairly easy to identify, and which are differentially incurred. Medical care is one obvious example. Equal distribution would be a very poor approximation to distribution according to needs in this kind of case, because people who were very sick might have to spend a great deal of their income to meet this need (thus having little left to satisfy their other needs) while people who were healthy would have to spend very little on this need. The solution is for society to provide directly for differentially incurred basic needs. (Direct provision need not exclude individual choice of personnel, methods, and so on.) This reintroduces the requirement of collective decision-making about needs, but the scope of that decision-making is greatly reduced and thus the task is much more manageable. All that society has to do is to identify those basic needs which are differentially incurred and to fund the provision of those needs directly. By combining this approach with that of equal distribution for the satisfaction of other needs, a society could actually achieve a rough approximation of the ideal of distribution according to needs.

The point of this digression was to show both that the original egalitarian model with its requirement of equal distribution was far more closely linked to the ideal of distribution according to needs than might first appear and that it is important to specify the ways in which distributional ideals are to be implemented. The usefulness of the egalitarian model does not depend, in the final analysis, on the merits of this particular argument or on the validity of either distributional ideal. The fundamental point to remember is that the use of moral incentives to separate the productive functions of the market from the distribution of income makes it possible to utilize *any* distributional principle that is regarded by the society as ideal, provided that there are social mechanisms for implementing the ideal which do not reestablish the link between production and distribution.

Collective Decision-Making and Communal Goals

As I observed at the beginning of this chapter, one important line of criticism of the egalitarian system focuses on its orientation towards private consumption. The system seems to provide no mechanism for making collective decisions or for setting communal goals. The emphasis on efficiency and productivity suggests that the public good can be defined simply in terms of economic growth. And the social duty to maximize pre-tax income seems to raise commodity fetishism to the height of a moral imperative.

In its original form, the egalitarian model is certainly vulnerable to these criticisms because the model was deliberately designed to replicate certain features of PPM systems. After all, the more conventional view is that individual free choice, responsiveness to consumer preferences, and economic growth are all good, and further that these desirable attributes of PPM systems would be jeopardized if distribution were severed from production. But assume now that the ideals of the critics are preferable. They want a politico-economic system that can make collective decisions, that can take a broad range of cultural values into account, that can pursue communal goals, that can set limits to economic growth, etc. What does the egalitarian model have to offer those who seek this kind of system?[8]

Prices and Conservation

In the first place, the egalitarian model, like any market system, offers a mechanism which greatly simplifies the task of systematically comparing the alternative uses to which resources can be put. More specifically, the market prices which emerge from the interactions of resource holders make it possible to compare the alternative inputs for any given output and induce producers to use whatever means of creating a given output will use up the fewest productive resources. Presumably, a conservation-oriented, no-growth society would want to perform this task more efficiently than most societies would. Methods of production which waste resources would hardly serve the purposes of such a society. Note that this general argument presupposes nothing whatsoever about the nature of the output. Outputs need not be private consumption goods. Mass transportation systems use resources, for example, and some ways of building and running mass transportation systems will use fewer resources than others. Market prices will reflect this.

Price distortions. Perhaps someone will object that market prices are distorted. I avoided this problem earlier by simply assuming that market prices were not distorted, but then I wanted to make the strongest possible case for the PPM system in order to make the task of constructing a comparably efficient egalitarian system more difficult. Now I want to consider the arguments of critics of PPM systems. The critics claim that market prices fail to take account of the fact that some resources are nonrenewable, fail to include the damage done to the environment in extracting raw materials, and so on. This may well be true in existing PPM systems, but solutions to these problems are theoretically available. Taxes can be placed on environmentally damaging activities and subsidies can be provided for ecologically beneficial forms of production so that prices do reflect real social costs and benefits. Of course, it may be difficult to implement reforms of this kind in existing systems, but this is not an essay on current policy. I have said throughout that the discussion would not be concerned with problems of transition. It is essential to abstract from the cultural and historical circumstances of existing PPM systems in order to appreciate the radical potential of the egalitarian model. The use of the market clearly does imply a social process of calculation. But calculation need not imply a narrow, materialistic set of values.

The market as a social device. In the egalitarian system the market mechanism is simply a social device adopted to serve the goals of the community. If property laws are drawn up which give some people certain rights over resources, this is done with the aim of achieving the goals of the community. The property laws have no a priori justification. They are justified only if they lead resource holders to act in ways that are beneficial to the community. Market prices are designed to facilitate decision-making by individuals and groups in ways that will serve the interests of the community. This is why prices can be regarded as indicators of social duty. The community is the ultimate judge of how well prices are performing this function. If the community concludes that certain prices do not accurately reflect social costs and benefits, it is appropriate for the community to alter these prices through taxes and subsidies. The community may also decide simply to prohibit some activities outright to ensure that market prices will not give socially undesirable signals (e.g., destruction of the habitat of the whooping crane). The use of taxes, subsidies, and prohibitions should not be exaggerated, however. If it were necessary to alter most prices, there would be no point in relying on the market mechanism to set them in the first place. The great advantage that the market offers is that prices can be determined spontaneously through interaction among resource holders. Thus the model makes sense only if it is possible to construct reasonably adequate property rules to govern resource holders in the first place. Assuming that taxes and subsidies can be used to correct for occasional deviations, the market will provide a way of coordinating productive activity which will minimize waste.

One possible objection to this line of argument is that members of the community may disagree with one another about how well property laws and prices are performing their functions. For example, some people may argue that the price of lumber under one set of property rules does not adequately reflect the social cost incurred when the natural beauty of a forest is destroyed. Others may argue that this value is given adequate weight in the prices emerging from the established set of property rules. There is no way to settle this type of argument on an a priori basis, and even in an ideal market system this kind of conflict is likely to occur often. What an ideal system requires therefore is some process for resolving such disagreements which the community regards as legitimate. For example, people might think that a majority of elected representatives should have the final say in deciding whether to change existing property rules or whether to impose taxes or grant subsidies in particular cases to make prices reflect real social costs and benefits. This particular method for settling such questions is only an illustration. Others could be used instead. In principle, the only requirement is that members of the community regard whatever method is used as legitimate. If people regard the decision-making method as legitimate, they would be justified in assuming that prices do reflect real social costs and benefits.

Communal Goals

Even if prices do reflect real social costs, how can the egalitarian system take a broad range of cultural values and communal goals into account? Is not the system indissolubly wedded to the privatistic values reflected in individual consumption decisions? The answer to these questions lies in the "planner sovereignty market system" discussed earlier in this chapter. We saw there how purchases of final products by government officials could be used to distribute goods according to needs. The same technique, governmental purchases of final products, could be used to substitute collective choices for the choices of individual consumers.

Suppose, for example, that a society wishes to encourage people with talent to devote their efforts to artistic and intellectual endeavors. The society may conclude that individuals will not spend enough in this way or that they will make poor choices when they do spend. The government can then simply spend money—providing grants to artists and scholars, purchasing their products, and the like. This is done even in existing PPM systems to some extent. In a variant of the egalitarian system, the money spent would not affect the after-tax income available to artists and scholars but it would affect the amount of resources available for their work and it would indicate to them the degree of importance which society attached to that work. The higher the pre-tax incomes available to artists and scholars, the greater the obligation talented people would feel to engage in artistic and scholarly activities. In principle, there is no reason why the amount spent on such endeavors need be as limited as it is in most PPM systems. Existing PPM systems often have a cultural bias against artistic and intellectual endeavors, and concern for the effect of taxes on incentives may limit governmental expenditures. But the latter constraint is eliminated in any variant of the egalitarian system, and the former is not a structural problem but a problem of transition. In principle, the government could spend however much it wished on these endeavors.

Some people might object that governmental expenditures would entail governmental control. Rich patrons, they might argue, are essential to creativity in the arts. It is only the few with highly cultivated tastes who can appreciate the truly innovative and who will encourage those who take chances.

Government-sponsored art would be monolithic and mediocre. Again, this is more a problem of culture than of structure. In our culture, people tend to assume that governmental expenditures should always be subject to public review and scrutiny while individual expenditures should be largely a matter of individual discretion. It is easy to forget that these are not natural laws. Imagine a culture in which skepticism about individual capacities to choose wisely would lead to severe restrictions on individual discretion in expenditures. Conversely, imagine a culture in which concern for integrity and innovation in the arts might lead the government to delegate decisions on how to spend funds intended for the arts to a number of mutually independent, autonomous individuals. Given the appropriate culture, such individuals could enjoy the same discretion (and power) that rich patrons have in PPM systems, despite the fact that they would be disbursing governmental funds. Even the selection of these "governmental patrons" could be delegated to nongovernmental individuals or groups to protect their autonomy. I am not arguing that this type of arrangement is necessarily desirable. I am only trying to indicate how flexible the egalitarian system can be, if one looks beyond the confines of the existing culture. From this brief discussion, it should be clear that a market system which was able to rely on moral incentives would be virtually unlimited in its ability to use governmental expenditures to substitute communal choices for individual preferences.

Governmental expenditures and the distribution of income. Someone might wonder whether such governmental expenditures would not violate the principle of equal distribution. There are two possible answers to this. First, it is by no means clear that such expenditures would violate that principle. How is one to measure the benefits of governmental expenditures? The task is difficult enough when it is a question of subsidies for external economies or expenditures on collective goods,[9] but both of these cases merely attempt to correct for the inability of the market to respond to certain kinds of individual preferences. By contrast, the governmental expenditures discussed in the last few paragraphs are an attempt to substitute collective choices for individual preferences. These expenditures are a form of parentalism, with the presumably wiser choices of the community replacing those of individuals for their own good. If such expenditures really are undertaken for the common good, there is no obvious basis for claiming that they benefit one individual more than another. On the other hand, governmental expenditures obviously could be used simply to benefit some particular group (those who like rock music). The problem is that people may disagree about whether a particular expenditure (on symphony orchestras) really fosters the common good or merely that of some members of the community. This leads to the second and more important answer.

Given the more flexible attitude adopted towards the egalitarian system in this chapter, the question of whether governmental expenditures violate the principle of equal distribution is not as important as it might seem. I have already shown earlier in the chapter that the egalitarian model could be modified to take account of other principles of distribution such as distribution according to need. Thus the crucial question for any ideal system utilizing the market and moral incentives is whether people believe that the ways of originating demand are legitimate. Demand may originate from individual consumer choices or from governmental expenditures (for any of a variety of reasons) or from both. As long as people think that the ways of originating demand are legitimate, the distributional consequences will also be perceived as legitimate.

People may disagree about what combination of ways of originating demand is ideal. For example, in my view it seems highly desirable to provide considerable scope for individual choice in consumption. Given equal income, why shouldn't people be able to choose what kinds of food, clothing, and shelter they want? What possible social gain is there in requiring people to adopt precisely the same tastes? Every individual is also a member of the community, and allowing each individual to spend his income as he wishes is one way of enabling the community to indicate what it wants produced. In a sense, the community delegates the decision to the individual. On the other hand, there are many areas, from seat belts to symphonies, where I think individual consumers are likely to be shortsighted or ignorant about what is in their best interests both as individuals and as members of a community. For this reason, I would also think an ideal system should make extensive provision for collective choice through governmental expenditures. And, as I indicated earlier, I believe there are certain kinds of differentially incurred basic needs for which the government should make direct provision. Nevertheless, the usefulness of the egalitarian system as a utopian model should not depend on the extent to which people agree with my particular views on the proper mix of consumer choice and governmental expenditures, for the model can accommodate other mixes just as well. Indeed, I would expect that even in an ideal system, the precise combination would not be permanently fixed and people would continue to disagree about what was best. It would be important therefore for there to be some process for settling this question which people would regard as legitimate. (Delegation of the decision to elected representatives would be one obvious possibility.) Similarly, it would be important for people to accept as legitimate the process by which governmental expenditures were determined. (Again, delegation to elected representatives would offer an obvious possibility.) Unless both processes were regarded as legitimate, there would be no reason to regard prices as indicators of social duty because prices will ultimately reflect the demands generated by the decisions to spend governmental funds on some things and to let consumers spend their equal income-shares on other things.

Summary

It should now be clear that the original egalitarian model is only one possible variation of a utopian market model utilizing moral incentives. In the original model, I assumed that prices reflected real social costs and that people accepted the principle of equal distribution. In this chapter I have tried to express the principles implicit in these assumptions in more general and explicit terms: In an ideal market system relying on moral incentives, people must accept as legitimate both the processes for determining prices and property laws and the processes for determining how demand is to be originated. Both of these types of process are essentially ways of establishing goals for the community. Thus, the ideal market model places collective decisions about the goals of the community at the heart of the system. If some decisions are delegated to individuals, including individual consumers, this is because the community has determined that this will serve the common good.

Prices and Social Duty

The preceding discussion of how the egalitarian model might be adapted to take account of a broad range of communal goals places me in a better position to address the question of why market prices should be taken as indicators of social duty in the original egalitarian model or in any of its variants. I have touched on this matter at various times earlier in the essay but for the most part have simply assumed that prices were indicators of social duty. Now it is easier to show why those assumptions make sense. In the ideal system, the community has created appropriate property rules and has adjusted prices where necessary so that prices reflect real social costs and benefits. Furthermore, the community has decided who will have the authority to originate demand (whether individual consumers or governmental agencies or both). The market then is simply a mechanism which makes it possible for the community to indicate to people what productive activities they can engage in if they wish to help the community achieve its goals. Prices are merely sources of information about what the community wants done. All of this was implicit in the original egalitarian model, but one can see now that "what the community wants done" need not be simply an amalgamation of the privatistic decisions of individuals. The obligation to maximize pre-tax income need not make commodity fetishism a moral imperative, as the criticisms outlined earlier claimed. Rather it makes service to the community a moral imperative. Community goals may be broadly defined and collectively determined, and prices will still play an essential role in indicating to individuals how they can help fulfill these goals.

Blind Idealism

To see the essential role played by prices as indicators of social duty, one need only imagine a society in which people are motivated by the desire to use their abilities and resources for the well-being of the community but in which there is no market mechanism. Fundamental problems of calculation and coordination have to be solved. Certainly the society does not want to waste the efforts of these committed people, nor does it want to waste its nonhuman resources. How will people be able to tell what the community wants done? In a simple society, this might not pose too difficult a problem, but in any complex society the community will want many different things done. How are people to tell which of the goals are more important and which are less important, and by how much? Furthermore, in a complex society most individuals will be able to use their abilities and resources in many different ways. Assuming they want to help the community, how can they tell what they should do? Just knowing what the community wants done will not be enough, even if it is possible to establish priorities among various community goals. Suppose, for example, that a person would be able to contribute a great deal towards the achievement of one of the community's lesser goals by doing one thing or could contribute a little towards one of the community's most important goals by doing another. He could simply decide to do what he thinks is best, but he wants to know what the community would prefer. How can he tell?

In my ideal market system, all these problems can be solved. The community communicates what it wants done by enabling certain individuals, agencies, and institutions, to spend money. The demand created by these initial expenditures ultimately sends signals to all of the participants in the society in the form of prices. The individual need not worry about the problem of comparing the relative importance of social goals and the relative value of his contributions to different tasks. The initial expenditures will reflect community priorities and will thus affect the amount of pre-tax income which can be gained at any particular task. The amount the individual can contribute to any particular activity will be reflected in the amount he can earn from engaging in that activity. Thus the relative usefulness of an individual's contributions to alternative tasks and the relative importance which society places on achieving various goals interact automatically in the market as supply and demand. And the individual can be confident that he will contribute the most he can to what the community wants done if he simply maximizes his pre-tax income.

The Uses of Limited Knowledge

Perhaps someone will object that imperfections in knowledge and in competition will develop in any market system and that prices may therefore fail at times to indicate accurately what the community wants. The objection is correct, but it does not alter the conclusion that people should regard prices as indicators of where their social duty lies. A realistic utopian market model presupposes that the government will do whatever it can to assure that the market functions properly, as we saw in the discussion of externalities in the preceding section. No real market system could ever function perfectly, but no other mechanism for communicating information can function perfectly either. If people are to make judgments about what actions of theirs will best serve the community, they must have criteria for these judgments. Under the conditions of the egalitarian model and its variants, prices provide such criteria. They are rough, approximate, and sometimes misleading. If they can be improved in particular cases (through taxes, antitrust laws, and so on), that is all to the good. But one could not encourage people systematically to doubt the reliability of prices without undermining their usefulness as guides. Nor can one assume that the fact that people are committed to serving society will enable them to discover and correct the inadequacies of prices as guides. One great temptation of utopian visions is to assume that all conflicts of goals and of judgments would be eliminated if people were simply motivated by concern for others. I have tried to avoid that temptation. That is why I argued in the preceding section that an ideal system would require methods of making decisions and resolving disagreements about property rules, taxes, and individual versus governmental expenditures, and that people must regard these methods as legitimate. The same principle applies here. Goodwill does not always lead to good results. The fact that a person seeks to do what the community wants is no guarantee that he has any understanding of what the community does in fact want. Prices, in an ideal market system, are at least the outcome of a process through which the community has attempted to express what it wants done. Thus, for all their defects, prices will provide better guides than the unsupported and subjective judgments of individuals about what the community wants.

Competition and Cooperation

The emphasis on prices as sources of knowledge about what the community wants done may help to clarify other aspects of what appears to be the odd marriage of moral incentives and the market. One objection raised against the invisible hand (whether in capitalist or socialist market systems) is that people in market systems cannot be concerned with the good of others if the market is to function properly. Miller puts it this way:

> Community depends on the intention that people have in acting, and merely knowing that your actions have good consequences is not the same as intending them. There must be a direct intention to benefit others for us to speak of fraternity or community. The reason for this is that community refers to the quality of relationships between people and our relationships to others depend on

our perception of their intentions towards us.... [M]arkets, far from creating community between people, actually prevent it from emerging by obliging people to act in a self-interested way even if they would prefer to be altruistic.[10]

Regardless of its merits when applied to ordinary markets, this argument clearly does not apply to a market system using moral incentives of the kind discussed in this essay. What people intend in maximizing pre-tax income is precisely service to the community. Market prices are not signals to individuals about their private financial advantage but rather about their public responsibility to their fellow citizens. In such a system, reliance on the market can enhance rather than diminish the sense of fraternity and community.

A second, related objection is that the competitive ethos of the market is fundamentally incompatible with the concern for others implicit in moral incentives. Emphasis on the "competitive ethos" of the market may be misplaced even when one is considering ordinary market systems. As Lindblom argues,

> "competitive" is a misleading term. No less than in a market system, people in authority systems compete for good jobs and other advantages. Democratic politics is also competitive. Socialist emulation in Cuba and China is competitive. Finally, many forms of market behavior called "competitive" in market systems are not competitive in the psychological sense. Wheat farmers, for example, are said to be competitive in a market system. But they do not rival each other, do not seek to displace each other. Each of them is largely indifferent to thousands of other wheat farmers, and to those in his own neighborhood he is tied by common interests and sociability rather than separated by rivalry.[11]

In the context of a market system which utilizes moral incentives, the argument can be taken still further. To maximize one's pre-tax income is simply to follow rules and patterns of behavior which have been explicitly designed for the good of the community as a whole. Like other rules, market rules require people to act on the basis of impersonal criteria, and this may lead to hardship in particular cases. For example, if a person introduces a technological innovation and lowers the cost of some product, he may drive other producers out of business. But what is the alternative? Would it show more concern for his fellow citizens, if he were to suppress the innovation? This might please the other producers, but what about the rest of the people who would have benefited from the reduced cost of the product? Suppose, for example, he had discovered a way to use fewer trees in making paper. What course of action demonstrates the most concern for his fellow citizens and for the community? And what guidelines can people use for making decisions in such cases? Genuine concern for others should not be confused with either favoritism or shortsightedness. The competition required by market activities is not incompatible with the concern for others implicit in moral incentives so long as prices are generally reliable indicators of what the community wants. Indeed, in this context, market competition is really the most effective form of social cooperation. The alternative is a blind altruism which benefits no one. "The Gift of the Magi" makes a good story but a bad social system.

The Individual vs. the System

Even if the egalitarian model is as effective in communicating communal goals for production as the preceding arguments contend, does it follow that everyone should always maximize pre-tax income? Should people be expected to devote all their energies to productive activities, no matter how broadly defined? Are there not other obligations, both social and personal, which are not captured by the prevailing price? And what about the individual who pits himself against the community? What about the struggling artist, for example, who believes in himself when no one else will, or even the individual who simply seeks work that is personally satisfying though less productive than other alternatives? Will not such people be regarded as moral shirkers in the egalitarian system because they fail to respond to market prices? If so, is not the system even more oppressive and more stifling to the individual than a conventional capitalist system where the only penalty for failure to respond to prices is a loss of money?

In considering these objections, I shall distinguish among three types of conflict between what prices indicate a person should do with his productive resources and what he wishes to do with them: conflicting judgments, conflicting obligations, and conflicting preferences. These distinctions should help to clarify the nature, extent, and justification of the obligation to maximize pre-tax income.

Conflicting Judgments about Social Good

One reason for choosing not to maximize pre-tax income would be that an individual might strongly believe that in his particular case prices fail to provide an accurate indication of where he can contribute the most to society. In the previous section, I showed how the egalitarian system could pursue a broad range of communal goals and I argued that prices would provide better guides to where people can contribute most to what the community wants than the subjective judgments of individuals. Nevertheless, prices and the processes by which they are determined are not infallible. Suppose an inventor is convinced that he can make a breakthrough in some important area but cannot persuade anyone else. Suppose a scientist or an artist is convinced that he is engaged in important work, the significance of which is simply not appreciated at this time. In each of these cases, the individual might choose to continue the work that he believes in, despite opportunities to earn more pre-tax income in some other type of endeavor. The individual would be making a conscious decision to substitute his personal judgment about what best serves the community in this case for the judgment which emerges from the established social processes.

The civil disobedience analogy. In many respects this type of deviance from the goal of maximizing pre-tax income is like a conscientious act of civil disobedience in a democratic society.[12] The person engaging in civil disobedience usually recognizes a prima facie obligation to obey the law. Similarly, in our case, the individual recognizes an obligation to use his productive resources in whatever way will contribute the most to society. Thus the basic obligation is not in dispute. Moreover, a citizen in a democratic society will usually feel an obligation to obey even those laws with which he disagrees, because the democratic process of establishing the laws is regarded as a legitimate way for resolving disagreements about what should be done. Similarly, our hypothetical individual presumably accepts as legitimate the processes by which property laws, prices, and governmental expenditures are determined. Normally, prices would provide reliable indicators of social duty. In both cases, what is at stake is an exception, a conscientious refusal to follow the outcome of processes which are normally regarded as imposing obligations and/or a plea to the community for reconsideration of the outcome of those processes. The civil disobedient hopes that the community will reconsider and change the law or policy. In the meantime, he has to endure the formal and informal sanctions imposed on lawbreakers. Similarly, the individual who chooses not to respond to prices because he believes them to be misleading appeals to the community to reconsider the adequacy of market indicators in this particular case, and, in the meantime, suffers the social disapproval visited upon those who fail to perform their social duty to use their productive resources to achieve communal goals.

I should not overstate the parallel. In the case of civil disobedience, one breaks a law. There is usually a relatively clear line between breaking the law and not breaking it. Questions of degree are usually not crucial. By contrast, questions of degree play a central role in determining the extent to which a person fulfills his social duty to maximize pre-tax income. Almost everyone would contribute some pre-tax income. Almost no one would actually maximize pre-tax income. The extent to which a person deviates from formally required social duty in conscientiously refusing to respond to prices depends upon the alternatives which he faces. The size of the gap between what the individual can earn from the occupation he thinks will contribute most to society and what the individual can earn from other available occupations will determine the seriousness of the deviation.

The fact that the egalitarian system would impose a penalty (social disapproval) on some who genuinely believed that they were acting in the best interests of the community may be seen as a defect. But the limitations of the egalitarian system in this area are limitations which all social systems will share. No system can ensure that pioneers of genius will be recognized as such immediately. In all systems, those who seek to challenge accepted social processes or to change fundamental values and perceptions are bound to encounter resistance and to pay some price for their innovative efforts. The egalitarian system is no worse than others in this regard and it is better than many. If the pioneer is convinced that he is right, he can hope that current judgments will be seen as incorrect at a later stage. In the egalitarian system, the pioneer suffers social disapproval but does not starve, and the conviction that he is acting on behalf of society may help to sustain him in the face of social disapproval.

Conflicting Obligations

A second reason for not maximizing pre-tax income is that the duty to acquire it may conflict with other social or personal obligations. For example, an individual's obligation to earn as much pre-tax income as possible may come into conflict with his obligation to be as good a parent as possible. If nothing else, time spent at work may be time spent away from one's family. At some point it may be necessary to choose between the two obligations. It is essential to recall here that the egalitarian system does not presuppose that people will devote themselves exclusively to acquiring pre-tax income. Duty in economic activity was defined in terms of maximization, that is, acquiring as much pre-tax income as one can, in order to give a clear and consistent direction, just as one might also say that an individual has an obligation to be as good a parent as he can. In practice, it is quite possible to have several competing obligations and to be unable to fulfill them all to the highest degree. The egalitarian system does not require that the duty to acquire pre-tax income be given the highest priority or indeed that it be given a very high priority at all. For example, it is quite possible to imagine an egalitarian system in which all individuals had an obligation to participate in political affairs and in which this political obligation was regarded as far more important than the obligation to contribute to economic production. The general expectation would be that the political obligation would normally take priority whenever the two obligations conflicted. People would then participate in public affairs even when this participation reduced their pre-tax incomes (e.g., by taking them away from their income-producing work).

The limits of market prices. Perhaps someone who has noted my earlier paeans to the flexibility of the market will wonder whether this kind of political obligation could not also be incorporated into the market and communicated through prices. But not all social values can be communicated through the market. Market prices make it possible to calculate relative scarcities, but there are some cases where we may wish to avoid such considerations. For example, if one wants the political obligation to participate in public affairs to fall equally upon all, then one will want to avoid any consideration of relative scarcities. If the absence of one individual from economic activity is more costly than the absence of another, one does not want to know about it in this context. But the function of prices is precisely to provide the kind of information which has been determined here to be irrelevant.

If the previous case seems too farfetched, simply consider military conscription. It is certainly possible to imagine a society which requires all its young people to be equally subject to the draft on the grounds that risking one's life for one's country should not be an obligation limited to those with lesser economic talents. The market is simply not suitable for the communication of this kind of obligation.

Calculation and alienation. To take the argument one step further, there are important areas of social life where the kind of conscious calculation which is implied by the use of market prices may destroy the very goal that one seeks. Some relationships in individual and community life depend upon feelings of trust and affection which can be undermined by excessive calculation. It is sometimes necessary to transcend calculation for the sake of solidarity. Relationships within the family are a familiar example.[13] Some people have argued that this principle should be extended to all human interactions. For this reason, they think that a fully human society will have to eliminate the use of money entirely, not merely because it creates a potential for inequality but because the use of money inevitably involves calculation and thus creates barriers between people.[14] In my view, this line of argument goes too far—at least for any utopia which seeks also to be realistic. In any large, complex society we must inevitably become involved in many interactions in which we treat other people primarily as means to an end (as bus drivers, store clerks, mail carriers), and we must serve as means for others. Money facilitates this type of interaction, but money does not cause it. Even if money were entirely eliminated, it would not be possible to enter into a "truly human" relationship with every person who contributes to one's material existence in a complex society.

The most obvious alternative to reliance on money and markets for this type of coordination is some type of authority system.[15] Bureaucracy offers one familiar and relatively efficient form of this, but bureaucratic relationships are certainly no more "human" than financial ones. As Weber put it,

> Its [bureaucracy's] specific nature ... develops the more perfectly the more bureaucracy is "dehumanized," the more completely it succeeds in eliminating from official business love, hatred, and all purely personal, irrational, and emotional elements which escape calculation.[16]

Participatory democracy offers another alternative. The relationships among members of a participatory democracy may entail less calculation, at least under some conditions, but participatory democracy is a method for organizing human affairs which can be used by only a relatively limited number of people for a relatively limited number of problems and which imposes severe demands on the time of those involved.[17] The greatest potential benefit of participatory democracy seems to lie in the organization of decision-making within the workplace. As a vehicle for coordinating activities among enterprises or for determining what kinds of consumer goods should be produced, it seems to offer far less promise.

If the end of alienation requires the elimination of calculation from human affairs, neither the egalitarian system nor any other model is likely to prove satisfactory. On the other hand, it is perfectly possible to imagine a variant of the egalitarian system which places great value on other social and/or personal duties, even when these conflict with the duty to acquire pre-tax income, and which excludes calculation and market considerations from important spheres of human activity.

Conflicting Preferences

The third type of reason for not maximizing pre-tax income is that individuals may have preferences for work or leisure which conflict with the obligation to maximize pre-tax income. For example, an individual may prefer a poorly paid but interesting job to a highly paid but dull one, or an individual may simply prefer to spend some of his time on leisure activities even though he will thereby forego some of his potential pre-tax income.

In considering this issue, we should begin by recalling again the discussion in Chapter 2 concerning trade-offs among alternative satisfactions. I explicitly argued there that the egalitarian system did not require a monolithic motivational schema and that people in the egalitarian system could be expected to pursue other satisfactions even when this reduced pre-tax income and thus social-duty satisfactions. Thus the formal duty to maximize pre-tax income serves more as a directional indicator for a certain kind of socially desirable behavior than as an actual goal which people would be expected to achieve.

Several points follow from this. First, people could choose

to pursue their preferences rather than their social duty when the two conflicted. If an individual could earn far more pre-tax income by working in a large corporation than by operating a corner grocery store but greatly values the autonomy which running his own business provides, he still may choose to run the store. It is important, however, for him to recognize the cost to society which this choice entails. The difference between the potential pre-tax income of the corporate job and that of the grocery communicates this cost to him. More of society's productive goals could be achieved if he took the corporate job. Note again the importance of degrees here. The cost to society and thus the obligation to take the higher-paying job is great if the gap between the incomes of the two jobs is great and small if the gap is small.

Second, in any egalitarian system, people would find that the satisfactions from pursuing personal preferences such as leisure would outweigh the marginal social-duty satisfactions from earning more pre-tax income at some point. Certainly, people would not be expected to work at every possible moment, though they might normally be expected to work "full time" (a standard which might vary a bit from one job to another as it does in existing systems). Some people might exceed the norm and others fall below it, surpassing or falling below the normal level of social regard as a consequence, but most people would simply work at an acceptable, expected level.

Third, the relative value placed on social-duty satisfactions would depend on the importance the society placed on those goals which could be achieved through economic production. Different egalitarian systems might place different values on these goals, just as PPM systems differ in the importance they attach to economic production. Theoretically it would be possible to have an egalitarian system in which people placed a relatively high value on meaningful work and on leisure and a relatively low value on economic production. In such a system the obligation to maximize pre-tax income would exist, but fulfilling this obligation would be regarded as less important than finding meaningful work and enjoying life.

Finally, it is important to recall from Chapter 3 that the

costs of not maximizing pre-tax income in the egalitarian system are not as different from the costs of not maximizing income in the PPM system as might first seem to be the case. Income in PPM systems provides satisfactions from social esteem and self-regard as well as financial benefits. Thus failing to maximize income in PPM systems reduces these nonfinancial satisfactions.

Despite these cautions and qualifications, it remains true that, other things being equal, the egalitarian system places more social pressure on people to maximize pre-tax income than does the PPM system. The egalitarian system by its nature imposes a direct and explicit obligation on people to acquire pre-tax income. Thus the fundamental question is, What justifies the imposition of such an obligation? Why should a person feel obliged to take less meaningful work simply because it provides more pre-tax income? Why should a person who enjoys both leisure and a simple life-style feel obliged to work "full time"? Granted that these people may still choose the more meaningful work or the more extensive leisure, and granted the importance of degrees in determining the strength of the obligation, what right does society have to visit them with any social disapproval and to try to make them feel at all guilty for these choices?

Justification of the Egalitarian System

A full answer to these questions would require an analysis of the foundations of social obligation far beyond the scope of this essay. What I can offer here is some indication of the kind of theory which might be used to justify it.

A Rawlsian Justification

One possible line of argument would be to attempt to apply Rawls's *Theory of Justice* to the egalitarian system.[18] Is the social duty to use one's productive resources in the ways desired by society an obligation which rational people would willingly assume if they were constructing social arrangements without any knowledge of how these arrangements would affect them as individuals? The answer seems to be yes, given the other conditions of the egalitarian system. Rawls himself argues that rational individuals choosing behind a veil of ignorance about their personal situations would start with equality as a benchmark and would agree only to accept departures from equality which would be to the advantage of the least well-off under conditions of inequality.[19] He suggests that economic inequalities which created incentives for greater productivity might be one form of inequality compatible with this principle.[20] But if a general obligation to use productive resources in the ways desired by society could be as effective as income differentials in inducing productive efforts, those who would be least well-off under conditions of economic inequality would seem to gain from an arrangement which relied on this obligation rather than on income differentials. Since those choosing behind the veil of ignorance are assumed to adopt the perspective of the least well-off, would they not accept the obligation to use productive resources in the ways desired by society as a fundamental component of the system in order to ensure that income could be distributed equally (or perhaps according to need)? The answer seems to be yes with two provisos. First, they would have to be confident that the obligation to use productive resources in the ways desired by society would be as effective as income differentials in inducing productive efforts. Second, they would have to believe that this obligation did not create greater inequalities than those which would exist if income differentials were used. This second proviso requires some elaboration. The obligation to use one's resources falls equally upon all, but some people may find this obligation more burdensome to fulfill than others because of the differences in the intrinsic satisfactions and dissatisfactions derived from different types of work.

The third chapter of this essay has shown that both of these provisos would be satisfied under the conditions of the egalitarian system. (1) Given appropriate conditions of socialization, the obligation to use resources for social goals would be as effective as income differentials in motivating productive activity. (2) Because the least well-paid jobs are also usually the least enjoyable, equal distribution would improve the position of those who would be least well-off under conditions of economic inequality and would not create a new class that was even worse-off.[21]

Many of the claims which Rawls puts forward on behalf of the difference principle seem to apply with equal or greater force to the obligation in the egalitarian system to use one's productive resources in the ways desired by society. Thus Rawls says: "the difference principle represents, in effect, an agreement to regard the distribution of natural talents as a common asset and to share in the benefits of this distribution whatever it turns out to be."[22] In imposing an obligation to maximize pre-tax income, the egalitarian system is treating natural talents as a common asset, and the system is even more effective than the difference principle in ensuring that all share in the benefits of these natural talents.

As justification for treating natural talents as a common asset, Rawls argues: "[I]t is clear that the well-being of each depends on a scheme of social cooperation without which no one could have a satisfactory life.... [W]e can ask for the willing cooperation of everyone only if the terms of the scheme are reasonable."[23] What could be a more reasonable basis for enlisting people's cooperation than ensuring that everyone will be equally obliged to cooperate and everyone will share equally in the benefits obtained through cooperation? Thus Rawlsian social-contract theory seems well suited to provide a justification for the requirements of the egalitarian system.[24]

Alternative Justifications

I do not mean to suggest that this brief summary of how Rawls's theory might be applied to the egalitarian system constitutes a fully developed theoretical justification of that system. I have simply tried to suggest one possible line of argument which could justify both the equal distribution of income and the imposition of an obligation to maximize pre-tax income. The connection to Rawlsian social-contract theory is not essential for the egalitarian system, however. In recent years an enormous literature has emerged dealing with the issues of justice, equality, freedom, and obligation. I have deliberately tried to avoid linking the egalitarian system too closely with any particular position in these debates. Obviously, the moral justification of the egalitarian system is incompatible with some of the positions which have been advanced. Robert Nozick's theory is a prime example.[25] The egalitarian system presupposes a need to take account of the patterned consequences of individual decisions. Obviously, it presupposes a commitment to egalitarian values. But there are many strains of thought within the egalitarian tradition, and my intention has been to construct the model with enough flexibility so that some variant of the egalitarian model would be compatible with most of the major strains in the egalitarian tradition, and thus with the moral justifications offered for these strains. For example, I have tried to show that the egalitarian model would be compatible either with distribution according to needs or with equal distribution. Need and equality have both served as important distributional principles within the egalitarian tradition, and the tensions and conflicts between the two principles have never been fully resolved even in theory. I wanted my egalitarian model ultimately to be compatible with either principle. Similarly, I expect that the obligation to maximize pre-tax income could be justified on intuitionist or utilitarian grounds as well as on contractarian grounds. To consider it from another perspective, the obligation to maximize pre-tax income is simply a more specific version of the traditional socialist expectation, "from each according to his abilities." Thus all of the arguments which have been used to justify this socialist requirement could be used to justify the obligation to maximize pre-tax income as well.

Conclusion

Whatever contribution this essay makes to our understanding of equality and justice will come not from its direct discussion of these topics but from its exploration of the structural possibilities of politico-economic organization. All too often, current theories either ignore questions about what is possible or construe the possible too narrowly. My hope is that this essay will encourage people both to think creatively about possible politico-economic arrangements and to pay careful attention to the ways in which ideals may be realized through social mechanisms. Ultimately, I hope that the essay will help to undermine the credibility of the five fat sheep in the epigraph at the beginning of this book, and thus enhance the prospects of the ninety-five thin.

Appendix
Saving from Equal Income Shares

In discussing the question of saving in Chapter 2, I adopted the following assumptions:

> Individuals in the egalitarian system believe that the obligation to earn as much pre-tax income as they are capable of earning does not extend to the use of their after-tax equal income shares, and, more specifically, they believe that they ought not to use savings from their equal income shares for the purpose of generating additional income.

I left open the question of whether individuals could save some of their equal income shares for other purposes. In this appendix I wish to examine the consequences of various possible rules about saving from equal income shares in the egalitarian system.

In a PPM system individuals are free to follow their own time preferences with respect to consumption (within the constraints imposed by their resources). Two individuals with the same income in a PPM system may thus adopt two quite different consumption patterns not only with respect to what they consume but also with respect to when they consume. For example, someone might want to spend very little money on a vacation one year in order to be able to afford an expensive vacation the next year. Another person might have the opposite time preference. He might like to borrow money this year for an expensive vacation and to pay it back the next year by spending less then. Moreover, one individual might spend his income on goods and services which retain no market value (vacations, food), while another with the same income might buy durable goods (cars, appliances) which can be resold at a lower price. Such consumer durables therefore represent a form of saving. Some consumer goods, such as houses, jewelry, or art, can even increase in value.

The question which an egalitarian system must face is how to arrange things so as to provide the greatest possible freedom of choice in consumption without undermining the principle of equal distribution. The logically necessary prerequisites of the egalitarian system do cover some points about consumption but they leave open some important questions, as we shall see.

The tax laws of the egalitarian system clearly impose one limit not found in the PPM system. If a person did save some of his equal income share, he could not lend these savings in return for interest which he could use to increase his future consumption. Apart from this, however, there is nothing to prohibit individuals from saving part of their equal income-shares if they choose to do so. The requirement that the egalitarian system provide virtually the same freedoms as a PPM system clearly extends to freedom of choice in consumption. And freedom of choice concerns not only *what* one consumes but *when* one consumes. If an individual wants to save some of his equal income share one year so that he can splurge the next year, he has not received any more or less income for consumption during either year than any other individual. This kind of choice should be treated simply as a matter of one's consumption preferences, like the choice about how much of one's equal income share one will spend on food, clothing, housing, and the rest.

As indicated in the text, there would have to be some administrative mechanism for distinguishing saving from equal income shares from the saving generated for investment, since individuals would be free to spend the former for consumption whenever they wanted while they would be prohibited from spending the latter on consumption. One simple solution for cash savings would be simply to establish special banks or at least special accounts for savings from equal income shares. (These banks or accounts could pay interest directly to the government, but that would not affect social-duty satisfactions, as we have seen.)

Saving from Equal Income Shares

One obvious way that people in the egalitarian system might choose to save would be through the purchase of durable goods such as cars. This would pose no new administrative problems since savings from pre-tax incomes cannot be held in forms which provide personal consumption benefits.

Suppose an individual decides to sell a used durable good. Should the money he receives from the sale be counted as taxable income? Assume that he receives less than he originally paid for the good. Clearly, in such a case, the money received should not be counted as taxable income. If he had saved part of his equal income share in the form of cash, it obviously could not be counted as taxable income when he later decided to spend it, or the effect would be to prohibit cash saving. Any money received from selling a used durable good below its original cost is simply another form of saving. Therefore it should not count as taxable income.

Suppose, however, that the individual is able to sell a consumer good for more than he originally paid for it. As noted, this frequently occurs in PPM systems with houses, art objects, and so on, and there is no reason to think that it could not occur in an egalitarian system. If one allowed individuals to keep such gains, then one would be tolerating a form of income inequality. Any money received above the original purchase price would be income, not savings. Thus it would seem obvious that the egalitarian system would have to tax away any net gains.

This policy would create certain dilemmas, if the tax were imposed only when the good was sold. Suppose, for example, that there were inflationary increases in the cost of housing throughout the egalitarian system. An individual who had bought a house for $30,000 might find that it would be worth $50,000 if he sold it. He would obviously have a strong financial incentive not to sell the house. If he were to sell it for $50,000 he would have to pay $20,000 in taxes and he would have only $30,000 to spend on new housing. Given a general increase in housing costs, this $30,000 would not purchase nearly as good a house as the one he was in. One consequence would be that some people would remain in the same housing when they would prefer to move and others would not be able to get the housing they would like to have. Another consequence would be that individuals might have strong income-consumption incentives not to move even when they could increase their pre-tax incomes by moving to another city to take another job.

These undesirable consequences could be largely eliminated if the tax were imposed on an annual basis on any increase in the market value of a consumer good, regardless of whether the good was kept or sold. Such a tax might be difficult to administer. If the tax were applied only to houses and land, however, the problem of administration would be greatly reduced. These are the two most obvious and most important types of consumer goods which increase in value, and their market value is relatively easy to determine. Under the proposed arrangement, each year's tax would establish a new base. A tax would be paid in the amount of the increase over the previous year (see table 10).

Table 10: **Tax on Increase in Housing Value**

	Housing Value	Increase	Tax Paid
Year 1	$25,000	—	—
Year 2	$27,000	$2,000	$2,000
Year 3	$30,000	$3,000	$3,000
Year 4	$30,000	$0	$0
Year 5	$31,000	$1,000	$1,000

Houses and land can also decrease in value. There would be two possible ways to deal with decreases. One would be to provide rebates for any taxes paid on previous increases. Then each year's assessment would provide the starting point for the calculation of the next year's tax or rebate. The original price paid would provide a floor beneath which no rebates would be granted. By the same token, if the market value fell below the original price, increases back up to the amount of the original price would not be taxed. The second way would be to treat decreases as costs to be absorbed by the owner, as with many other consumer goods. In this case, however, no new tax would be imposed unless the market value of the house surpassed its previous high. Table 11 represents the first alternative and table 12 the second.

Table 11: Tax with Rebate for Decrease in Housing Value

	Housing Value	Increase or Decrease	Tax or Rebate
Year 1	$25,000	—	—
Year 2	$29,000	+$4,000	$4,000 (T)
Year 3	$26,000	−$3,000	$3,000 (R)
Year 4	$24,000	−$2,000	$1,000 (R)
Year 5	$30,000	+$6,000	$5,000 (T)

Table 12: Tax without Rebate for Decrease in Housing Value

	Housing Value	Increase or Decrease	Tax
Year 1	$25,000	—	—
Year 2	$29,000	+$4,000	$4,000
Year 3	$26,000	−$3,000	$0
Year 4	$24,000	−$2,000	$0
Year 5	$30,000	+$6,000	$1,000

Either of these arrangements would be compatible with the egalitarian requirement that gains be taxed, and either of them eliminates any incentive to hold on to land or housing simply because it has increased in value. In effect, the tax ensures that each individual will have to pay at least what his housing is currently worth. Therefore the incentives for holding on to housing which one does not really want are virtually eliminated. (The only remaining incentive of this kind one might have would be the opportunity to recoup losses resulting from decreases. These incentives would be stronger and more widespread under the second arrangement.)

So far in the discussion of housing and of durable goods, I have focused on the question of saving in the egalitarian system. The other question to be considered is whether individuals in the egalitarian system would be able to borrow. This is an obvious question to introduce in this context since it is very common to borrow in PPM systems when purchasing durable goods and almost unheard of not to borrow when purchasing housing. People may simultaneously borrow and save when purchasing consumer durables and housing.

None of the logically necessary prerequisites of the egalitarian system provides any reason for prohibiting borrowing, and the need for freedom of choice in consumption seems almost to require that borrowing be permitted. Borrowing for consumption purposes in the egalitarian system would work as it does in the PPM system. Individuals would have to pay interest in order to borrow money. Paying interest does not violate the principle that income for consumption be equally distributed, since one is paying for a consumption benefit. (Receiving interest on savings from one's equal income share would violate the principle of equal distribution, as we have seen.)

One of the classic dilemmas for all utopian egalitarian systems has been the problem of how to maintain equality over time without so restricting the options available to individuals that the value of equality is undermined. In permitting saving and borrowing, I have opened up the possibility that some individuals in the egalitarian system will acquire more wealth than others simply by saving more. The importance of potential differences in wealth is greatly reduced, however, by the fact that individuals cannot use their savings to increase their incomes and wealth either through interest or capital gains. The wealth has to be entirely saved from the equal income share. The rules adopted so far would thus be likely to create a relatively high degree of equality of wealth among individuals starting at the same point in time in the egalitarian system. Yet these rules have not significantly restricted freedom of choice in consumption (beyond the basic restriction that no one can acquire more after-tax income than anyone else).

There is one important respect in which the egalitarian system would have to restrict freedom of choice in order to maintain equality over time. Individuals would not be free simply to give things to others. More precisely, gifts and inheritances would have to be considered taxable income in the egalitarian system. Obviously there would be no need to apply this principle to gifts of relatively small value. But if the basic rule were not adopted, then some individuals would be likely to acquire much more wealth than others simply through the accident of birth. An only child with several unmarried aunts and uncles might stand to inherit a substantial estate in the egalitarian system, if gifts and inheritances were not taxed. He would have a great economic advantage over the child with several siblings and many cousins. Over time some families might build up substantial amounts of inherited wealth. This could lead to differences in standards of living far greater than the variations made possible by allowing individuals to dispose of their own equal income shares as they wished. Thus, the egalitarian system would have to restrict the individual's freedom to pass on what he saves.

Notes

Chapter 1

1. Alexis de Tocqueville, *Democracy in America,* trans. Henry Reeve (1835; reprinted, New York: Schocken Books, 1961), I, lxxi.
2. Irving Kristol, "Equality as an Ideal," *International Encyclopedia of the Social Sciences* (New York: Macmillan, 1968), 5:110.
3. George Halm, *Economic Systems,* 3d ed. (New York: Holt, Rinehart and Winston, 1968), pp. 7–8.
4. Arthur M. Okun, *Equality and Efficiency: The Big Tradeoff* (Washington, D.C.: The Brookings Institution, 1975), p. 47.
5. Ibid., p. 48.
6. Ibid., p. 119. In fairness to Okun, I should note that his essay is primarily concerned with the contemporary American politico-economic system, that he proposes a variety of programs which would increase both efficiency and equality in the American context, and that he is clearly *not* in favor of always sacrificing equality to efficiency. Nevertheless, the statements I have quoted were not taken out of context and do seem to me to represent Okun's views on the limits of theoretically possible politico-economic arrangements.
7. Brian Barry, *The Liberal Theory of Justice* (Oxford: Clarendon Press, 1973), p. 162.
8. Thomas Nagel, "Equal Treatment and Compensatory Discrimination," *Philosophy and Public Affairs* 2 (1973): 354, 363.
9. Ibid., p. 363.
10. A private-property market system could also be called a capitalist system. I have chosen to use the phrase "private-property market system" instead of "capitalist system" for two reasons. First, the phrase "capitalist system" has normative connotations for many people (some positive and some negative). The phrase "private-property market system" is less apt to carry such connotations. Second, the phrase "private-property market system" draws attention to the *structural* features of this type of politico-economic

system (as opposed to its historical origins, for example). These structural features are what will concern us in this essay.

11. See, for example, Martin Bronfenbrenner, *Income Distribution Theory* (Chicago: Aldine-Atherton, 1971), pp. 36–37.

12. Michael Young, *The Rise of the Meritocracy* (Baltimore: Penguin Books, 1958), p. 158.

13. Titmuss argues that income inequality in Britain is much greater than the statistics on money-income distribution indicate because of the loose definition of business expenses and the extensive provision of goods and services provided for "business purposes." The upper-income groups receive many more of these perquisites than do the lower-income groups. See Richard M. Titmuss, *Income Distribution and Social Change* (London: George Allen and Unwin, 1962), esp. pp. 169–86.

14. Equal distribution of income for consumption does not mean that people in the egalitarian system would have to consume all of their equal income shares each year. See the Appendix for a discussion of saving from equal income shares in the egalitarian system.

15. See, for example, Richard Lowenthal, "Development vs. Utopia in Communist Policy," in *Change in Communist Systems,* ed. Chalmers Johnson (Stanford: Stanford University Press, 1970), and G. William Skinner and Edwin A. Winckler, "Compliance Succession in Rural Communist China: A Cyclical Theory," in *A Sociological Reader on Complex Organizations,* ed. Amitai Etzioni, 2d ed. (New York: Holt, Rinehart and Winston, 1969), esp. pp. 411–12.

16. Robert Dahl and Charles Lindblom, *Politics, Economics, and Welfare* (New York: Harper and Row, 1953), p. 224.

17. Friedrich Hayek, *The Road to Serfdom* (Chicago: University of Chicago Press, 1944), pp. 124–25.

18. On the theory of market socialism, Lange's essay in Oscar Lange and Fred Taylor, *On the Economic Theory of Socialism* (Minneapolis: University of Minnesota Press, 1938), is still the standard text. For a survey of the major theoretical issues on the topic, see Abram Bergson, "Market Socialism Revisited," *Journal of Political Economy* 75 (1967): 655–73.

The possibility of introducing more market elements into the Soviet economy was widely discussed as a result of proposals made by E. G. Liberman. The views of Liberman and others are to be found in *Value and Plan,* ed. Gregory Grossman (Berkeley: University of California Press, 1960).

Yugoslavia has made much more extensive use of the market in practice than any other socialist state. For a discussion of the role of the market in the Yugoslav economy, see Svetozar Pejovich, *The Market-Planned Economy of Yugoslavia* (Minneapolis: University of Minnesota Press, 1966).

19. Michael Polanyi, "The Determinants of Social Action," in *Roads to Freedom,* ed. Erich Streissler (London: Routledge and Kegan Paul, 1969), p. 177. See also Israel M. Kirzner, *Competition and Entrepreneurship* (Chicago: University of Chicago Press, 1973).

20. See Bergson, "Market Socialism Revisited."

21. There are some exceptions. Lange contends that under market socialism the income inequalities are only compensatory, reflecting the different utilities attached to different kinds of work (Lange, *On the Economic Theory of Socialism,* pp. 101–2). Lange is clearly mistaken in this view. As I shall show, prices in a market system—even a socialist market system—must reflect relative scarcities. For example, certain qualities needed in production (e.g., intelligence) may be in relatively short supply and others (e.g., physical prowess) may be more widely available and/or less in demand. These factors will influence labor prices and therefore incomes under Lange's system of market socialism. See Halm, *Economic Systems,* pp. 220–22, on the same point.

22. See Tjalling C. Koopmans, *Three Essays on the State of Economic Science* (New York: McGraw-Hill, 1957), p. 84.

23. Gordon Bjork stresses this aspect of efficiency in his *Private Enterprise and the Public Interest* (Englewood Cliffs, N.J.: Prentice-Hall, 1969), chap. 5, but the argument that a PPM system is efficient in this respect can be traced back to Adam Smith.

24. In the next few paragraphs I borrow from Paul A. Samuelson, *Economics,* 7th ed. (New York: McGraw-Hill, 1967), p. 42. Samuelson's description and my own leave out the familiar and necessary assumptions about the absence of monopoly, the absence of externalities, etc., in order to simplify the presentation.

25. The argument here follows Halm, *Economic Systems,* p. 62.

26. See Okun, *Equality and Efficiency,* p. 54.

27. Halm, *Economic Systems,* p. 62.

28. Empirical studies suggest that the actual negative effects of progressive marginal taxes on willingness to work in real PPM systems are quite small. This is partly because such taxes create contradictory income and substitution effects. That is, on the one hand the tax makes the cost of leisure lower, creating an incentive for one to substitute leisure for work, but on the other hand the tax lowers the individual's income and thus creates an incentive for him to increase work in order to maintain a higher standard of living. In

practice, the two effects seem to cancel each other out to a large degree. These empirical studies cannot be used to support the claim that equal distribution would have little or no effect on effort, however, since the people studied still usually gain substantial income benefits from more work. In the egalitarian system all such income benefits would be eliminated entirely. For a summary of the relevant literature, see George F. Break, "The Incidence of Economic Effects of Taxation," in *The Economics of Public Finance* (Washington, D.C.: The Brookings Institution, 1974), pp. 180–91.

29. See n. 19 above.

30. See Bronfenbrenner, *Income Distribution Theory*, p. 133.

31. See Dahl and Lindblom, *Politics, Economics, and Welfare*, pp. 160–61, and James Meade, *Efficiency, Equality, and the Ownership of Property* (Cambridge: Harvard University Press, 1965), p. 38.

32. For example, Wilbert Moore, "The Utility of Utopias," *American Sociological Review* 31 (1966): 765–72, and Herbert Gans, *More Equality* (New York: Pantheon Books, 1973), pp. 193–94. Gans does give some indication of how he thinks such research should proceed and presents a few utopian "scenarios" (pp. 195–223), but he does not discuss the methodological questions in any detail.

33. The term is borrowed from John C. Harsanyi, "Rational-Choice Models of Political Behavior vs. Functionalist and Conformist Theories," *World Politics* 21 (1969): 513–38.

34. The definition of rationality is adapted from Harsanyi, "Rational-Choice Models," p. 515, and Anthony Downs, *An Economic Theory of Democracy* (New York: Harper and Row, 1957), p. 6. Downs has a more extensive, technical discussion of the conditions of rationality than this brief definition indicates, and Kenneth Arrow explores the conditions of rationality in even more detail in the first two chapters of his *Social Choice and Individual Values,* (New York: John Wiley and Sons, 1951; 2d ed., 1963). These refinements are not necessary for the purposes of this essay, however.

35. Buchanan points out that the term "choice" is actually a misnomer in this context, since the behavior of the individual is logically determined by the assumptions. See James M. Buchanan, "Is Economics the Science of Choice?" in *Roads to Freedom,* ed. Streissler, p. 49. The usage is common and convenient, however, and we shall continue it.

36. Harsanyi, "Rational-Choice Models," pp. 536–37.

37. W. G. Runciman adopts a similar approach by simply imag-

ining a hypothetically just Britain with the same resources as the real Britain of today in *Relative Deprivation and Social Justice* (Middlesex, England: Penguin Books, 1972), p. 340, and he notes on pp. 344–45 that the question of transition raises a host of other problems. On the problems connected with the transition to utopia, see George Kateb, *Utopia and Its Enemies* (New York: Schocken Books, 1972), pp. 21–67.

38. Melvin Tumin, "On Inequality," *American Sociological Review* 28 (1963): 21.

Chapter 2

1. This technique of constructing parallel rational-actor models which differ only in certain specified ways is not uncommon. See, for example, W. S. Vickrey, "Utility, Strategy, and Social Decision Rules," *Quarterly Journal of Economics* 74 (1960): 507–35. Most authors, however, assume certain differences and then trace out the consequences of these differences. My approach is somewhat unusual since I specify not only a difference between the two systems but also the conclusion which I wish ultimately to infer (that the egalitarian system is no less efficient than the PPM system), and I leave for investigation the specification of the difference which would make it possible to infer this conclusion.

2. I have included the word "net" in the phrase "pre-tax income" simply to indicate that individuals in the egalitarian system would be expected to deduct any business expenses which they pay for themselves from gross income in calculating the value of their pre-tax incomes. To avoid repetition, I shall generally leave this term out of the rest of the discussion.

3. For the moment, there is no need to specify the nature of these satisfactions, but it should not be assumed that they are purely "altruistic." I shall show in the next chapter that under certain conditions individuals could receive such satisfactions as self-esteem and social approval for performing their social duty. Moreover, I shall show that these satisfactions are in some respects quite like the satisfactions derived from acquiring income for consumption.

4. The absence of inherent constraints on economic institutions, methods of organization, and so on, is also an absence of inherent requirements. In the thought experiment, the egalitarian system need have only those features which I assume the parallel PPM system to have. The particular features of one imaginary PPM system which I use here for purposes of illustration and analysis

should not be regarded as intrinsic characteristics of all possible PPM systems. The importance of this point will become clear in Chapter 4.

5. To avoid repetition the phrase "after-tax income" will be used to mean "after-tax income for consumption" unless the context clearly indicates otherwise.

6. Again, one should take note of the heuristic function which the assumption of identity of demand serves. Some organizations commonly found in PPM systems might not exist in an egalitarian system simply because there would be no demand for them. For example, in an egalitarian system there would be no need for individuals to make pension arrangements. However, this does not affect the basic thrust of the argument about the organizational flexibility of the egalitarian model. There would be no *rules* preventing the existence of any organizations found in PPM systems.

7. Mancur Olson stresses the point that the effectiveness of incentives in controlling behavior depends on the extent to which the incentives are selective, that is, on the extent to which they reward (or punish) only those who respond (or fail to respond) to them. See Mancur Olson, Jr., *The Logic of Collective Action* (New York: Schocken Books, 1968), esp. pp. 51 and 61. The social-duty incentives of the egalitarian system are selective incentives in Olson's sense.

8. In this chapter I am emphasizing the compatibility of inequalities in power, prestige, and opportunity with equality in the distribution of after-tax income, because these other inequalities may affect efficiency and it is important to distinguish their impact from that of income distribution. Nevertheless, it is important not to assume that the egalitarian system requires such inequalities by its very nature. What is required in a given egalitarian system in this thought experiment depends upon what is assumed about the PPM system to which it is parallel. Again, I shall develop this point in more detail in the final chapter.

9. Some of those involved in the debate about the consequences of the separation of ownership and control in the modern corporation have tended to assume that owners who actually manage their enterprises would necessarily be profit-maximizers. Actually a good case can be made for the view that it is only the "functionless" absentee stockholder who closely approximates this motivational model, and that owners who are actually involved in the running of a business might deviate from the profit-maximizing model as much or more than hired managers. See Gordon Tullock, "The New

Theory of Corporations," in *Roads to Freedom,* ed. Streissler, esp. p. 294. For my purposes, however, the debate is not of great importance. As can be seen from the text, my egalitarian model is compatible with a view which attaches an important function to property owners, and, a fortiori, the model would be compatible with a view which attached little or no importance to owners.

10. I should note again that, in the end, one cannot ignore income-consumption satisfactions entirely in the egalitarian system, and I shall discuss this issue later in the chapter. Here, however, it simplifies the exposition to ignore income-consumption satisfactions.

11. As I indicated at the beginning of the chapter, I intend to treat effort as a constant when discussing the question of price changes and resource allocation in this section. Nevertheless, it is useful to refer to the trade-off between leisure and other satisfactions when analyzing the nature of trade-offs among satisfactions in the PPM and egalitarian systems because the income-leisure trade-off plays such a major role in economic analysis.

12. A complete analysis of an individual's full earning capacity would have to take into account both his long-term prospects and the risks associated with alternative allocations. Both of these factors will be taken into account later in the book. I have excluded them here in accordance with my initial description of the order of exposition of the argument.

13. The assertion that income-consumption satisfactions are simply a function of the amount of income acquired is an oversimplification, since there is an extensive empirical literature on relative deprivation and reference groups which indicates that the amount of satisfaction people receive from a given amount of income is significantly affected by the comparisons they choose to make with other people's incomes. See Runciman, *Relative Deprivation and Social Justice,* and Herbert Hyman and Eleanor Singer, eds., *Readings in Reference Group Theory and Research* (New York: The Free Press, 1968). Nevertheless, the oversimplification seems appropriate here since it makes the case for the egalitarian system more difficult and since income-consumption satisfactions are not directly tied to earning capacity. Income-consumption satisfactions may also be affected by changes in the cost of living, as we shall see later in the chapter.

14. To the extent that "effort" involves the type or the quality of work done, it is covered by the discussion of resource allocation in the previous section.

15. "Automatically" here means "assuming rationality."

16. A reduction in one's wage would also affect the relative attractiveness of one's job, as we saw earlier, but I am not concerned with those effects here. I wish to focus only on the effects of such a price change on the trade-off between income and leisure in a given job.

17. A price increase might have other effects (such as creating incentives for Jane to alter her consumption patterns), but, again, I am focusing here only on the way the price change affects the trade-off between leisure and income.

18. From this it can be seen that the satisfactions of consumption are not formally identically with the satisfactions of acquiring income for consumption (what I have called income-consumption satisfactions). Indeed the two are actually in conflict to some degree in a PPM system at any given point in time, since it is possible to acquire more income-consumption satisfactions by foregoing consumption satisfactions, and vice versa. Nevertheless, the distinction between the two kinds of satisfactions is not important for most purposes.

19. The most obvious factor—risk—will be discussed later in the chapter. Other factors could play a role, too, though. For example, friendship could influence a decision about loaning one's savings.

20. One important consequence of this in real-world PPM systems is that the amount people wish to save may not coincide exactly with the amount people wish to invest. Inflation or unemployment may result from this imbalance. Government fiscal and monetary policies can be adjusted in an attempt to correct the imbalance.

21. Again, risk is also a key factor affecting investment decisions, but I am deferring discussion of this until later in the chapter.

22. The main reason it seems likely that such an arrangement would not work is that the individuals who saved would be foregoing significant income-consumption satisfactions, but I am deferring discussion of the role of income-consumption satisfactions in the egalitarian system until later in the chapter.

23. See the Appendix regarding the dilemmas which personal saving creates for an egalitarian system.

24. The purchase of existing stocks does not constitute an investment in the sense defined earlier, since it creates no new capital. If new stocks are issued to generate funds for the purchase of capital goods, then buying such stocks counts as an investment.

25. This would not eliminate the need for the government to use

the conventional fiscal and monetary controls characteristic of PPM systems, although it might reduce their importance to some degree. This general control over the level of savings does not enable the government to stimulate investment directly and/or in specific problem areas, as conventional fiscal controls do.

26. On the virtues of decentralized control over resources, see, for example, Friedrich Hayek, "The Price System as a Mechanism for Using Knowledge," in *Comparative Economic Systems,* ed. Morris Bornstein, rev. ed. (Homewood, Ill.: Richard D. Irwin, 1969), pp. 21–32. See also Polanyi, "Determinants of Social Action," in *Roads to Freedom,* and Kirzner, *Competition and Entrepreneurship.* One argument which obviously could not be applied to the egalitarian system is that individual resource-holders should have the right to decide by themselves what the level of savings will be and that the government should not try to intervene directly or indirectly. See Henry Wallich, *The Cost of Freedom* (New York: Collier Books, 1960), pp. 42–43.

27. As we shall see shortly, success or failure in risky allocations would affect other satisfactions in the egalitarian system even though it would not affect social-duty satisfactions.

28. This does not imply that an individual necessarily adopts the same attitude toward risk in all cases. An individual might take risks with some kinds of satisfactions and try to avoid risks with others. For example, he could be a gambler in business dealings and cautious in personal relationships—or the reverse.

29. See, for example, Gary Becker, *Human Capital* (New York: Columbia University Press, 1964). Real individuals almost never make the careful, explicit, complicated calculations which Becker's model seems to suggest.

30. The distinction drawn earlier between income-consumption satisfactions and consumption satisfactions is irrelevant in this context because the two are not in conflict and indeed are not really distinguishable in cases such as this where it is a question of income in kind.

31. In ordinary language we might speak of people "investing" in these commodities, but the term "investment" is reserved here for the purchase of new capital goods.

32. It could be argued that this assumption is implicit in the original stipulation about equal distribution, but it seems worth making it explicit here because of the role played by income-consumption satisfactions.

33. Howard Sherman has developed a model of "partial com-

munism" in which goods and services are distributed in a highly egalitarian manner but in which choice in consumption is greatly restricted. It is this lack of choice which Peter Wiles makes the focal point of his critique of Sherman. See Howard Sherman, "The Economics of Pure Communism," *Soviet Studies* 22 (1970): 24–36, and Peter Wiles, "A Comment but Not a Rejoinder," *Soviet Studies* 22 (1970): 37–43.

Chapter 3

1. Robert Merton, *Social Theory and Social Structure*, rev. ed. (New York: The Free Press, 1968), pp. 186–87.
2. Alex Inkeles, *What Is Sociology?* (Englewood Cliffs, N.J.: Prentice-Hall, 1964), p. 50.
3. Alex Inkeles, "Social Structure and Socialization," in *Handbook of Socialization Theory and Research,* ed. David Goslin (Chicago: Rand McNally, 1969), p. 627.
4. Daniel Miller, "Psychoanalytic Theory of Development: A Re-evaluation," in *Handbook,* ed. Goslin, p. 499.
5. See, for example, the articles by Gewirtz, Bandura, Aronfreed and LeVine in *Handbook,* ed. Goslin.
6. Wilbert Moore, *Order and Change* (New York: John Wiley and Sons, 1967), p. 182.
7. See Jean Piaget, "Developmental Psychology: A Theory," *International Encyclopedia of the Social Sciences* (New York: Macmillan, 1968), 4:140–47.
8. The argument that the obligation to acquire pre-tax income makes sense presupposes that the market is functioning properly, i.e., that prices are not (badly) distorted as a result of externalities, imperfect competition, and so on.
9. See Lawrence Kohlberg, "Moral Development," *International Encyclopedia of the Social Sciences,* 10:483–94.
10. Wilbert Moore, "Occupational Socialization," in *Handbook,* ed. Goslin, p. 866.
11. Ibid., p. 862.
12. Alfred Kuhn, *The Study of Society: A Unified Approach* (Homewood, Ill.: Richard D. Irwin, 1963), pp. 98–99.
13. See, for example, the citation from Inkeles above and also Talcott Parsons, *The Social System* (Glencoe, Ill.: The Free Press, 1951), p. 32. Even the critics of this view agree that it is the dominant one. See, for example, Dennis Wrong, "The Oversocialized Conception of Man in Modern Sociology," *American Sociological Review* 26 (1961): 183.

14. See especially Wrong, "Oversocialized Conception of Man."
15. See, for example, the articles in *Motivation,* ed. Dalbir Bindra and Jane Stewart, 2d ed. (Middlesex, England: Penguin, 1971), and C. N. Cofer and M. H. Appley, *Motivation: Theory and Research* (New York: John Wiley and Sons, 1964).
16. See, for example, William McDougall, *An Introduction to Social Psychology* (London: Methuen, 1908); Henry Murray, *Explorations in Personality* (New York: Oxford University Press, 1938); Abraham Maslow, "A Theory of Human Motivation," *Psychological Review* 50 (1943): 370–96; and Amitai Etzioni, "Basic Needs, Alienation, and Inauthenticity," *American Sociological Review* 33 (1958): 870–85.
17. Albert Cohen, *Deviance and Control* (Englewood Cliffs, N.J.: Prentice-Hall, 1966), p. 60.
18. Philip Slater, "Social Bases of Personality," in *Sociology,* ed. Neil Smelser (New York: John Wiley and Sons, 1967), p. 557.
19. Ibid.
20. See Parsons, *Social System,* p. 27, and Inkeles, "Social Structure," p. 631.
21. George Homans, *Social Behavior,* rev. ed. (New York: Harcourt Brace Jovanovich, 1974), p. 42.
22. Ibid.
23. Ibid., p. 27.
24. In support of this view, see Talcott Parsons and Neil Smelser, *Economy and Society* (New York: The Free Press, 1956), p. 182; James C. Davies, *Human Nature in Politics* (New York: John Wiley and Sons, 1963), p. 7; Cofer and Appley, *Motivation,* p. 14; Homans, *Social Behavior,* pp. 42–43.
25. See pp. 104–5 above and also Parsons, *Social System,* p. 27.
26. Maslow, for example, lists this as the most fundamental of the five basic needs. See Maslow, "Theory of Motivation," p. 371.
27. These are described in Davies, *Human Nature,* pp. 11–15.
28. Such a claim would, of course, be similar to the Marxist claim that abundance is a prerequisite for the achievement of full communism.
29. See Amitai Etzioni, *A Comparative Analysis of Complex Organizations* (New York: The Free Press, 1961), pt. II.
30. See J. Dollard and N. E. Miller, "Learned Drive and Learned Reinforcement," *Personality and Psychotherapy* (1950), excerpted in Bindra and Stewart, *Motivation,* p. 91.
31. Talcott Parsons, "Levels of Organization and the Mediation of Social Interaction," in *Institutions and Social Exchange,* ed. Her-

man Turk and Richard Simpson (Indianapolis: Bobbs-Merrill, 1971), p. 29.

32. Frederik Barth, "Economic Spheres in Dafur," in *Themes in Economic Anthropology,* ed. Raymond Firth (London: Tavistock, 1967), p. 153.

33. Ibid., p. 156.

34. Barth made a rough calculation of relative value based on the cost of millet, which was the basic raw material for the beer and which was available for sale in local markets.

35. See Karl Polanyi, *The Great Transformation* (New York: Rinehart, 1944); Karl Polanyi, C. Arensberg, and Harry Pearson, eds., *Trade and Market in the Early Empires* (Glencoe: The Free Press, 1957); Paul Bohannan and George Dalton, *Markets in Africa* (Evanston, Ill.: Northwestern University Press, 1962); George Dalton, "Economic Theory and Primitive Society," *American Anthropologist* 63 (1961): 1–25.

36. See especially, Scott Cook, "The Obsolete 'Anti-Market' Mentality," *American Anthropologist* 68 (1966): 323–45.

37. See Leopold Pospisil, *Kapauku Papuan Economy,* Yale University Publications in Anthropology, no. 67 (New Haven: Yale University Press, 1963).

38. Manning Nash, "The Organization of Economic Life," in *Tribal and Peasant Economies,* ed. George Dalton (New York: Anchor Books, 1967), p. 9. See also Percy Cohen, "Economic Analysis and Economic Man," in *Economic Anthropology,* ed. Firth, pp. 92, 96.

39. See P. Cohen, "Economic Analysis," p. 113.

40. Max Weber, *The Protestant Ethic and the Spirit of Capitalism,* trans. Talcott Parsons (1930; reprint ed., New York: Charles Scribner's Sons, 1958), p. 71.

41. See, for example, Robert Bellah, *Tokugawa Religion* (Glencoe, Ill.: The Free Press, 1957), and Robert E. Kennedy, Jr., "The Protestant Ethic and the Parsis," *American Journal of Sociology* 68 (1962): 11–20.

42. Kingsley Davis, "Social and Demographic Aspects of Economic Development in India," in *Economic Growth: Brazil, India, Japan,* ed. Simon Kuznets, Wilbert T. Moore, and Joseph Spengler (1955), p. 294, cited by Neil Smelser, *The Sociology of Economic Life* (Englewood Cliffs, N.J.: Prentice-Hall, 1963), pp. 41–42.

43. David C. McClelland and David G. Winter, *Motivating Economic Achievement* (New York: The Free Press, 1969), p. 23. Emphasis added.

44. Homans, *Social Behavior,* pp. 27–28.

45. See, for example, Robert Opsahl and Marvin Dunnette, "The Role of Financial Compensation in Industrial Motivation," *Psychological Bulletin* (1966), reprinted in *Management and Motivation,* ed. Victor Vroom and Edward Dei (Middlesex, England: Penguin, 1970), p. 129. See also William F. Whyte, *Money and Motivation* (New York: Harper and Row, 1955).

46. Parsons and Smelser, *Economy and Society,* p. 23.

47. Merton, *Social Theory,* pp. 190–91.

48. Ibid., p. 221. See also Whyte, *Money and Motivation,* p. 210; Albert Lauterbach, *Man, Motives and Money,* 2d ed. (Ithaca, N.Y.: Cornell University Press, 1959), p. 45.

49. See Talcott Parsons, "The Motivation of Economic Activities," *Canadian Journal of Economics and Political Science* 6 (1940), reprinted in Talcott Parsons, *Essays in Sociological Theory,* rev. ed. (Glencoe, Ill.: The Free Press, 1954).

50. This point would obviously not apply to deviant subgroups. I am referring here to a goal which would generally be accepted in the society as a whole.

51. See Parsons, "The Motivation of Economic Activity."

52. See the discussion of these arguments in Alasdair MacIntyre, "Egoism and Altruism," *The Encyclopedia of Philosophy* (New York: Crowell, Collier, and Macmillan, 1967), 2:462–66, and Thomas Nagel, *The Possibility of Altruism* (Oxford: Clarendon Press, 1970).

53. For a sustained argument supporting the position that altruism can be a distinct type of motivation, see Nagel, *The Possibility of Altruism.*

54. See Ludwig Wittgenstein, *Philosophical Investigations,* trans. G. E. M. Anscombe, 2d ed. (New York: Macmillan, 1958), p. 33, par. 68.

55. MacIntyre, "Egoism and Altruism," pp. 465–66.

56. Some people might object that the egalitarian system requires competitive rather than cooperative interaction. I discuss this question in Chapter 4.

57. Moore, *Order and Change,* p. 185.

58. I am assuming that it is a question of a deliberate refusal to earn pre-tax income. If a person were involuntarily unemployed, he would not be deviating from his social duty.

59. A number of studies have shown that many individuals will even give answers which they believe to be false in response to questions in order not to disagree with the rest of the group. See, for example, Solomon Asch, "Effects of Group Pressure Upon the

Modification and Distortion of Judgments," in *Group Dynamics: Research and Theory,* ed. Dorwin Cartwright and Alvin Zander (New York: Harper and Row, 1953).

60. Leonard Goodwin, *Do the Poor Want to Work?* (Washington, D.C.: The Brookings Institution, 1972).

61. See M. Boskin, "The Effects of Taxes on the Supply of Labour: With Special Reference to Income Maintenance Programs," *Proceedings of the 64th Annual Conference on Taxation* (Columbus, Ohio: National Tax Association, 1971), pp. 687–89; Harold Watts and Glen Cain, "Basic Labor Responses from the Urban Experiment," *Journal of Human Resources* 9 (1974): 156–278; and Joseph Pechman and P. Michael Timpane, eds., *Work Incentives and Income Guarantees: The New Jersey Negative Income Tax Experiment* (Washington, D.C.: The Brookings Institution, 1975). In contrast to these findings, however, recent results from an HEW study of an experiment in Seattle do seem to indicate that income grants had some negative effect on incentives to work. See the report in the *New York Times,* May 21, 1978, p. 50; November 16, 1978, p. 23.

62. Merton, *Social Theory,* p. 187.

63. In some societies a trend in the direction of such a norm seems to be developing already. Wesotowski reports that 65 percent of the respondents in one survey of the rural population in Poland said they thought income differences should be small. See Wladzimierz Wesotowski, "Some Notes on the Functional Theory of Stratification," *Polish Sociological Bulletin* 3–4 (1962), reprinted in *Class, Status, and Power,* ed. Reinhard Bendix and Seymour Lipset (New York: The Free Press, 1966), p. 67, n. 1. But contrast Robert E. Lane, "The Fear of Equality," in *Political Ideology* (New York: The Free Press, 1962).

64. M. McMullan, "A Theory of Corruption," *Sociological Review* 9 (1961), reprinted in *Readings on Economic Sociology,* ed. Neil Smelser (Englewood Cliffs, N.J.: Prentice-Hall, 1965), p. 154.

65. Ibid.

66. See Robert A. Dahl, *After the Revolution?* (New Haven: Yale University Press, 1971), pp. 40–56.

67. Merton, *Social Theory,* p. 394.

68. Kenneth Prewitt and Alan Stone, *The Ruling Elites* (New York: Harper and Row, 1973), p. 233.

69. Robert E. Lane and David O. Sears, *Public Opinion* (Englewood Cliffs, N.J.: Prentice-Hall, 1964), pp. 49–50.

70. See Merton, *Social Theory,* p. 394.

71. Ibid., p. 187.
72. See Robert A. Dahl and Charles E. Lindblom, *Politics, Economics, and Welfare* (New York: Harper and Row, 1953), p. 288.
73. Ibid., p. 389.
74. For a list of the definitional characteristics of polyarchy, see Robert A. Dahl, *A Preface to Democratic Theory* (Chicago: University of Chicago Press, 1956), p. 84.
75. This argument obviously presupposes that issues can play an important role in elections. There is considerable debate about how important a role issues do play in actual elections in existing polyarchal systems. See, for example, Richard Niemi and Herbert Weisberg, eds., *Controversies in American Voting Behavior* (San Francisco: W. H. Freeman, 1976), esp. pp. 161–75.
76. For a description of the role-playing model of popular control, see Norman Luttbeg, ed., *Public Opinion and Public Policy*, rev. ed. (Homewood, Ill.: Dorsey Press, 1974), p. 8. Empirical studies of legislators' behavior in existing polyarchies suggest, however, that most legislators do not perceive themselves as delegates and also that it might not matter much even if they did. See the studies cited in Luttbeg, pp. 393–95.
77. Dahl and Lindblom, *Politics, Economics, and Welfare*, p. 41.
78. See H. L. Wilensky, "The Uneven Distribution of Leisure: The Impact of Economic Growth on 'Free Time,'" *Social Problems* 9 (1961): 32–56. This does not apply to professionals and independent businessmen, however (see pp. 37ff.). The issue is complicated by the fact that some "leisure" time has to be used for housekeeping chores and by the fact that people may choose to work more in order to gain income to buy goods and services which reduce the amount of time needed for household work. See Stefan Linder, *The Harried Leisure Class* (New York: Columbia University Press, 1970). This tendency reinforces the conclusion in the text, however.
79. On this, and on other constraints which industrial requirements impose on choices concerning the amount one works, see E. P. Thompson, "Time, Work-Discipline, and Industrial Capitalism," *Past and Present* 38 (December, 1967): 56–97.
80. Most of the questions I shall consider in this section involve interpersonal comparisons of utilities, at least to some extent. The objections to such interpersonal comparisons are well known. (See, for example, Lionel Robbins, *An Essay on the Nature and Significance of Economic Science*, 2d ed. [London: Macmillan, 1935], pp. 138–41.) Nevertheless, in this section I intend to ignore such

objections for two reasons. First, I am trying to anticipate potential criticisms of the egalitarian system and to meet these criticisms on their own grounds, as it were. If I were to accept the extreme position on the noncomparability of the satisfactions, it would have the effect of ruling out the potential criticisms in advance on methodological grounds. I might justly be suspected of ducking the issues. Second, it seems to me that the extreme position on the noncomparability of satisfactions is wrong. As Little has observed, such a position is, in the end, a form of solipsism. See I. M. D. Little, *A Critique of Welfare Economics,* 2d ed. (Oxford: Oxford University Press, 1960), p. 55. While certain cautions are clearly appropriate, people can and do make frequent interpersonal comparisons of subjective feelings. For example, public opinion surveys depend in the final analysis on the assumption that people's subjective feelings are comparable. For a discussion of the question and a defense of the proposition that interpersonal comparisons are possible, see J. L. Simon, "Interpersonal Welfare Comparisons Can Be Made—and Used for Redistribution Purposes," *Kyklos* 27 (1974): 63–98.

81. This presupposes, however, that one retains sufficient time for consumption. This is not always the case. See Linder, *The Harried Leisure Class.*

82. The qualification is necessary because, as was noted before, socialization is never perfect. There are subgroups in PPM systems which reject the dominant cultural goals to a greater or lesser extent, and within these subgroups social approval and self-esteem may be based on values somewhat different from the values of the mainstream. See Frank Parkin, *Class Inequality and Political Order* (London: Paladin, 1972), esp. chaps. 2 and 3, and Runciman, *Relative Deprivation and Social Justice,* esp. chaps. 5 and 11. Nevertheless, the dominant values remain dominant. See Parkin, pp. 68–69.

83. Edward Bellamy, *Looking Backward* (1888; reprinted, New York: New American Library, 1960), p. 76. Emphasis added. While my egalitarian system closely resembles Bellamy's in relying on social duty as a source of motivation and in measuring compliance with duty in relation to capacity, Bellamy's system depends upon a centrally directed, command economy rather than on the market mechanism.

84. Ibid.

85. Melvin Tumin, "On Inequality," *American Sociological Review* 28 (1963): 20–21.

86. Ibid., p. 23. Emphasis added.

87. Ibid., p. 24, and Melvin Tumin, *Social Stratification* (Englewood Cliffs, N.J.: Prentice-Hall, 1967), pp. 110–11.

88. In contrast to my claim that socialization determines one's view of justice, David Miller has argued that an egalitarian concept of justice requires a solidaristic and relatively undifferentiated community. He suggests that emphasis on economic efficiency will require specialization of work roles and formal, impersonal relationships which will tend to undermine the egalitarian concept of justice and to replace it with a sense of justice based on desert (some variant of contribution to production). But the major evidence Miller offers in support of this view is that in some Israeli kibbutzim which have developed highly rational modes of production, managers are generally less satisfied with their roles than are ordinary workers. The dissatisfaction is attributed to a conflict between the official commitment of the kibbutz to equality in distribution and the managers' sense that their work is more highly skilled and ought to be more highly rewarded (although it does not appear that the managers themselves have articulated their dissatisfaction in this way). Even if the sources of managerial dissatisfaction are correctly identified, it is impossible to dissociate their attitudes from the fact that the kibbutzim are islands of egalitarianism in a sea of inequality, the larger Israeli society. The managers know that their kind of work is more highly rewarded in the larger society and, in many cases, they probably would have personal opportunities to take advantage of this if they left their kibbutzim. The reference groups with which individuals compare themselves play a crucial role in affecting their levels of satisfaction with economic rewards and with work roles. (See the discussion in the next section of this chapter and especially the references in n. 98, below.) If all of Israeli society shared an egalitarian mode of distribution and an egalitarian view of justice, the managers on the kibbutzim might be far less likely to be dissatisfied with their work roles and with an egalitarian mode of distribution. See David Miller, *Social Justice* (Oxford: Clarendon Press, 1976), pp. 332–35.

89. This is a point much emphasized by Milton Friedman in *Capitalism and Freedom* (Chicago: University of Chicago Press, 1962), chap. 10.

90. The qualification is necessary because more work might be available to some people than to others.

91. The category of "work satisfactions" should be understood to include all remaining nonmonetary rewards, including prestige and power.

92. This would be possible even if the executive job offered more power and prestige than the secretary's, because some people actively dislike exercising power and may not particularly desire prestige. Moreover, some people might find an executive's job too demanding and pressure-filled, even though these are the qualities which make it attractive to other people.

93. This argument assumes that the income difference between Sandra and Jim would not overcompensate her for the lower work-satisfactions to such an extent that the inequality of satisfactions would be greater in the PPM system than in the egalitarian system.

94. Okun's comment is typical. "In actual practice the income premiums that are equalizing—compensating for the lower attractiveness of a job—are swamped by income differentials that accentuate such non-monetary differentials as social status and recognition." Arthur Okun, *Equality and Efficiency: The Big Tradeoff* (Washington, D.C.: The Brookings Institution, 1975), p. 72. See also Tibor Scitovsky, *The Joyless Economy* (Oxford: Oxford University Press, Galaxy Books, 1976), pp. 91–101, and Robert Blauner, "Work Satisfaction and Industrial Trends in Modern Society," in *Labor and Trade Unionism,* ed. W. Galenson and S. M. Lipset (1960), reprinted in *Class Status and Power,* ed. Bendix and Lipset, pp. 473–87.

95. One of the most striking pieces of evidence in support of the argument that equal distribution would decrease net inequality of satisfactions is the fact that there is a very strong correlation between the level of one's income relative to the income of others in the same society and the level of self-rated happiness. This holds true both within the same society over time and across different societies. See Simon, "Interpersonal Welfare Comparisons," p. 86, and Richard Easterlin, "Does Money Buy Happiness?" *The Public Interest,* no. 30 (Winter 1973): 3–10. One could hardly expect those with higher incomes to consider themselves happier so consistently unless income differences tended to be additive rather than compensatory. Nevertheless, this evidence does not actually separate income-consumption satisfactions from work satisfactions.

96. See Runciman, *Relative Deprivation;* Martin Patchen, "The Effect of Reference Group Standards on Job Satisfactions," *Human Relations* 11 (1958), reprinted in *Readings in Reference Group Theory and Research,* ed. Herbert Hyman and Eleanor Singer (New York: The Free Press, 1968), pp. 325–38; and William H. Form and James A. Geschwender, "Social Reference Basis of Job Satisfac-

tion: The Case of Manual Workers," *American Sociological Review* 27 (1962), also reprinted in *Readings,* ed. Hyman and Singer, pp. 185–98. One should note that all of these studies tend to confirm rather than contradict the general argument that income differences tend to be additive rather than compensatory. However, these studies do show that some people who are objectively worse-off in terms of income (and indeed social status) receive more work satisfactions than people who are better-off because the worse-off compare themselves with those who are even worse-off while the better-off compare themselves with those who are even better-off.

97. Moore suggests that an equal distribution of income would be likely to lead to actual increases in other social inequalities. See Wilbert Moore, "But Some Are More Equal than Others," *American Sociological Review* 28 (1963): 16–17. Moore does not indicate why he believes this.

98. Since prestige is a form of social approval it may seem puzzling for me to assert that the egalitarian system could tolerate essentially the same differences in prestige as can be found in a PPM system. To clarify the point, it may be useful to distinguish between "esteem" and "prestige." As Kingsley Davis puts it, "[E]steem [is] the kind of approval that comes with the faithful fulfillment of the duties of a position. The approval that comes with *having* a position, i.e., approval attached to the position and not to the degree of faithfulness in performing its duties, is called *prestige.*" "Reply to Tumin," *American Sociological Review* 18 (1953), reprinted in *Class, Status, and Power,* ed. Bendix and Lipset, p. 61.

The social approval associated with social duty in the egalitarian system is a form of esteem, not prestige. (The position whose duties are being fulfilled is simply that of an adult member of the egalitarian society.) Other kinds of esteem would presumably be available in the egalitarian system as well. Moreover, whatever factors would cause a position to enjoy prestige in the PPM system would also cause it to enjoy prestige in the egalitarian system (except the characteristic that the position entitled one to a higher than average amount of income for consumption).

99. Even Davis and Moore, who insist on the functional inevitability of stratification, agree that some societies are far more egalitarian than others. See Kingsley Davis and Wilbert Moore, "Some Principles of Stratification," *American Sociological Review* 10 (1945), reprinted in *Class, Status, and Power,* ed. Bendix and Lipset, p. 52.

100. John Echols presents data on several different dimensions of inequality in "Does Communism Mean Greater Equality?—A Comparison of East and West Along Several Major Dimensions" (paper delivered at the 1976 Annual Meeting of the American Political Science Association in Chicago). While Echols focuses on East-West comparisons, the data presented on inequalities within the West does not indicate that those Western countries with more egalitarian distributions of income are less egalitarian in other dimensions. See esp. pp. 31–33.

101. Ibid. See also Runciman, *Relative Deprivation*.

102. Runciman, *Relative Deprivation*, p. 387 and passim.

103. Ibid.; Thomas Pettigrew, "Actual Gains and Psychological Losses," in *A Profile of the Negro American* (1964), reprinted in *Readings*, ed. Hyman and Singer, pp. 339–49; and Tumin, *Social Stratification*, pp. 98–100.

104. For example, some inequalities of power seem an inevitable consequence of the need for an organized government in any large society. Anarchists, however, would not see organized government as inevitable and radical democrats might argue that equal participation in decision-making would be possible.

105. Compare Pettigrew, "Actual Gains," and Runciman, *Relative Deprivation*, pp. 344–45.

106. See Runciman, *Relative Deprivation*, p. 344.

107. The principle of distribution according to work is, of course, more egalitarian than the principle of distribution according to ownership. For more on the relationship between equality and distribution according to need, see Chapter 4.

108. The Soviet Union did engage in a brief experiment with egalitarianism during the period of War Communism from 1918 to 1921, but it never pursued the policy as systematically as China or Cuba, and since that time has insisted on the necessity of relying on material incentives and on the principle of distribution according to work. See Margaret Dewar, *Labor Policy in the USSR, 1917–1928* (New York: Royal Institute of International Affairs, 1956), and Maurice Dobb, *Soviet Economic Development Since 1917* (New York: International Publishers, 1948).

109. The Cubans and the Chinese sometimes use the term "moral incentives" much more broadly than I have in this essay. For example, sometimes moral incentives can include public honors and even tangible awards such as vacations. See Robert M. Bernado, *The Theory of Moral Incentives in Cuba* (University, Ala.: University of Alabama Press, 1971), pp. 54–55, and Charles

Hoffmann, *The Chinese Worker* (Albany, N.Y.: State University of New York Press, 1974), pp. 110–17. The dominant use of the term, however, is compatible with my definition of moral incentives as incentives based on the desire to serve society.

110. For discussions of the Chinese experiments with moral incentives, see Hoffman, *Chinese Worker,* esp. pp. 93–122; Carl Risken, "Workers' Incentives in Chinese Industry," in *China: A Reassessment of the Economy, A Compendium of Papers Submitted to the Joint Economic Committee of the Congress of the United States* (Washington, D.C.: U.S. Government Printing Office, 1975), pp. 199–224; Jan Prybyla, *The Chinese Economy* (Columbia, S.C.: University of South Carolina Press, 1978), esp. pp. 108–36; Christopher Howe, "Labour Organization and Incentives in Industry, Before and After the Cultural Revolution," in *Authority, Participation, and Cultural Change in China,* ed. Stuart Schram (Cambridge: Cambridge University Press, 1973), pp. 233–56; Donald J. Munro, *The Concept of Man in Contemporary China* (Ann Arbor: University of Michigan Press, 1977), esp. pp. 142–57; Barry M. Richman, *Industrial Society in Communist China* (New York: Random House, 1969), esp. pp. 309–21 and 809–17; Charles Hoffman, *Work Incentive Practices and Policies in the People's Republic of China* (Albany, N.Y.: State University of New York Press, 1967), esp. pp. 58–78 and 117–21.

111. For discussions of the Cuban experiment with moral incentives, see Bernado, *Moral Incentives,* passim; Archibald Ritter, *The Economic Development of Revolutionary Cuba* (New York: Praeger, 1974), esp. pp. 259–306 and 326–34; Carmelo Mesa-Lago, *The Labor Sector and Socialist Distribution in Cuba* (New York: Praeger, 1968), esp. pp. 116–50; and Carmelo Mesa-Lago, *Cuba in the 1970's,* rev. ed. (Albuquerque: University of New Mexico Press, 1978), pp. 44–49.

112. See especially Richard Lowenthal, "Development vs. Utopia in Communist Policy," in *Change in Communist Systems,* ed. Chalmers Johnson (Stanford: Stanford University Press, 1970); Ritter, *Revolutionary Cuba,* pp. 294–306; and Prybyla, *Chinese Economy,* pp. 130–32.

113. Bernado, *Moral Incentives,* pp. 76–79; Hoffmann, *Work Incentive Practices,* pp. 76–77.

114. See Richard R. Fagen, *The Transformation of Political Culture in Cuba* (Stanford: Stanford University Press, 1969), and Richard H. Solomon, *Mao's Revolution and Chinese Political Culture* (Berkeley: University of California Press, 1971).

115. See Hoffmann, *Chinese Worker,* p. 188.
116. Charles E. Lindblom, *Politics and Markets* (New York: Basic Books, 1977), p. 287.
117. Bernado, *Moral Incentives,* p. 26; Hoffmann, *Chinese Worker,* p. 186.
118. It should be noted that in the Cuban and Chinese experiments moral incentives have been much more than a device to get people to work. Moral incentives are seen as a way of encouraging participation, creativity, and initiative. The ultimate goal is much more than achieving economic efficiency without maldistribution. It is an attempt to transform the moral and spiritual character of all social relations. My egalitarian model is considerably more pedestrian, but, for the reasons indicated in Chapter 4, it still may have something important to offer to those who set their sights on higher goals.
119. The figures on absenteeism are taken from Ritter, *Revolutionary Cuba,* pp. 282–83.
120. Ibid., pp. 285, 287, and 303.
121. Ibid., pp. 277–82; Hoffmann, *Chinese Worker,* p. 111.
122. Solomon argues that certain features of the Chinese methods have deep roots in Chinese political culture. See Solomon, *Mao's Revolution,* p. 326. But these particularities are not crucial for my purposes because I am focusing on the broad characteristics of the methods which are quite similar in the Cuban and Chinese cases.
123. See Orville Brim, "Adult Socialization," *International Encyclopedia of the Social Sciences* (New York: Macmillan, 1968), 14:558–59.
124. Slater, "Social Bases," p. 570.
125. Moore, *Order and Change,* p. 185.
126. Slater, "Social Bases," pp. 572–76.
127. Moore, *Order and Change,* pp. 3–19, esp. pp. 17–18.
128. See, for example, André Beteille, "The Decline of Social Inequality," in *Social Inequality,* ed. André Beteille (Middlesex, England: Penguin, 1969), p. 366, and Talcott Parsons, "Commentary," in *Institutions and Social Exchange,* ed. Turk and Simpson, p. 393.

Chapter 4

1. For variants of this argument, see William Leiss, *The Limits to Satisfaction* (Toronto: University of Toronto Press, 1976); Walter Weisskopf, *Alienation and Economics* (New York: Dutton, 1971);

Fred Hirsch, *Social Limits to Growth* (Cambridge: Harvard University Press, 1976); and Tibor Scitovsky, *The Joyless Economy* (Oxford: Oxford University Press, 1976).

2. The quotation is from Jeremy Bentham as cited in Weisskopf, *Alienation and Economics,* p. 77.

3. For one version of such a system, see James Meade, *Efficiency, Equality, and the Ownership of Property* (Cambridge: Harvard University Press, 1965).

4. See Paul Blumberg, *Industrial Democracy* (New York: Schocken, 1969). Harry Braverman has argued that inequalities of power in capitalist enterprises are used to maintain class control rather than to enhance efficiency. See Harry Braverman, *Labor and Monopoly Capital* (New York: Monthly Review Press, 1974).

5. The proviso is needed because even in an ideal market system it seems impossible to implement some distributional ideals, like compensation for the relative disutility of work, without reestablishing the link between production and distribution and thereby interfering with the functioning of moral incentives. See the discussion of this issue in Chapter 3.

6. Charles E. Lindblom, *Politics and Markets* (New York: Basic Books, 1977), p. 98.

7. Ibid., pp. 98–99. Lindblom does not directly address the question of how to induce workers if the government purchases all of the final products, but he seems to presuppose the existence of income inequalities and he suggests that the government can establish a separate market for consumer goods. Even if the prices in this market reflected governmental judgments about needs rather than the actual marginal costs of production (e.g., food priced lower than cost and luxuries higher), those with higher incomes would enjoy advantages which would bear no necessary relation to their needs. Thus Lindblom's version of the "planner sovereignty market system" would not meet the goal which I have adopted here, distribution according to need.

8. For the sake of simplicity I shall henceforth use the terms "egalitarian system" and "egalitarian model" to refer both to the original egalitarian model and to any of its variants, even though some of the variants may have distributional goals other than strict equality (e.g., distribution according to needs).

9. For an illustration of some of the difficulties in measuring the benefits of governmental expenditures, see W. Irwin Gillespie, "Effects of Public Expenditures on the Distribution of Income," in *Essays in Fiscal Federalism,* ed. Richard Musgrave (Washington,

D.C.: The Brookings Institution, 1965).

10. David Miller, "Socialism and the Market," *Political Theory* 5 (1977): 478. For a similar view, see Robert Heilbronner, "What is Socialism?" *Dissent* 25 (1978): 343–44.

11. Lindblom, *Politics and Markets,* p. 94n.

12. For discussions of civil disobedience in a democracy, see Peter Singer, *Democracy and Disobedience* (Oxford: Oxford University Press, 1974), and John Rawls, "The Justification of Civil Disobedience," in *Civil Disobedience,* ed. Hugo Bedau (New York: Pegasus, 1969).

13. Fred Hirsch develops this theme in a chapter winningly titled "Bought Sex Is Not the Same," in *Social Limits to Growth.* Richard Titmuss has also argued that great benefits can be gained from social arrangements which preclude personal calculations of cost and benefit. See Richard M. Titmuss, *The Gift Relationship* (New York: Random House, 1972).

14. Marx's powerful critique of the tendency of capitalism to reduce all human relationships to the "cash nexus" has played an important part in shaping the view that an ideal society would be one in which money played no role. In the late 1960s and early 1970s the Cuban leadership deliberately reduced the role of money in everyday life in order to move in the direction of a more fully human society. See Martin Kenner and James Petras, eds., *Fidel Castro Speaks* (New York: Grove Press, 1969), pp. 199–200, 287, 291–93.

15. Lindblom, *Politics and Markets,* pp. 11–13 and passim.

16. Max Weber, "Technical Advantages of Bureaucratic Organization," in *From Max Weber,* ed. Hans Gerth and C. Wright Mills (New York: Oxford University Press, 1946), pp. 215–16.

17. See Robert Dahl, *After the Revolution* (New Haven: Yale University Press, 1970).

18. John Rawls, *A Theory of Justice* (Cambridge: Harvard University Press, 1971).

19. Ibid., pp. 150–61.

20. Ibid., p. 151.

21. Rawls thinks that inequalities in primary goods tend to be highly correlated although he pays little attention to the relative satisfactions of different kinds of work. See *A Theory of Justice,* p. 94.

22. Rawls, *A Theory of Justice,* p. 101.

23. Ibid., p. 103.

24. Technically, it is necessary to note that Rawls assumes that

people in the original position will know only "general facts about human society." Although Rawls is never very clear about what counts as a "general fact," it may be that the kind of knowledge I am assuming here about the possibilities of effective socialization and about the relative attractiveness of different kinds of work belongs at a later stage, such as the constitutional stage or the legislative stage, where people are assumed to know a bit more about their particular society although not about their positions as individuals within that society. The basic argument that Rawlsian principles would justify the arrangements of my egalitarian model remains unaffected by this qualification. See Rawls, *A Theory of Justice*, pp. 137–38 and 200.

25. Robert Nozick, *Anarchy, State, and Utopia* (New York: Basic Books, 1974), especially Chapter 7.

Index

Absenteeism, in Cuba, 169
Achievement, need for, 112–13
Additive effects of income inequality. *See* Inequality of income, compensatory versus additive effects
After-tax income, 4; and income in kind, 6; and saving, 72–73. *See also* Equal income share
Alienation, 178, 204–6
Allocation of resources: as an element of efficiency, 12; and equal distribution, 14–15; and moral incentives, 27–49. *See also* Prices; Market
Altruism, 2, 120–24, 199, 225 n. 3
Arts, in egalitarian system, 191–92

Barry, Brian, 2
Barth, Frederik, 110
Bellamy, Edward, 153–54, 236 n. 83
Borrowing, in egalitarian system, 217–18
Bureaucracy: in egalitarian system, 102; as alternative to market, 205. *See also* Decentralization; Market
Business expenses, 7, 88–89, 140, 222 n. 13, 225 n. 2

Calculation, 189, 196, 204–6. *See also* Alienation; Knowledge of relative prices; Market
Capitalist system, 221 n. 10. *See also* PPM system
Central planning, xi
China, 164–73, 240 n. 109, 242 n. 118
Civil disobedience analogy, 201–3
Cohen, Albert, 105
Collective decision-making, 186–95

Commodity fetishism, 179, 187, 195
Communal goals in egalitarian system, 187–95
Community, 178, 180, 196–97, 200–208
Compensatory effects of income inequality. *See* Inequality of income, compensatory versus additive effects
Competition, 13–14, 178, 198, 199–200
Conservation, and market prices, 188–90
Consumer durables, as form of saving, 214–19
Consumer preferences, 24–25, 91, 178, 180, 187–88. *See also* Commodity fetishism; Freedom, of choice in consumption
Consumption, personal, 6; in egalitarian system, 8, 88–89. *See also* Equal income share; Freedom, of choice in consumption
Cooperation, 178, 198–200; *See also* Altruism
Corruption, 137–38
Cost of living, 56–58
Cuba, ix, 164–73, 240 n. 109, 242 n. 118
Cultural Revolution, in China, 165, 168

Dahl, Robert, x
Dalton, George, 110–11
Davis, Kingsley, 112
Decentralization: of governmental expenditures, 192; and the market, x, 10; of saving, 75; of socialization, 119–20, 130

247

Demand: assumed identity of, 24–25; legitimacy of, 193–97; and supply, in egalitarian system, 48–49. *See also* Market; Prices
Developmental models of socialization, 99–101
Deviance, 101, 129–38
Difference principle, 210
Differentially incurred basic needs, 186–87
Distribution, according to need(s), 5–6, 164, 178, 180, 184–87, 211, 243 n. 7
Distributional flexibility, of the egalitarian system, 183–87

Earning capacity, in egalitarian system, 36–38, 227 n. 12; and effort, 58–66; and inequalities, 151–53, 158–60; and inflation, 53–54; and investment, 69–72; knowledge of, by others, 124–27; long-term, 70–71; and risk, 82–86; and tradeoffs among satisfactions, 39–49
Economic decline, in egalitarian system, 65–66, 102, 145–51, 176
Economic growth, in egalitarian system, 65–66, 145–51, 187, 188–89. *See also* Saving; Investment
Efficiency: definition of, 12; in egalitarian system, 4, 80–82, 87–88, 145, 179, 181–83, 221 n. 6
Effort, in egalitarian system, 12, 15, 26, 50, 145–51
Egalitarian system: collective decision-making and communal goals in, 187–95; definition of, 4; deviance in, 129–38; distributional flexibility of, 183–87; effects of economic growth and decline on effort in, 145–51; elites in, 138–45; freedom in, 90–93; income-consumption satisfactions in, 86–89; and the individual, 200–208; inequalities in, 151–64; and innovation, 203; interaction with other systems assumed away, 21, 173; justification of, 208–12; organizational flexibility of, 24, 28, 32, 180–83, 225 n. 4, 226 n. 6; price changes and allocation in, 43–49; rationality of, 99–100, 123–24; requirements of, 4–18; socialization in, 104, 118–20; as utopian ideal, 178–80, 182; variability of satisfactions in, 41–42
Egalitarian socialist tradition, xi, 178, 179, 211
Elites, 102, 120, 138–45, 149–51, 176
Empirical social theory, as source of empirically necessary prerequisites, 20–21, 94, 166
Empirically necessary prerequisites, 96, 108, 118–19, 127, 128, 135, 137, 141, 150, 175–77
Equal distribution: deviance from, 134–38; and elites, 138–45; and governmental expenditures, 192–94; as norm, 135–37, 163, 176–77; as requirement of the egalitarian system, 4–5, 183–87
Equal income share: definition of, 6; and income-consumption satisfactions, 87–88; and saving, 73, 213–19, 222 n. 14
Equality and Efficiency, 2
Equilibrium point, as basis of comparison between PPM and egalitarian systems, 13, 43, 50
Esteem. *See* Social approval
Externalities, 220 n. 8

Freedom, 2, 90–93, 187, 200–208; of choice in consumption, 2, 91, 187, 214–18, 219, 229 n. 33; as requirement of egalitarian system, 4, 17–18; and socialization, 18, 118–20, 155, 169–71
Functional distribution, 14–15
Functionalist sociologists, x

Governmental expenditures and distribution of income, 192–94
Great Leap Forward, 165

Halm, George, 2, 15

Index

Harsanyi, John, 19
Hayek, Friedrich, 9
Homans, George, 106–7, 114
Honest officials, as prerequisite of egalitarian system, 137–38, 176
Housing, 215–17
Human capital, investment in, 16, 70–72
Human nature, ix, 103–8

Identity, assumption of, 23–25, 42, 180–82, 226 n. 6
Incentives. *See* Income-consumption satisfactions; Moral incentives; Social-duty satisfactions
Income and substitution effects, 55–57, 145–47, 223 n. 28
Income-consumption satisfactions, 25; and consumption satisfactions, 228 n. 18; and earning capacity, 37–38; in egalitarian system, 26–27, 86–89, 139, 227 n. 10; and income, 227 n. 13; and investment, 68–69; and motivation, 34, 101, 109–11, 114–18; and price changes, 43–49; and relative values, 32–33; and risk, 77–78; and saving, 67; and saving in egalitarian system, 228 n. 22; and tradeoff with leisure in PPM system, 50, 52, 54, 55–58, 64–66; and tradeoff against work satisfactions, 43–45; individual versus community, 200–208
Inequality: decline in legitimacy of, 1, 172–73; in egalitarian system, 8, 30–32, 102, 151–64, 178, 226 n. 8, 238 n. 95; of income, compensatory versus additive effects, 156–60, 223 n. 21, 238 n. 94, 239 n. 96; and justification of egalitarian system, 209–10
Income in kind, 6
Inflation, 51–55, 228 n. 20
Inheritance, 30, 181, 218–19
Inkeles, Alex, 97
Interpersonal comparison of utilities, 235 n. 80
Investment, 12, 16, 26, 66–72, 157, 228 n. 24, 229 n. 31
Israeli kibbutzim, 237 n. 88

Kohlberg, Lawrence, 99–100
Knowledge: and earning capacity, 85–86; of relative prices, 101, 124–29, 152, 176; uses of limited, 197–98
Kristol, Irving, 1
Kuhn, Alfred, 104–5

Labor productivity. *See* Economic growth
Lane, Robert, 140
Lawmakers in egalitarian system, 139–45, 177
Leisure, 8, 50, 55–58, 133–34, 146–48, 235 n. 78
Lindblom, Charles E., x, 168, 184
Logic, of the egalitarian system, 42, 50–51; *See also* Logically necessary prerequisites
Logically necessary prerequisites, 20, 25, 73–74, 86, 89, 94–95, 174–75
Looking Backward, 153–54

McClelland, David, 112–13
MacIntyre, Alasdair, 122–23
McMullen, M., 137
Market: administrative advantages of, x, 168; and communal goals, 196–98; and community, 198–200; and compensation for relative disutilities, 156–60; competition and cooperation through, 200; defects of, 178–79, 204; definition of, 10; and inequality of income, 10, 11; planner sovereignty model, 184–85, 191–92, 243 n. 7; as requirement of egalitarian system, 4, 10–11; as social device for comparing alternative uses of resources, 188–90. *See also* Egalitarian system; Moral incentives
Market capitalism, x, 1. *See also* PPM system
Market socialism, 11, 222 n. 18, 223 n. 21

Index

Material incentives, 165–66. See also Income-consumption satisfactions
Maximization of pre-tax income: as directional indicator of social duty, 34–36, 206–8; and socialization, 104; as strategy in face of risk, 78–85. See also Earning capacity; Social duty
Medical care, 186–87
Merton, Robert, 96–98, 115–16, 119, 135, 139, 141
Miller, Daniel, 97–98
Miller, David, 198
Monetary success, as goal of American culture, 115–16
Money: and alienation, 205, 244 n. 14; and equal distribution, 6. See also Equal income share; Income-consumption satisfactions
Moore, Wilbert, 98, 103, 130
Moral incentives: and altruism, 120–24; in Cuba and China, ix, 165–71, 240 n. 109, 242 n. 118; definition of, 8; and market, x–xi; in planner sovereignty system, 184–85; as requirement of egalitarian system, 8–10; and resource allocation, 27–49; role of, in egalitarian system, 4, 26, 34, 183. See also Egalitarian system; Social-duty satisfactions
Motives for economic activity, in primitive societies, 110–11; in industrial societies, 111–13. See also Income-consumption satisfactions; Social-duty satisfactions; Socialization

Nagel, Thomas, 2, 3
Nash, Manning, 111
Needs, differentially incurred basic, 186–87, 194. See also Distribution according to need(s)
Nozick, Robert, 211

PPM system, 4, 221 n. 10; contrasted with market socialism, 11; deviance in, 131–33; earning capacity in, 37–38; effects of growth and decline on effort in, 146–47; efficiency of, 12–14; freedom in, 17–18; income-consumption satisfactions in, 109, 114–18; inequalities in, 152, 156–62, 180–81; inflation and unemployment in, 228 n. 20; knowledge of prices in, 124–29; and pursuit of public interest, 9; and risk, 77–78; saving in, 67–68; social approval in, 124–25; and thought experiment, 23–25; and tradeoffs among satisfactions, 35; variability of value in, 130–31
Parentalism, 193
Parsons, Talcott, 109, 115
Participatory democracy, 205–6
Personal distribution, 14–15. See also Equal income share
Piaget, Jean, 99
Planner sovereignty market system, 184–85, 191–92, 243 n. 7
Polanyi, Karl, 110–11
Polanyi, Michael, 11
Political leadership, in egalitarian system, 150
Political obligation, 204
Politics, Economics, and Welfare, x
Polyarchy, 142, 143–45
Power, inequality of, 8, 30–32, 102, 144–45, 161–64, 180–83, 226 n. 8
Preferences, conflicting, 206–8
Prerequisites, of egalitarian system, 4, 18–21. See also Logically necessary prerequisites; Empirically necessary prerequisites
Prestige: inequalities in, 8, 30–32, 102, 161–64, 226 n. 8; distinguished from esteem, 239 n. 98
Pre-tax income: for artists and scholars, 191; and contribution to community, 195–200; deviation from maximization, 35–49, 129–34, 202; and earning capacity, 36–38; effect on after-tax income, 30; as indicator of value of economic contribution, 153; net, 225 n. 2; and profits, 29; and return on investment, 71–72; and risk, 78–80; and social good, 201–3. See also Prices; Social duty

Prewitt, Kenneth, 139
Prices: changes in, 35, 43–49, 49–66; distortion of, 188–89, 230 n. 8; functions of, in ideal market system, 195–98; functions of, in PPM system, 13; as indicators of social duty, 185, 189, 194, 195–200, 202; limits of, 204. *See also* Income-consumption satisfactions; Market; Pre-tax income; Social-duty satisfactions
Primary goods, 244 n. 21
Production, separated from distribution, 179, 183
Profit-maximization, 27–30, 226 n. 9
Protestant Ethic and the Spirit of Capitalism, 113
Property, in egalitarian system: ownership of, 27–32, 180–81; laws regarding, 189, 190, 195

Rational-choice model (or rational-actor model), 18–19, 23, 85–86, 94, 224 n. 34, 225 n. 1
Rawls, John, 208–10
Relative deprivation, 227 n. 13
Relative prices, knowledge of. *See* Knowledge, of relative prices
Relative scarcity, 48–49, 184, 204
Relative values, assumption about, 25, 32–35, 39–43
"Revolutionary Offensive," in Cuba, 165, 166, 168, 169
Rise of the Meritocracy, 7
Risk, 12, 16–17, 26, 75–85, 157, 229 n. 29
Runciman, W. G., 162

Sanctions, for deviance from social duty, 132–33
Saving: and efficiency, 12, 15; in egalitarian system, 72–75; and equal income shares, 73, 213–19; in PPM system, 67–68; permissible forms of, 74, 88–89, 140. *See also* Investment
Sears, David, 140
Self-esteem, 98–99, 116; and knowledge of relative prices, 127–29; inequalities in, in egalitarian system, 151–56, 159–60
Self-interest, ix, 120–24
Slater, Philip, 105
Smelser, Neil, 115
Social approval, 96–99, 116, 118; and distinction between prestige and esteem, 239 n. 98; and economic contribution, 153–55; inequalities in, in egalitarian system, 151–56, 159–60; and knowledge of relative prices, 124–27. *See also* Social-duty satisfactions
Social costs and benefits, reflected in prices, 190
Social duty to acquire pre-tax income: and commodity fetishism, 179, 187; and conflicting obligations, 203–4; and conflicting preferences, 206–8; extreme deviance from, 131–34; and earning capacity, 151–53; and individual judgment, 201–3; justification of, 208–12; limits on, 34–35; as logically necessary prerequisite of egalitarian system, 25; long-term perspective on, 70–71; and prices, 189–90, 195–200; as product of socialization, 96–101; and risk, 78–79. *See also* Pre-tax income; Moral incentives; Social-duty satisfactions
Social-duty income and substitution effects, 59–65
Social-duty satisfactions, 25; and earning capacity, 36–38, 53–55, 151–53; and effort, 49–66; and freedom, 90; inequalities in, 151–56; and investment in egalitarian system, 69–72; nature of, 99; and price changes, 43–48; and relative values, 33–35; and resource allocation, 27–49; and risk, 79–85; and saving, 72–75; and tradeoffs with leisure, 50, 52–55, 58–66; and tradeoffs with work satisfactions, 39–49, 158–60. *See also* Moral incentives; Self esteem; Social approval
Socialization: and attitudes towards

contribution and reward, 155; and changes in values, 172–73; in Cuba and China, 169–71; as empirically necessary prerequisite, 96–101, 155, 175, 177; and freedom, 18, 118–20, 155, 169–71; intensity of, 108–24; limitations on, 101; and norm of equal distribution, 135–37, 140; in PPM system, 115–16; and plasticity of human nature, 103–8; and self-interest, 120–24; and social duty, 96–101; spontaneous changes in, 147–48, 150; variability of, 106–7, 172, 236 n. 82

Stone, Alan, 139
Stratification, inevitability of, x
Substitution effects. *See* Income and substitution effects
Supply and demand, in the egalitarian system, 48–49. *See also* Market; Prices

Tax laws, in egalitarian system, 23, 87, 175–76; and deviance, 135–38; and elites, 138–45; and loopholes, 88–89, 134; and saving, 73–74
Taxes: to correct price distortions, 189–90; on profits from housing, 215–17; progressive, on income, 15, 223 n. 28
"The Gift of the Magi," 200
Theory of Justice, A, 208–10
Tocqueville, Alexis de, 1, 172
Tradeoffs among satisfactions, 34, 35–49, 50, 145–51, 206–8. *See also* Income-consumption satisfactions; Leisure; Social-duty satisfactions; Work satisfactions
Transition to egalitarian system, excluded, 21, 95, 164, 167, 170–71, 173, 189, 191, 224 n. 37
Trustee analogy, 29–30
Tumin, Melvin, 21, 154, 155

Unemployment, 146–47, 228 n. 20, 233 n. 58
Utilitarian calculus of value, as characteristic of markets, 178, 180
Utopian model: egalitarian system as, 178–79, 194; realistic, 185, 197–98, 205; and nature of inquiry, 3, 18, 224 n. 32

Values, changes in: in Cuba and China, 169–71; in egalitarian system, 172–74
Variability of satisfactions in egalitarian system, 31, 41–42, 129–31, 157–58. *See also* Income-consumption satisfactions; Social-duty satisfactions; Work satisfactions

Wages: and resource allocation, 14–15, 38–49; and effort, 55–60. *See also* Pre-tax income; Prices
Waste, avoidance of, 188–90, 196
Weber, Max, 112, 205
Work satisfactions, 39–48, 133–34, 157–60, 237 n. 91. *See also* Leisure; Tradeoffs among satisfactions
Workers' participation, 182

Young, Michael, 7